CW01483594

THE UNITED NATIONS, INTRA-STATE
PEACEKEEPING AND NORMATIVE CHANGE

MANCHESTER
UNIVERSITY PRESS

New Approaches to Conflict Analysis

Series editor: Peter Lawler, Senior Lecturer in International Relations, Department of Government, University of Manchester

Until recently, the study of conflict and conflict resolution remained comparatively immune to broad developments in social and political theory. When the changing nature and locus of large-scale conflict in the post-Cold War era is also taken into account, the case for a reconsideration of the fundamentals of conflict analysis and conflict resolution becomes all the more stark.

New Approaches to Conflict Analysis promotes the development of new theoretical insights and their application to concrete cases of large-scale conflict, broadly defined. The series intends not to ignore established approaches to conflict analysis and conflict resolution, but to contribute to the reconstruction of the field through a dialogue between orthodoxy and its contemporary critics. Equally, the series reflects the contemporary porosity of intellectual borderlines rather than simply perpetuating rigid boundaries around the study of conflict and peace. *New Approaches to Conflict Analysis* seeks to uphold the normative commitment of the field's founders yet also recognises that the moral impulse to research is properly part of its subject matter. To these ends, the series is comprised of the highest quality work of scholars drawn from throughout the international academic community, and from a wide range of disciplines within the social sciences.

PUBLISHED

M. Anne Brown
Human rights and the borders of suffering:
the promotion of human rights in international politics

Karin Fierke
Changing games, changing strategies:
critical investigations in security

Tami Amanda Jacoby and Brent Sasley (eds)
Redefining security in the Middle East

Deiniol Jones
Cosmopolitan mediation?
Conflict resolution and the Oslo Accords

Jan Koehler and Christoph Zürcher (eds)
Potentials of disorder

Helena Lindholm Schulz
Reconstruction of Palestinian nationalism:
between revolution and statehood

David Bruce MacDonald
Balkan holocausts?
Serbian and Croatian victim-centred propaganda and the war in Yugoslavia

Jennifer Milliken
The social construction of the Korean War

Ami Pedahzur
The Israeli response to Jewish extremism and violence:
defending democracy

Tara Väyrynen
Culture and international conflict resolution:
a critical analysis of the work of John Burton

The United Nations, intra-state peacekeeping and normative change

EŞREF AKSU

Manchester University Press

MANCHESTER AND NEW YORK

distributed exclusively in the USA by Palgrave

Published by Manchester University Press
Oxford Road, Manchester M13 9NR, UK
and Room 400, 175 Fifth Avenue, New York, NY 10010, USA
www.manchesteruniversitypress.co.uk

Distributed exclusively in the USA by
Palgrave, 175 Fifth Avenue, New York,
NY 10010, USA

Distributed exclusively in Canada by
UBC Press, University of British Columbia, 2029 West Mall,
Vancouver, BC, Canada V6T 1Z2

British Library Cataloguing-in-Publication Data
A catalogue record for this book is available from the British Library

Library of Congress Cataloging-in-Publication Data applied for

ISBN 0 7190 6748 0 *hardback*

First published 2003

11 10 09 08 07 06 05 04 03   10 9 8 7 6 5 4 3 2 1

Typeset in Photina
by Action Publishing Technology Ltd, Gloucester
Printed in Great Britain
by Bell & Bain Ltd, Glasgow

CONTENTS

Contents

ACKNOWLEDGEMENTS

This book heavily draws on my PhD project completed at La Trobe University, Melbourne, Australia. I owe a special debt of gratitude to Joe Camilleri. Without his excellent supervision, intellectual support and generous friendship this project could not have materialised. I also would like to thank all colleagues and friends who, in different ways and capacities, knowingly and unknowingly, have continuously stimulated my thoughts about the issues that this book tries to wrestle with: Hugh Dyer, Richard Falk, John Groom, Yekti Maunati, Wendy Mee, Nicole Oke, Taha Parla, Hugh Smith and Ünsal Sönmezler.

ABBREVIATIONS

AAPSO	Afro-Asia Peoples' Solidarity Organisation
ABAKO	Alliance des Bakongo (Alliance of the Bakongo People)
ANC	Armee Nationale Congolaise (Congolese National Army)
APEC	Asia-Pacific Economic Cooperation
ARRK	Agricultural Relief and Rehabilitation in Kampuchea
ASC	American Security Council
ASEAN	Association of South-East Asian Nations
BLDP	Buddhist Liberal Democratic Party
CCC	Cooperation Committee for Cambodia
CCPM	Joint Political-Military Commission
CENTO	Central Treaty Organization
CGDK	Coalition Government of Democratic Kampuchea
CIEC	Conference on International Economic Cooperation
COMECON	Council for Mutual Economic Assistance
CONAKAT	Confederation des Associations Tribales du Katanga (Confederation of Tribal Associations of Katanga)
CSCE	Conference on Security and Cooperation in Europe
DOMREP	Mission of the Representative of the Secretary-General in the Dominican Republic
ECOSOC	Economic and Social Council
ECOWAS	Economic Community of West African States
ECSC	European Coal and Steel Community
EEC	European Economic Community
EU	European Union
FAA	Forças Armadas Angolanas (Angolan Armed Forces)
FNLA	Frente Nacional de Libertação de Angola (National Front for the Liberation of Angola)
FUNCINPEC	Front Uni National pour un Cambodge Indépendant, Neutre, Pacifique et Coopératif (United National Front for an Independent, Neutral, Peaceful and Cooperative Cambodia)
GAOR	General Assembly Official Records
GATT	General Agreement on Tariffs and Trade
G7	Group of Seven
ICBM	Inter-continental ballistic missile
IGO	Inter-governmental organisation
INTERFET	International Force in East Timor

KPNLF   Khmer People's National Liberation Front
MAD   Mutual Assured Destruction
MINUGUA   Misión de Verificación de las Naciones Unidas en Guatemala (UN Verification Mission in Guatemala)
MINURSO   Misión de las Naciones Unidas para el Referéndum del Sáhara Occidental (UN Mission for the Referendum in Western Sahara)
MNC   Mouvement National Congolais (Congolese National Movement)
MONUA   Mission D'Observation des Nations Unies en Angola (UN Observer Mission in Angola)
MONUC   Mission de l'Organisation des Nations Unies en République Démocratique du Congo (UN Organization Mission in the Democratic Republic of the Congo)
MPLA   Movimento Popular de Libertação de Angola (Popular Movement for the Liberation of Angola)
NAFTA   North American Free Trade Agreement
NAM   non-aligned movement
NATO   North Atlantic Treaty Organization
NGO   Non-governmental organisation
NIEO   New International Economic Order
OAS   Organization of American States
OAU   Organization of African Unity
OECD   Organization for Economic Cooperation and Development
ONUC   Opération des Nations Unies au Congo (UN Operation in the Congo)
ONUCA   Observadores de las Naciones Unidas en Centroamerica (UN Observer Group in Central America)
ONUMOZ   Operación de las Naciones Unidas en Mozambique (UN Operation in Mozambique)
ONUSAL   Observadores de las Naciones Unidas en El Salvador (UN Observer Mission in El Salvador)
ONUVEH   Observadores de las Naciones Unidas para la Verificatión de las Elecciones en Haiti (UN Observer Group for Verification of the Elections in Haiti)
ONUVEN   Observadores de las Naciones Unidas para la Verificación de las Elecciones en Nicaragua (UN Observer Mission for Verification of the Elections in Nicaragua)
OPEC   Organization of the Petroleum Exporting Countries
OSCE   Organization for Security and Cooperation in Europe
PADEK   Partnership for Development in Kampuchea
PDK   Party of Democratic Kampuchea (the Khmer Rouge)

PRK	People's Republic of Kampuchea
PSA	Parti Solidaire Africain (African Solidarity Party)
SALT	Strategic Arms Limitation Talks
SCOR	Security Council Official Records
SDI	Strategic Defense Initiative
SEATO	Southeast Asia Treaty Organization
SNC	Supreme National Council
SOC	State of Cambodia
SWAPO	South West African Peoples' Organisation
UAR	United Arab Republic
UCAH	Unidade de Coordenação para Assistencia Humanitaria (UN Humanitarian Assistance Coordination Unit)
UNAMIC	United Nations Advance Mission in Cambodia
UNAMIR	United Nations Assistance Mission for Rwanda
UNAMSIL	United Nations Assistance Mission to Sierra Leone
UNASOG	United Nations Aouzou Strip Observer Group
UNAVEM I	First United Nations Angola Verification Mission
UNAVEM II	Second United Nations Angola Verification Mission
UNAVEM III	Third United Nations Angola Verification Mission
UNCI	United Nations Commission for Indonesia
UNCIP	United Nations Commission for India and Pakistan
UNCRO	United Nations Confidence Restoration Operation in Croatia
UNCTAD	United Nations Conference on Trade and Development
UNDOF	United Nations Disengagement Observer Force
UNDP	United Nations Development Programme
UNEF I	First United Nations Emergency Force
UNEF II	Second United Nations Emergency Force
UNESCO	United Nations Educational, Scientific and Cultural Organization
UNFICYP	United Nations Peacekeeping Force in Cyprus
UNGOMAP	United Nations Good Offices Mission in Afghanistan and Pakistan
UNHCHR	United Nations High Commissioner for Human Rights
UNHCR	United Nations High Commissioner for Refugees
UNIFIL	United Nations Interim Force in Lebanon
UNIIMOG	United Nations Iran–Iraq Military Observer Group
UNIKOM	United Nations Iraq–Kuwait Observation Mission
UNIPOM	United Nations India–Pakistan Observation Mission
UNITA	União Nacional para a Independência Total de Angola (National Union for the Total Independence of Angola)
UNITAF	Unified Task Force in Somalia
UNMIBH	United Nations Mission in Bosnia and Hercegovina

UNMIH	United Nations Mission in Haiti
UNMIK	United Nations Interim Administration Mission in Kosovo
UNMOGIP	United Nations Military Observer Group in India and Pakistan
UNMOP	United Nations Mission of Observers in Prevlaka
UNMOT	United Nations Mission of Observers in Tajikistan
UNOGIL	United Nations Observation Group in Lebanon
UNOMIG	United Nations Observer Mission in Georgia
UNOMIL	United Nations Observer Mission in Liberia
UNOMSA	United Nations Observer Mission in South Africa
UNOMUR	United Nations Observer Mission in Uganda–Rwanda
UNOSOM I	First United Nations Operation in Somalia
UNOSOM II	Second United Nations Operation in Somalia
UNOVER	United Nations Observer Mission to Verify the Referendum in Eritrea
UNPREDEP	United Nations Preventive Deployment Force
UNPROFOR	United Nations Protection Force
UNPSG	United Nations Civilian Police Support Group
UNSCOB	United Nations Special Committee on the Balkans
UNSF	United Nations Security Force in West New Guinea (West Irian)
UNTAC	United Nations Transitional Authority in Cambodia
UNTAES	United Nations Transitional Administration for Eastern Slavonia, Baranja and Western Sirmium
UNTAET	United Nations Transitional Authority in East Timor
UNTAG	United Nations Transition Assistance Group
UNTEA	United Nations Temporary Executive Authority in West Irian
UNTSO	United Nations Truce Supervision Organization
UNYOM	United Nations Yemen Observation Mission
WFP	World Food Program
WHO	World Health Organization
WTO	World Trade Organization

1

The UN and intra-state conflicts: problematising the normative connection

WIDESPREAD INTRA-STATE CONFLICT is not a new phenomenon. Its rise to the centre of attention in international policy circles is. UN involvement in intra-state conflicts is not new either. What is new is the increasing systematisation of UN involvement in conflict-torn societies. It is these two novelties of the post-Cold War world that shape the main concerns of this study. What is problematised here is the connection between the UN's evolving approach to intra-state conflicts and the value system of the international community.

There should be little doubt that the UN's frequent involvement in domestic conflicts contributes to gradual change in several international norms. As is the case with any systematised practice, the UN's intra-state peacekeeping is certainly capable of creating, modifying, and eroding established international norms to varying degrees. The more interesting connection, however, lies in the question of whether the UN's intra-state peacekeeping (quite apart from being either a 'cause' or 'consequence') mirrors a deep-running and more profound normative change in world politics, which is probably the manifestation of much bigger influences exerted on international actors and which has considerable impact on how violent conflicts are perceived, contextualised and addressed. Has the UN's relationship with intra-state conflicts always reflected, and rested on, the same configuration or interpretation of significant international norms? If not, what has changed in the way the international community links the UN with intra-state conflicts, and how? Equally importantly, does the suspected change hint at the possibly evolving normative significance of the UN in world politics?

This study takes issue with the relatively reductionist explanations of what the UN is and how it relates to peace and security. The post-Cold War systematisation of UN involvement in intra-state conflicts, similar to any other UN activity, has been variously attributed (implicitly or explicitly) to a number of factors, including, among others, the particular geopolitical change that the end of the Cold War brought about; the usual pragmatism of the international community in the absence of a more suitable mechanism for dealing with destabilising effects of domestic conflicts; the distinct organisational relevance, culture and experience of the UN; and the UN's own efforts to assume a special identity and role in world politics. A closer examination of the evolution of UN peacekeeping in intra-state conflicts – especially between the two most active and critical periods of UN peacekeeping: the early 1960s and the early 1990s – suggests that the role assigned to the UN in intra-state conflict management begs more than the explanations offered so far. It suggests in the first place that the UN's evolving approach to conflict involves a number of normative changes in addition to the several empirical changes which have been the subject of much scholarly research in the post-Cold War period. More importantly, it suggests that this evolving approach indicates a deeper and gradual, though highly obscured, normative shift that gives the UN a new institutional meaning, a new *raison d'être*.

Although the UN is at the centre of much empirical and normative research, its possibly evolving relationship to the wider international value system remains largely under-explored. More notably, despite the radical changes in the global political setting and in the UN's scope of activities over the years, what exactly the UN stands for is not all that clear. We do know that the UN has a vast mandate and is based on a great many principles. Yet we do not quite know – apart from our 'first impressions' – whether, and to what extent, international actors prioritise any of the UN's objectives and principles over others, and whether there has been a change in their priorities, possibly impacting on the UN's evolving identity.

It has long been argued that many potential contradictions are inherent in the UN Charter – for instance, that between peace and justice.[1] Perhaps more immediately noticeable are the perceived tensions between what might be labelled 'state-centric'[2] and 'human-centric'[3] principles embedded in the Charter.[4] Roberts and Kingsbury observe that the principles of territorial integrity and self-determination may prove irreconcilable, as was demonstrated in the case of the former Yugoslavia.[5] At times, the principles of non-intervention and human rights may come into conflict.[6] The ongoing debate on the right to humanitarian intervention, for instance, revolves mainly around a perceived normative dilemma embedded in the Charter. As the Carnegie Commission puts it: 'The contradiction between respecting national sovereignty and the moral and ethical imperative to stop slaughter within states is real and difficult to resolve.'[7] Examples of such normative difficulties can be multiplied. The principle of peaceful settlement of conflicts, for instance, may be at odds with human rights and self-determination.[8] It is possible to argue that even peace and security may sometimes contradict each other.[9]

To complicate matters, there are common and enduring 'beliefs' about the UN, the accuracy of which must be questioned in the light of contemporary developments. A classical example is the idea that the UN is 'of, by, and for governments'.[10] Another example, which is closely connected and perhaps more vital, is the view that the UN's primary objective is maintenance of *international* peace and security. No doubt, these beliefs find some support from the wording of the Charter. However, does the UN's actual practice not raise serious doubts about their correctness? The organisation's active involvement in intra-state conflicts is a case in point. It may well be the case that international players are redefining the UN's 'normative basis', that is its ideal(ised) objectives, functions and authority – all three of which are key analytical concepts utilised in this study – without touching the wording of the Charter.[11] In the process, the impact of some crucial Charter principles, among them state sovereignty, human rights,[12] and socio-economic development, may be changing.

Still more significant are the wider implications of such possible change for 'governance' and for the UN's role in it.[13] Originally the UN was devised by victorious states to regulate 'inter-national' behaviour following World War II. In that sense, the organisation was intended to play a regulatory role in inter-governmental governance, with a special emphasis on peace and security. The Charter embodies states' scepticism as to potential UN intrusion into governance *within* their internal sphere. Perhaps the best indicator of such scepticism is the principle of UN non-intervention, which finds its expression in Article 2.7.[14] It may well be the case, though, that the UN is increasingly allowed, encouraged and indeed expected to play an active role in governance within what has been hitherto considered the exclusive political domain of states. The changes that have taken place over time in the UN's actual practice *vis-à-vis* intra-state conflicts are certainly significant enough to provoke interest in whether these are indicative of a corresponding normative shift, involving the UN's overall role in world politics.

Addressing normativity

What the UN is and is not, what it does and does not do, are at some level deeply connected with the international community's collective expectations of and prescriptions for the UN. The world organisation's involvement in intra-state conflicts, as epitomised by its intra-state peacekeeping activities, cannot be adequately understood if treated in isolation from the normative domain. It is for this reason that this study persistently addresses the issue of normativity; and it is in this sense that the study engages in 'normative research'. This conscious choice needs a brief elaboration.

Normativity, with its multiple meanings and implications, has already become a central concern in the study of international relations. The terms 'norm' and 'normative' suffer, of course, from non-consensual usage by social scientists. The distinctions to be drawn between norm/normative and such related concepts as value/value judgement, morality/moral, ethics/ethical, are, to say the least, blurred in the literature. Definitional usage generally seems to lack a clear conceptualisation. This is perhaps the first difficulty which besets any exploration of the normative domain. The difficulty is compounded by the fact that 'norm' and 'normative' are also frequently used in combination with related terms, some of which have already been mentioned. We find, for example, such expressions as 'normative rules', 'ethical norms', and 'normative principles'. Despite their solid place and frequent application in social scientific discourse, norm and normative seem to be used in academic writings with much the same flexible, broad and multiple connotations we encounter in everyday language.[15]

Apart from the absence of consensual definition and conceptualisation, there is also the added difficulty posed by the expression 'normative research/ theory'. This difficulty does not necessarily arise from the definition or meaning of norm and normative. Normative theory seems to refer to three distinct types of intellectual activity, which are not, however, always or entirely mutually exclusive. The first type involves notions of what should be done. We may consider this to be the classical concern of normative theory, which is usually associated with *normative ethics*, that is the traditional subdiscipline of moral philosophy, which aims to guide actions.[16] Here the act of normative theorising is equated with thinking systematically about what is good and what is bad, what is right and what is wrong. Consequently the theorist arrives at, or at least hopes to arrive at, a set of standards which could and should be applied to distinguish between that which is right/good and that which is wrong/bad.[17] It is this classical understanding of normative theory which presents itself as the opposite of 'empirical' theory. Normative theorising in this sense deals with the 'ideal', whereas empirical theorising is interested in the 'real'.[18] While the use of the term *classical* or *traditional* in social science may implicitly suggest that the approach has somehow been transcended or undermined,[19] the classical understanding of normative theory is not necessarily outmoded. Many contemporary works still have substantial elements which owe much to this classical understanding – though they may adopt, for example, a postmodernist stance.[20]

The second type involves enquiry into norms which either already exist or are in the making. According to this understanding, the task of normative theory is to discover, describe and explain empirically the communal[21] standards and perceptions as to right and wrong. The task is, further, to explain the relationship between norms and other phenomena. How discovery, description and explanation of norms (as in the case of other 'facts' or 'phenomena') can best proceed is a different and ongoing debate between differing epistemological and methodological approaches to science. This second understanding of normative theory has no doubt some affinity with the positivist school of thought. Put differently, if a positivist were interested in norms and claimed to be conducting normative research, it is this second understanding of normative theory that he would have in mind. A multitude of such studies are to be found in the contemporary literature.[22]

The last type of intellectual activity designated by 'normative theory' pertains to the very nature of the act of theorising and research. In recent years many scholars have prefaced their studies by explicitly admitting the impossibility of non-normative theorising, even though their preference might be to remain in one or other of the two traditions outlined above.[23] Accordingly, the normativity of a theory does not stem merely from the *intention* (as in the first understanding) or *object* (as in the second understanding) of analysis, but also from the inescapable fact that the very act of theorising/research itself involves normative approaches, reflections and judgements. The theorists as well as the communities around which the act of theorising takes place are not immune to norms and normative influences. Research activity (including observation of facts, perception of 'reality', general reasoning, mental processing of data, and even the formulation of descriptive statements) is itself largely shaped by the normative influences to which the researcher is subject.[24] Therefore, explicit normative theory[25] is that in which the theorist problematises the normative nature of any theorising and seeks to offer a methodology capable of overcoming this difficulty.[26]

The ontological and epistemological tensions between the second and third approaches to normativity are apparent. Is there such an 'objective' reality as a norm? If norms exist only 'intersubjectively' – that is to say, not independently of one's mind – how can one adopt an epistemological position that is almost positivist in orientation?[27] Proponents of both approaches are today very much aware of the criticisms levelled against their stance.[28] The issue is far from resolved.

This study is concerned to explore the 'normative' domain. The normative dimension of the study addresses neither its purpose nor its nature. Rather, it addresses the *object* of analysis, namely the development and impact of norms in the international realm. The crucial point here is that we are examining *international actors*' value preferences (crudely put: the object) in a conceptual framework that *we ourselves* have drawn in accordance with our own research interests and approach to reality (our perception of object). This study, then, adopts the second approach outlined above – without necessarily embracing the positivist stance with all its wider ontological implications – and at the same time situates itself consciously in the third approach.[29]

In analytical terms, we are concerned to identify the perceptions and normative preferences of relevant players as to what *should* be the UN's objectives, functions and authority *vis-à-vis* intra-state conflicts. The word 'should' points to the expectations that key players have of the UN, and in that sense expresses the ideals of the UN. Discussions at the UN usually involve two types of 'should'. While the first type relates to ideals, regardless of practical constraints,[30] the second type takes into account a range of practical constraints. It should be apparent that the two are not always or easily separable. Nevertheless, the study tries to distinguish between the two types as carefully as possible, and to focus on the former rather than the latter.[31]

Norms, interests, time and governance

International norms, peacekeeping, intra-state conflicts, and the UN have each been the subject of a great number of studies.[32] A brief examination of the literature that combines these broad areas of research points to a growing interest in human rights, humanitarianism and the erosion of the sovereignty principle, especially during the 1990s. Much research has been done on whether an international norm of humanitarian intervention is emerging under the UN's auspices.[33] Change in international norms, in this sense, has been central to post-Cold War studies, though its wider implications for the UN and for the international value system have not been adequately explored. Perhaps as a consequence, the analysis of the *dynamics* underlying the triangular relationship between the UN, intra-state conflicts and relevant actors' conceptions of governance is largely absent in the literature. Two crucial factors are at play here: the nexus between interests and normative preferences, and the time dimension.

The role that is envisaged for the UN in governance can be usefully considered a function of the complex interplay between interests and norms.[34] It is especially in this respect that this study hopes to make an advance on our understanding of the UN's evolution. It problematises relevant actors' expectations of and prescriptions for the UN in relation to intra-state conflicts. More specifically it seeks to establish how these actors interpret or at least relate to those few crucial norms that may be said to constitute the backbone of the UN's legal/normative texture. More explicitly still, the study contextualises actors' value preferences in relation to significant Charter principles, as reflected in both rhetoric and practice, and as they emerge in the context of the structural political change over time.[35] In other words, throughout the study particular attention is devoted to the identification of the interests and normative preferences of relevant actors that have constituted complex, hardly separable, wholes in the specified time periods. The way such interest-norm complexes[36] have impacted on the UN's normative approach to intra-state conflicts specifically, and on the organisation's possibly evolving role in global governance generally, will shed light on the dynamics and patterns of change.

Another feature of this study is its sensitivity to a factor that is crucial to understanding any social institution – namely time.[37] International relations as a field of enquiry has for too long underestimated the centrality and implications of the time dimension. On the one hand, the discipline has been full of ahistorical accounts.[38] On the other hand, it has suffered from what might be called a 'vulgar mode' of historicism.[39] This study ranges over a timespan that is relatively short in the lifetime of any institution (i.e. not more than three decades), and attempts to identify the continuities and discontinuities between two sets of interest-norm complexes in the international realm, one corresponding to the early 1960s, the other to the early 1990s. If profound normative changes have indeed occurred in such a relatively short period, a careful account of the political and structural dynamics at work may shed useful light on the recent past and point to instructive implications for the future.

The UN's activities in the Congo or its 'transitional authority' in West Irian were radical moves once. Some three decades later came the Namibia operation, which would have been unimaginable even a few years earlier. El Salvador, Cambodia, and Bosnia, to cite but a few, were each more 'daring' than the missions that came before. Yet the extent and modalities of UN involvement in intra-state conflicts, and ultimately governance, have proved ever more remarkable. What exactly was the UN trying to do in Kosovo or East Timor in the late 1990s? Is the UN's concern in those and similar places exclusively over international peace and security? More to the point, the dynamic that facilitates and limits this apparent change in the scope of UN activity is not amenable to easy description, let alone explanation. International norms and accompanying interests may well be giving rise to evolving modes of governance. The contemporary world may be in the process of creating new forms of governance, in which the UN is only one, though uniquely placed, actor.

The UN's intra-state peacekeeping serves our research purposes as a useful and powerful symbol for overall UN involvement in intra-state conflicts. Our focus is on those intra-state conflicts where the UN's objectives, functions and authority were partially if not wholly embodied in and delegated to UN peacekeeping operations. The normative views expressed or implied by different actors on the eve and in the wake of UN peacekeeping form the focal point of our enquiry. Setting up a peacekeeping operation frequently attracts normative judgements on UN peacekeeping *per se*. To the extent possible, we need to distinguish between attitudes to the UN in general and attitudes to UN peacekeeping in particular. Consequently, this study takes into account actors' views on what the objectives, functions and authority of UN peacekeeping should be in the context of intra-state conflicts, and attempts to discern the implications of these expectations for the role ascribed to the UN and for the broader normative context within which that role is (re)defined.

Two points that arise out of the preceding introduction need to be clearly underlined. First, while dealing with intra-state peacekeeping, this study puts the emphasis more on 'intra-state' than on 'peacekeeping', because what begs the explanations we are seeking is the UN's systematised active involvement in intra-state conflicts rather than the tools used for that purpose. Secondly, the emphasis of the study will be on the peacekeeping *environments* in which field operations take shape, and not on field operations *per se*. 'Peacekeeping environments', as understood here, encompass as much the global political setting as the specific conditions prevailing on the ground. Peacekeeping environment refers not only to the geographical or territorial space in which UN and non-UN field operations are conducted, but also to the political space within which normative views are expressed. It refers to the larger milieu within which international actors present, exchange and negotiate their overall value preferences and their views on the UN's relationship to these value preferences. The study is interested, then, in characterising the normative preferences that UN peacekeeping environments reveal, and the UN's prescribed role in relation to this normative framework.

Roland Paris has correctly identified a prevailing problem in the peace-keeping literature: 'the study of peace operations has generated a great deal of microtheory but very little macrotheory'.[40] If we are to make sense of the 'very existence' of UN peace operations, and of its relevance to governance, there is a need to marry the peacekeeping research with the more theoretical body of literature. Though ours is not primarily a study of international relations theory, it draws on theoretical insights, and hopes to contribute to the bridg-ing of the gap between formal theory and its applicability to empirical research. Making use of the conceptual tools provided by the 'historical struc-tural' approach, as will be introduced in Chapter 2, we set out to gain a better understanding of the UN's organisational role in world politics. We place particular emphasis on global structural changes and their impact on collec-tive expectations of the UN as an actor (and ultimately as an institution).

Chapter 2 not only clarifies our theoretical position, but also elaborates on the key concepts used in the study and develops the overall analytical frame-work. Chapter 3 establishes, then, the historical structural context within which the UN's response to intra-state conflicts took shape. The purpose of this scene-setting chapter is to convey something of the enormous complexity of the political conditions within which violent conflict, and the UN's response to it, emerge. Without adequate visualisation of the structural landscape, the normative discussion on which we are about to embark would lose much of its explanatory utility. Against this backdrop, Chapter 4 deals specifically with the range of cases where the UN was actively involved in intra-state conflicts to the point of conducting a peacekeeping operation. Here UN peacekeeping in intra-state conflicts is situated within the broader political context. Attention is focused on the normative basis of such UN involvement, and on its relationship with the political changes discussed in the historical structural context chapter.

In the subsequent four chapters we further develop the argument by concentrating on four comprehensive case studies: the Congo, Cyprus, Angola and Cambodia. We explore the interest-norm complexes within which those cases were handled by the UN. The aim is to demonstrate in detail how relevant actors' normative preferences, which were closely entwined with their political calculations in the wake of existing structural configurations, were resolved in specific peacekeeping environments where the UN was especially active in addressing intra-state conflicts.

NOTES

1 See D. Bratt, 'Peace over justice: developing a framework for UN peacekeeping operations in internal conflicts', *Global Governance: A Review of Multilateralism and International Organizations*, 5:1 (Jan–Mar 1999), 63; and A. C. Arend and R. J. Beck, 'International law and the recourse to force: a shift in paradigms', in C. Ku and P. F. Diehl, *International Law: Classic and Contemporary Readings* (Boulder, CO: Lynne Rienner, 1998), p. 328.

2 Perhaps the major state-centric norm is state sovereignty, which is closely connected with the principles of territorial integrity, political independence, non-intervention and self-help. Stedman considers the last two as the 'fundamental rules of sovereignty': see S. J. Stedman, *International Actors and Internal Conflicts* (New York: Rockefeller Brothers Fund, 1999), p. 21.

3 Knight notes that the principles of state sovereignty and non-intervention are embodied in Articles 2(4) and 2(7), while the principles of human rights protection and humanitarian intervention are incorporated to the preamble, Articles 1(3), 13, 55, 56, 62, 68, and 76(c): see W. A. Knight, 'The changing human rights regime, state sovereignty, and Article 2(7) in the post-Cold War era', in A. Williams *et al.*, *Article 2(7) Revisited*, available online at www.brown.edu/Departments/ACUNS/New_publications/2.7/2.7.TOC.shtml (16 December 2000).

4 Damrosch speaks of two 'clusters of values' which underpin the Charter: 'state system values' and 'human rights values': see L. F. Damrosch, 'Introduction', in L. F. Damrosch (ed.), *Enforcing Restraint: Collective Intervention in Internal Conflicts* (New York: Council on Foreign Relations Press, 1993), pp. 8, 93.

5 A. Roberts and B. Kingsbury, *Presiding Over a Divided World: Changing UN Roles, 1945–1993* (Boulder, CO: Lynne Rienner, 1994; IPA Occasional Paper Series), pp. 61–2.

6 See also A. Eknes, 'The United Nations and intra-state conflicts', in M. Heiberg (ed.), *Subduing Sovereignty: Sovereignty and the Right to Intervene* (London: Pinter, 1994), p. 100.

7 Carnegie Commission on Preventing Deadly Conflict, *Final Report* (Washington, DC: Carnegie Corporation of New York, 1997), p. 136.

8 Roberts and Kingsbury, *Presiding Over a Divided World*, pp. 61–2.
9 For some actors, requirements of peace and requirements of security may not be the same. One needs only to recall the famous motto of the former Israeli Prime Minister Netanyahu: 'peace *with* security'.
10 R. Thakur, 'Human rights: Amnesty International and the United Nations', *Journal of Peace Research*, 31:2 (1994), 143.
11 The Charter as well as the UN's rules of procedure may even be 'eroding' by actual practice: see Y. Z. Blum, *Eroding the United Nations Charter* (Dordrecht: Martinus Nijhoff, 1993).
12 'Human rights', as understood here, are inseparable from 'humanitarianism'. The technical (and, admittedly, often practical) distinction between the 'human rights law' and 'humanitarian law' is not relevant to our problematisation. In any case, the two bodies of law are converging at an increasing pace.
13 'Governance' can be loosely defined as 'the sum of the many ways individuals and institutions, public and private, manage their common affairs': see Commission on Global Governance, *Our Global Neighbourhood: The Report of the Commission on Global Governance* (New York: Oxford University Press, 1995), p. 2.
14 Article 2.7. specifically relates to *the UN*'s non-intervention in states' internal affairs: 'Nothing contained in the present Charter shall authorize the United Nations to intervene in matters which are essentially within the domestic jurisdiction of any state or shall require the Members to submit such matters to settlement under the present Charter; but this principle shall not prejudice the application of enforcement measures under Chapter VII.'
15 While adherence to everyday connotations poses an 'analytical' difficulty, this is not necessarily or always detrimental to academic endeavour. 'Understanding' (*Verstehen*) and tackling the issue of normativity may not be possible without adopting the common social/communal expressions of it. Our notions of norm and normativity in this study will be clarified in Chapter 2. Suffice it to say at this stage that we do not find it useful to introduce artificial distinctions between three terms which are used in this study more or less synonymously: 'norm', 'principle' and 'value'. Nevertheless, with reference to Milton Rokeach's classical definition of value as 'an enduring belief that a specific mode of conduct or end-state of existence is personally or socially preferable to an opposite or converse mode of conduct or end-state of existence' (M. Rokeach, *The Nature of Human Values*, New York: The Free Press, 1973, p. 5), we need to note that our usage of 'norm' and 'principle' tends to point to *behavioural prescriptions* involving 'specific modes of conduct'. 'Value', on the other hand, relates more to preferred 'end-states of existence', the verbal expressions of which need not involve proper 'ought to' sentences. To give an example, the expression 'state sovereignty' would perhaps qualify more as a value, whereas 'State sovereignty should be protected' would indicate a corresponding norm/principle.
16 P. Singer, *Ethics* (Oxford: Oxford University Press, 1994), pp. 4, 10.
17 Leading examples in the last thirty years include C. R. Beitz, *Political Theory and International Relations* (Princeton, NJ: Princeton University Press, 1979); S. Hoffman, *Duties Beyond Borders: On The Limits and Possibilities of Ethical International Politics* (Syracuse, NY: Syracuse University Press, 1981); J. Rawls, *A Theory of Justice* (London: Oxford University Press, 1973); H. Shue, *Basic Rights: Subsistence, Affluence, and U.S. Foreign Policy* (Princeton, NJ: Princeton University Press, 1980). Contemporary theoretical approaches in international relations, including neoliberalism and constructivism, have not 'engaged in normative thinking *per se*'. They have not 'addressed questions of the ought and should variety': see R. Shapcott, 'Solidarism and

after: global governance, international society and the normative "turn" in international relations', *Pacifica Review*, 12:2 (June 2000), 154–5.

18 At the roots of this understanding lies the presumed distinction between 'factual' and 'normative' statements. For useful discussions see F. M. Frohock, *Normative Political Theory* (Englewood Cliffs: Prentice Hall, 1974), pp. 1–43; and W. D. Hudson (ed.), *The Is-Ought Question: A Collection of Papers on the Central Problems in Moral Philosophy* (London: Macmillan, 1969).

19 Well-known examples in international relations are 'classical' realism and liberalism as opposed to neo-realism and neo-liberalism.

20 An example is C. Douzinas and R. Warrington, *Justice Miscarried: Ethics and Aesthetics in Law* (New York: Harvester Wheatsheaf, 1994). While postmodernism is usually presented as being irreconcilable with ethics, Bauman notes that as a result of systematic inquiries to the postmodern condition, 'the chances of "moralization" of social life may – who knows? – be enhanced': see Z. Bauman, *Postmodern Ethics* (Oxford: Blackwell, 1993), p. 3.

21 The community in question may be the 'international community' as well.

22 It would not be incorrect to argue that a major part of contemporary normative research in international relations, ranging from the 1980s regime theories to the latest constructivist programme, is based on this conception. This approach is both exemplified and quickly surveyed in M. Finnemore and K. Sikkink, 'International norm dynamics and political change', in P. J. Katzenstein, R. O. Keohane and S. D. Krasner (eds), *Exploration and Contestation in the Study of World Politics* (Cambridge, MA: MIT Press, 1999), pp. 247–77. While the burgeoning norm-sensitive constructivist research agenda in international relations theory increasingly draws on interpretivist insights, there are notable arguments that it is in fact based on a positivist epistemology: see D. Dessler, 'Constructivism within a positivist social science', *Review of International Studies*, 25 (1999), 123–37.

23 An example is Richard Price's article 'Moral norms in world politics', *Pacifica Review*, 9:1 (1997), 45–72.

24 The origins of this approach can be traced back to Max Weber, Wilhelm Dilthey and Ludwig Wittgenstein. This idea was systematically introduced into social theory by Peter Winch in *The Idea of A Social Science*: see M. Frost, *Toward a Normative Theory of International Relations: A Critical Analysis of the Philosophical and Methodological Assumptions in the Discipline with Proposals toward A Substantive Normative Theory*, (Cambridge: Cambridge University Press, 1986), ch. 1.

25 Since this third understanding excludes the possibility of non-normative theory, the most proper distinction in this understanding could perhaps be only between 'explicit' and 'implicit' normative theories, where the latter refers to theories which are either not aware of their own normative nature or do not deal with the problem of normativity.

26 Depending on one's normative approach, of course, this may be perceived and presented as a 'richness in our understanding of the world', for example, rather than a 'difficulty to overcome'.

27 Some implications for the study of international organisation are hinted at by F. Kratochwil and J. G. Ruggie in their seminal article 'International organization: a state of the art on an art of the state', reproduced in F. Kratochwil and E. D. Mansfield, *International Organization: A Reader* (New York: HarperCollins College Publishers, 1994).

28 For a sophisticated and relatively recent defence of what we call 'the second approach', see M. Nicholson, *Causes and Consequences in International Relations: A Conceptual Study* (London: Pinter, 1996).

29 As such, this study has a degree of affinity to 'critical approaches'.

30 These are perhaps better captured in 'ought to' formulations.

31 Boutros-Ghali's following statement is a very good example encapsulating both types of 'should': 'I am firmly committed to the concept of peace enforcement. It is essential if we are to strengthen international peace and security. But there is a new reality: member states are not ready for it. I must accept reality. I also must continue to give you my view'; cited in J. N. Rosenau and M. Durfee, *Thinking Theory Thoroughly: Coherent Approaches to An Incoherent World* (Boulder, CO: Westview Press, 1995), p. 117.

32 The following studies provide very useful literature reviews. On normative research in international relations, see G. A. Raymond, 'Problems and prospects in the study of international norms', *Mershon International Studies Review* 41 (1997), 205–45. On peacekeeping, see C. Collins and T. G. Weiss, *An Overview and Assessment of 1989–1996 Peace Operations Publications* (Providence, RI: The Thomas J. Watson Jr. Institute for International Studies, Occasional Paper No. 28). On intra-state conflicts, see D. Balch-Lindsay and A. J. Enterline, 'Killing time: the world politics of civil war duration, 1820–1992', *International Studies Quarterly*, 44 (2000), 615–42; and C. Peck, *Sustainable Peace: The Role of the UN and Regional Organizations in Preventing Conflict* (Lanham, MD: Rowman & Littlefield, 1998), pp. 25–44.

33 Examples include J. Chopra and T. G. Weiss, 'Sovereignty is no longer sacrosanct: codifying humanitarian intervention', *Ethics and International Affairs*, 6 (1992); T. B. Knudsen, 'Humanitarian intervention revisited: post-Cold War responses to classical problems', *International Peacekeeping*, 3:4 (Winter 1996); P. Laberge, 'Humanitarian intervention: three ethical positions', *Ethics and International Affairs*, 9 (1995); O. Ramsbotham, 'Humanitarian intervention 1990–5: a need to reconceptualize?', *Review of International Studies*, 23 (1997); A. Roberts, 'Humanitarian war: military intervention and human rights', *International Affairs*, 69:3 (1993); and the special issue of the *International Journal* on Humane Intervention: 48:4 (Autumn 1993).

34 This interplay attracts systematic attention at a growing rate from a group of international relations scholars ('constructivists') who put greater emphasis on the role played by norms. A representative volume is P. J. Katzenstein (ed.), *The Culture of National Security: Norms and Identity in World Politics* (New York: Columbia University Press, 1996).

35 In his discussion of human rights, Ruggie points to the importance of interests and context: 'Human rights *are* more than a mere rationalization of structures of power. Yet their international normative status remains closely dependent upon the projection of power, the defense of interests, and the nature of political community existing among states.': see J. G. Ruggie, 'Human rights and the future international community', *Daedalus*, 12:4 (Fall 1983), 99–100.

36 This is not an analytical category that we propose to use in this study, but a phrase that usefully designates the nexus in question.

37 There are relatively few analytical studies which 'problematise' change in the context of the UN. Those which attempt to discern the dynamics of and realistic possibilities for change are even rarer. Notable examples include M. Bertrand, 'The process of change in an interdependent world and possible institutional consequences', in J. P. Renninger (ed.), *The Future Role of the United Nations in an Interdependent World* (Dordrecht: Martinus Nijhoff, 1989), pp. 39–70; W. A. Knight, *A Changing United Nations: Multilateral Evolution and the Quest for Global Governance* (Houndmills: Palgrave, 2000); Roberts and Kingsbury, *Presiding Over a Divided World*.

38 Perhaps the classical example is the ahistorical analytical stance taken by the neorealist school.

39 'Historicism', as popularised and criticised by Popper, refers to the deterministic idea that there must be fixed laws of historical progress: see K. R. Popper, *The Poverty of Historicism*, 2nd edn, (London: Routledge and K. Paul, 1960). The 'modernisation school' of the 1950s and 1960s is a good example for this tendency in political theory.
40 See R. Paris, 'Broadening the study of peace operations', *International Studies Review*, 2:3 (Fall 2000), 30–2.

2

Rethinking the UN through intra-state peacekeeping: the analytical framework

U NTIL THE LATE 1980s, international relations theory had a rather crude attitude towards normative research in general. Although, after decades of neglect, norms had finally found their way into mainstream international relations through the study of institutions in the early 1980s, the realist and liberal 'paradigms' of international relations, and for that matter, their 'neo' variants, pursued their rival research programmes on strikingly similar premises. They shared the same assumptions as they engaged in empirical research, and, as a by-product, either continuously re-created the same 'reality' in their findings[1] or were entrapped by shared dilemmas.[2] They proceeded, as Keohane aptly puts it, on a number of key 'rationalistic' assumptions, including rationality on the part of actors (mainly states), scarcity of and competition over resources, exchange theory, and transaction-cost arguments.[3] These epistemological, and ultimately ontological, premises have been increasingly challenged by what Keohane loosely calls 'reflective' approaches, the shared characteristic of which can be said to include their rejection of fixed identities and preferences.[4]

In a highly original study of the UN's evolution, Knight draws on Keohane's rationalistic-reflective distinction (reworded slightly as 'rationalist' and 'reflectivist'), and utilises a particular analytical approach which he implicitly associates with the reflectivist camp, namely Cox's 'historical structural' approach.[5] While he sets out to 'understand and explain multilateral evolution and the related question global governance' through the method of historical structures,[6] his study has also an explicit prescriptive quality. It places the UN as an organisation in the broader context of the evolution of multilateralism (understood as a deep organising principle which may have several concrete manifestations – institutions), pays particular attention to the social processes that constitute and tend to transform world orders, examines the UN's responses to exogenous and endogenous pressures, and concludes that the UN is capable of changing.[7] Viewed from the historical structural perspective, 'the UN system can be conceived as evolving and changing, not in any predetermined direction but according to the demands and challenges of international society at any given time'.[8]

Knight's research is noteworthy in that it seeks to apply a highly sophisticated body of theoretical literature to the study of multilateral institutions through an examination of the UN. Especially important for us is his application of historical structural 'insights' to the study of institutional evolution, with a constant focus on social forces and pressures that impact on the UN's organisational change.[9] The notion of 'historical structures', as we shall demonstrate below, provides a particularly promising avenue to investigate the normative connection between the UN and intra-state conflicts. While this notion is utilised by Knight to explore possibilities, potentials and prospects in the evolution of multilateralism, it is not adequately applied to the analysis of past change. Rather it is heavily complemented, indeed occasionally substituted, by a semi-constructivist 'learning' approach, revolving around the UN's 'reflexive (non-purposive) adaptation' and 'planned (purposive) change' in response to pressures.[10] In other words, the nature of power configurations and of change is not adequately emphasised. The structural element as a constraint and facilitator is certainly taken into account. However, since the main preoccupation is to develop a reform agenda for the UN, voluntarist arguments are given more prominence. That is to say, the emphasis is put on the availability of the best possible options given the limitations. Equally importantly, change in actors' ideas, values, preferences *vis-à-vis* the UN – that is, the focal point of our study – is only tangential to Knight's purposes. While mindful of Knight's work, therefore, we propose to bring more of Cox's analytical model to the fore. This does not mean, however, that this study exemplifies a direct adoption and application of the historical structural method. Rather, it means that our approach to the meaning and implications of normative change draws on historical structural insights.

Exploring normative change with 'historical structures' in mind

In contrast to several other structuralist approaches, Cox conceives of structures as 'limited totalities' which do not incorporate everything, but rather represent a particular sphere of human activity in its historically located totality. A 'historical structure' (borrowed from Braudel) is merely a 'framework for action'[11] – though a considerably influential one – which consists of a particular configuration between material forces, ideas and institutions at a given moment in time. Such a triangular configuration, according to Cox, 'does not determine actions in any direct mechanical way but imposes pressures and constraints. Individuals and groups may move with the pressures or resist and oppose them, but they cannot ignore them.'[12] The relationship between the agency and structure, therefore, can be seen as 'open-ended' within limits. The relationship between the three corners of the triangle, that is, material capabilities, ideas and institutions is also open-ended in that the direction and extent of influence between these factors depend on the historical context within which the structure takes shape.

'Material capabilities', the first corner of the triangular structure, include dynamic productive capabilities (such as technology) as well as accumulated resources. They at least implicitly refer to 'interests' in the realist sense of the word. 'Ideas', the second corner, comprise not only intersubjective meanings and interpretations of the world, which can be seen as bonding individuals and groups, but also rival collective images of social order based on such separating characteristics as ethnicity and religion. Cox is less nuanced on the meaning of 'institutions',[13] but seems to refer to both types of institutions suggested by Keohane: general patterns of activity and specific exemplars of patterns of activity (including international organisations).[14]

Historical structure is an illuminating concept for our study in a number of respects. First, it is well suited to examine the relationship between norms, interests, and the UN, which arguably correspond or, at least, directly relate to the three corners of historical structure. This point will be further clarified during our discussion of the UN Charter below. Secondly, the idea that there are *multiple* historical structures[15] which succeed each other by a process of structural transformation provides useful insight for the comparison envisaged between the early 1960s and the early 1990s. Thirdly, the notion that cohesion and contradiction are both inherent in historical structures sheds light on the countervailing tendencies that emerge and grow in the context of historically situated power configurations, yet manage to bring about the end of those structures in favour of new ones. Finally, the notions of hegemonic versus counterhegemonic tendencies and hegemonic versus non-hegemonic structures illuminate changes in actors' thought patterns, including their general value preferences and their specific normative responses to institutions.

Cox's notion of hegemony (borrowed from Gramsci) is more sophisticated than the state-driven hegemony as can be found, for instance, in hegemonic stability theory. Hegemony, as used by Cox, refers to:

> a coherent conjunction or fit between a configuration of material power, the prevalent collective image of world order (including certain norms) and a set of institutions which administer the order with a certain semblance of universality (that is, not just as the overt instruments of a particular state's dominance) . . . The notion of hegemony as a fit between power, ideas, and institutions makes it possible to deal with some of the problems in the theory of state dominance as the necessary condition for a stable international order; it allows for lags and leads in hegemony. For example, so appealing was the nostalgia for the nineteenth

century hegemony that the ideological dimension of the *pax britannica* flourished long after the power configuration that supported it had vanished.[16]

In other words, although power configurations may well be at the root of hegemony, their influence is exercised by the particular historical structure to which they are incorporated. By implication, then, the *direct* impact of a state or group of states on the rest of the world ceases to be a requirement for hegemony to last. What is more, any one of the three corners of a given historical structure may be more enduring than the other two: this suggests itself as a particularly interesting analytical tool in understanding potential discrepancies (lags and leads) between interests, norms and institutional practices. A given institution, to give an example, may persist over time and find its way into the next historical structure, even if the interests and norms to which it was originally tied have disappeared.

Our analysis will benefit from the historical structural approach, but it should be re-emphasised that our normative enquiry is by no means intended as a study of international relations theory. Reference to theory is being made here primarily in three ways, to further three specific purposes. In the first place, it is used to explore the nature of the postulated normative change and grasp its wider meaning. Secondly, theory is used to complement and illuminate the empirical aspects of our study. Our overviews and detailed case studies will gain explanatory utility to the extent that they interact with theoretical insights. Thirdly, we will use theory to reflect conceptually on the trends that emerge from our study. In other words, theory will help us to situate the wider implications of our findings. With our theoretical premises clarified, we shall now introduce the main concepts that inform this study.

Drawing the boundaries of the normative domain

'Norms', as applied in this study, refer to 'collective expectations about proper behaviour for a given identity'.[17] But exactly whose expectations of whom do we have in mind? Normative international relations theory has generally put the emphasis on collective expectations that states have of each other. It is central to our argument that, conceptually, certain norms may pertain to a single, unique actor, for it is perfectly possible that a 'given identity' may belong to no one but a unique player.[18] In its various capacities as forum, instrument and actor in its own right, the UN is a unique entity mirroring (but also influencing) the political and normative processes in the entire international community. This study focuses on the expectations which relevant actors have of the UN in relation to intra-state conflicts as can be discerned by examining peacekeeping environments.[19]

The 'UN' is used in this study to refer to any actor who has the capacity,

17

stemming from the Charter or from a peacekeeping mandate, to take decisions and actions (at the political, strategic, operational or tactical level, as appropriate)[20] on behalf of the United Nations. The UN as defined encompasses a great many actors including the Security Council and the General Assembly at the top of the hierarchy, through to the Secretary-General and his Special Representatives, all the way down to a peacekeeper or a field officer. Depending on the case, the UN may also include representatives of the subsidiary bodies and the wider UN system (e.g. the United Nations High Commissioner for Refugees (UNHCR), the United Nations Development Programme (UNDP) or the World Health Organization (WHO)), provided that they are relevant to the mission mandated by the deliberative bodies.

Thus far we have referred more than once to the normative expectations by 'relevant actors' of the UN. What makes an actor 'relevant'? Simply put, any attribute of an actor (e.g. aims, interests, power, history, geography) which is likely to make it influential, directly or indirectly, in shaping the UN's involvement in a given intra-state conflict. Particularly 'relevant' from this perspective are three principal constituents of the UN itself: the Security Council, the General Assembly and the Secretariat. While each of these constituents is important in its collective capacity, the Permanent Five in the Security Council, influential permanent or *ad hoc* coalitions in the General Assembly, and the Secretary-General clearly stand out as deserving of closer scrutiny. These actors have obvious and substantial bearing on the UN's objectives, functions and authority *vis-à-vis* intra-state conflicts. This study will therefore systematically focus on all these actors, though, depending on the case, one may deserve more attention than another.

It is nevertheless possible to identify other actors who may be said to exercise lesser but none the less significant influence. The following actors will be taken into account to the extent that they prove influential in shaping the UN's response to a given intra-state conflict: first, states as represented by their governments; secondly, inter-governmental organisations (IGOs) with global or regional focus and membership; thirdly, the members of the wider 'UN system', which are frequently active in peacekeeping environments; fourthly, a variety of transnational actors, including several non-governmental organisations (NGOs)[21] and media organisations; finally, internal parties to violent conflicts.

Over and above the Permanent Five, there may be reason to examine the role of a number of other states. Those states which are most directly affected by a given intra-state conflict would be particularly relevant, for they would be likely to press for a specific course of UN action. Those which supply personnel for a given UN peacekeeping operation would also require attention, since they could exert influence both in the peacekeeping theatre and on the floor of the General Assembly. Regional IGOs almost always express opinions as to

18

how intra-state conflicts in their respective regions should be handled and what role the UN should play. In addition, such inter-/trans-national players as the UNHCR,[22] the WHO[23] and CARE International[24] frequently become involved in environments of intra-state conflict, express normative preferences and embody expectations of the UN. The media may deserve particular attention. The 'CNN factor' has now become part of the commonplace explanation of the US involvement in Somalia.[25] As for the internal parties to a conflict, their views as to the UN's role prove crucial in shaping or changing international prescriptions in certain peacekeeping environments. The study will, therefore, attempt to take into account the role of a wide array of actors to the extent that they exercise discernible influence in the conflicts under consideration.

Normativity centred around the UN Charter

In this study, we are particularly interested in how potentially incompatible Charter principles are resolved by relevant actors, and how this resolution reflects on their prescriptions for the UN. Whether this resolution undergoes periodic change – presumably in response to changing circumstances – is another crucial matter deserving of attention. In other words, the 'normative', for our purposes, refers primarily to the express purposes and principles enshrined in the Charter and interpreted by relevant actors. To make the scope of this study clearer, it is worth re-emphasising that the domain of the 'normative' neither begins nor ends with the Charter. Even within the relatively limited terrain of international politics, norms are not confined to those enunciated in the Charter. Such aims as the 'preservation of the society of states' or the 'maintenance of balance of power', for instance, have also been proposed as international norms.[26] To the extent that international actors consider the achievement of such aims as contributing to the international common good, those principles may indeed be regarded as constituting part of the normative domain of international politics. The approach we adopt here is deliberately confined to the principles explicitly pertaining to the functioning of the UN system, not least because they provide a common discourse within which international actors express and even negotiate their value preferences.[27]

The Charter has hardly changed since the inception of the UN.[28] As the 'constitutional' foundation of the UN system, it enshrines several general prescriptive guidelines which each member of the organisation – by virtue of signing and ratifying the Charter – has accepted to follow. While the Charter entails certain expectations *by* member states *of* each other, it also provides the prescriptive basis for actions by each principal organ, subsidiary body or affiliated agency within the UN system. Hence, it lays out the general standards for judging the acts and actions attributable to the UN as an actor. The Charter, then, can be considered as the overall prescriptive framework which a significant number of key actors have explicitly embraced.[29]

One particularly important feature of the Charter is that it can be considered as the meeting point of 'ideas' and 'institution' – that is, two of the three corners in a historical structure. The Charter reflects a set of ideas, values and preferences that prevailed in the international community at a particular moment in time. To be more precise, the ideas that are introduced into the Charter (that are constitutive of the Charter) necessarily derived from those which were in circulation at the time of the UN's creation. The Charter itself, however, is the embodiment or, to be more precise, the institutionalisation, of those ideas. The UN, by virtue of its Charter, is an institution, in that it 'involves persistent and connected sets of rules that prescribe behaviour, roles, constrain activity, and shape expectations'.[30] The UN, furthermore, is the/an institution of a particular historical structure. The ideas/values and the power configuration in the international community at a particular historical juncture found their expression in a corresponding institution, that is, the Charter (which also gives life to the UN as an organisation and actor). It is with this notion in mind that we problematise the principles enshrined in the Charter.

The *problematique* of this study can be expressed in reference to a simplified model of historical structure. The institution (for our purposes: the Charter) has not changed over time. Yet, the interpretations of the Charter may well have changed. Put differently, a structural change may have taken place, with the institution lagging behind the material capabilities and ideas. The ideas, values and preferences of international actors (i.e. the 'ideational' corner of the triangle) may now be different from what they were in earlier periods. The international community may be relating to the Charter in a radically different way than before. Put still differently, actors' normative preferences may not correspond to the Charter the way they did in earlier periods, yet they would still need to be in close interaction with both the Charter and the new or evolving power configuration, since all of these would be part and parcel of a new strong, change-resistant, constraining factor: another historical structure.

The Charter reflects several international values, the most important of which is 'peace and security'. Our research is based on the premise that this principle is the least contested within the scope of the Charter. Not only does it figure prominently in the first two paragraphs of the Charter's first article,[31] but it is the overriding international value in the sense that virtually no actor then or since has questioned its desirability or even primacy. Whatever the UN does, it does it, at least in part, in order to protect and promote peace and security. But it would be interesting to know how relevant players problematise this overriding and uncontested value, especially in relation to other important principles in the Charter.

On close inspection it becomes evident that most principles scattered through the Charter cluster around three other basic values and are closely associated with them:[32] state sovereignty, human rights and socio-economic development. State sovereignty and human rights seem to be especially relevant to the formulation of the UN's response to intra-state conflicts. As such these two values deserve our systematic attention, though socio-economic development also needs to be taken into account to the extent that it is integrated into normative prescriptions for UN peacekeeping. How do international players resolve potential inconsistencies between these broadly conceived principles as they manifest themselves in intra-state conflicts? Which of these Charter values inform UN peacekeeping in intra-state conflicts, and to what extent? What are the collective expectations of and prescriptions for the UN that emerge in the process? These questions go right to the heart of the normative framework on which is based the definition or interpretation of the UN's role in intra-state conflicts.

Problematising UN peacekeeping in intra-state conflicts

Peacekeeping is only one of the possible modes of UN involvement in intra-state conflicts, but it has become the most visible and topical one. First we shall briefly introduce UN peacekeeping and problematise its application to intra-state conflicts, bearing in mind that our focus is not on peacekeeping *per se* but on peacekeeping environments in which actors' normative views are expressed.

The exact meaning of peacekeeping is open to debate. This is largely a definitional problem, as different notions of peacekeeping have gained currency at different times and places.[33] Different scholars and practitioners refer to different phenomena as peacekeeping.[34] The International Peace Academy defines peacekeeping as 'the prevention, containment, moderation and termination of hostilities between or within states through the medium of third-party intervention, organised and directed internationally, using multinational military, police, and civilian personnel to restore and maintain peace'.[35] This broad definition is useful at least in that it encompasses practically all of the activities which have been referred to as peacekeeping in various contexts.[36]

For our purposes it is unnecessary to elaborate on peacekeeping *per se*. We concentrate instead on a particular subset of peacekeeping, which occupies the central place among all peacekeeping activities: UN peacekeeping. Although the origins of peacekeeping can be found in the League of Nations experience, the term itself came properly into use only with the creation of a

21

UN-authorised mission in 1956,[37] and was formalised when the UN General Assembly established the Special Committee on Peacekeeping Operations[38] in February 1965 to deal with peacekeeping matters.[39]

UN peacekeeping: an ambiguous enterprise

The UN's peacekeeping doctrine, although relatively more developed, suffers nevertheless from the same definitional problems. To begin with, we find no mention of peacekeeping in the Charter.[40] One study maintains that the UN Mission for the Referendum in Western Sahara (MINURSO) had a peacekeeping component in addition to the other two components (i.e. civilian police and voter identification).[41] That study clearly reserves the term peacekeeping for deployment of military personnel in a given conflict. Today, however, UN operations consisting solely of unarmed civilian police forces are also considered peacekeeping: the UN Civilian Police Support Group (UNPSG) in Croatia's Prevlaka Peninsula is a good example. What is more, the Mission of the Representative of the Secretary-General in the Dominican Republic (DOMREP) back in the 1960s has long taken its place in the UN's semi-official list of peacekeeping operations, although it consisted of nothing more than a few observers.[42] So who are UN peacekeepers, and what kinds of tasks constitute peacekeeping in the context of the UN? It is partly this ambiguity which makes UN peacekeeping an especially relevant focal point for our research. The different – at times vastly different – notions of UN peacekeeping entertained by different actors make it possible to explore the complex normative framework within which their prescriptions for the UN take shape. The objectives, functions and authority assigned to the UN through peacekeeping are necessarily closely connected with actors' normative views.

UN peacekeeping was developed essentially as an *ad hoc* mechanism[43] to deal with threats to peace and security in the Cold War environment where the Charter's vision of collective security seemed unattainable. It resulted from the pragmatic approach by the UN's international civil servants who, despite the unfavourable political environment, wished the organisation to perform its basic function: maintenance of peace and security. It is against this background that the founding fathers of UN peacekeeping, Dag Hammarskjöld and his team, tried to develop guidelines within which this mechanism could safely operate, presumably in full accordance with Charter principles.

The most commonly suggested understanding of UN peacekeeping seems to have been derived from the Hammarskjöld–Pearson recipe[44] for UN peacekeeping in the 1950s.[45] This understanding of UN peacekeeping is premised upon five basic principles,[46] the exact meaning and implications of which have been continuously debated ever since they were first proposed. First, UN peacekeepers cannot be deployed without the consent of the parties to the conflict (principle of consent). Secondly, UN peacekeepers should not themselves become a party to the conflict and not favour one party to another (principle of neutrality/impartiality).[47] Thirdly, UN peacekeepers are not allowed to use force except in self-defence (principle of non-use of force). Fourthly, UN peacekeepers should be made up of voluntary contributions of contingents from small, neutral countries. And finally, day-to-day control of the UN operation should belong to the UN Secretary-General. The first three of these peacekeeping norms are especially important for they provide behavioural guidelines for an 'ideal' UN peacekeeping operation. Consent, neutrality/impartiality and non-use of force may even be treated as 'constitutive norms'[48] of peacekeeping, given the belief that operations lacking any of these three principles cannot be called peacekeeping.[49]

The original doctrine notwithstanding, there is no agreement in the peacekeeping literature as to which missions constitute 'peacekeeping'. Although many studies, typologies and classifications of UN peacekeeping seem to share a substantial subset of individual instances, their discrepancies are significant enough to thwart any straightforward conceptualisation.[50] UN peacekeeping, when used in a broad sense, seems to include three more or less distinct types of mission.

First are the relatively small-scale UN fact-finding and/or peace observation missions. One UN publication clearly distinguishes between two categories of UN peacekeeping operations: 'observer missions' and 'peacekeeping forces'.[51] Yet, not all UN-initiated small-scale observer missions are universally thought to belong to the domain of UN peacekeeping. The UN Special Committee on the Balkans (UNSCOB, 1947–54), for example, is cited by some sources as the first UN peacekeeping mission.[52] Others disagree, arguing that UNSCOB members were not operating under the Secretary-General's authority.[53]

The second category consists of those UN operations which are also often labelled 'UN peace enforcement'. UN missions authorised – whether in part or at a certain stage – to take enforcement measures in certain conflicts have been frequently included in the realm of UN peacekeeping.[54] It is this category of UN operations which gave rise to the conception of 'wider peacekeeping'.[55] This category also includes those non-enforcement operations which have nevertheless been actively supplemented by auxiliary UN-authorised enforcement operations.[56] These operations also contributed to the extensive and still continuing debate on 'humanitarian intervention'.[57]

A brief review of the literature suggests that UN peace enforcement as such is usually conceived of in two different ways: either with reference to the actual coercive nature of the operation in the field, or with reference to the constitutional basis of any mission. The second approach puts the emphasis on whether or not a given mission has been mandated under Chapter VII.[58] There are clear-cut cases where a mission, at least in part or at a certain stage, was explicitly mandated under this chapter (e.g. Somalia). For the proponents of the second approach, however, there are also a number of unclear cases, where the mandate requires special interpretation. Whether or not a given mandate emanated from Chapter VII was not always explicitly stated by the authorising organ of the UN.[59]

The third category, which may be said to constitute UN peacekeeping in the narrower sense, has its own conceptual difficulties. It is now common-place to refer to two UN peacekeeping operations as instances of 'classical' UN peacekeeping: the United Nations Emergency Forces in Sinai (UNEF I and II: 1956 and 1973 respectively).[60] Having been deployed between the armed forces of the belligerent states, their main, and perhaps sole, function was to supervise an agreed-upon cease-fire and deter any possible breaches of it.[61] The great majority of UN peacekeeping operations, especially in (but not limited to) the post-Cold War period, on the other hand, had more ambitious mandates. Moreover, these operations did not deal with purely inter-state conflicts – a fact which has long challenged earlier interpretations of the Charter, where the emphasis was on the meaning and implications of 'international' peace and security.

Perhaps the most distinctive feature of UN peacekeeping in the narrow sense is its ambiguous constitutional basis. Hammarskjöld's well-known description of UN peacekeeping as 'Chapter VI and $1/2$' operations is informative in two respects. On the one hand, UN peacekeeping operations are distinguishable from relatively small-scale observer/fact-finding missions insofar as the latter cannot operate outside the framework of Chapter VI. As far as their operational objectives and their personnel strengths are concerned, it is neither possible nor necessary for observer/fact-finding missions to pass the Chapter VII threshold.[62] On the other hand, it may not be appropriate to refer to missions which have been authorised (explicitly or by implication) under Chapter VII as *peacekeeping*.[63] According to the original doctrine, UN peacekeeping forces are not supposed to 'impose' peace on the combatants, though they do contain a clear element of deterrence. After all, UN peacekeeping generally makes use of military personnel. None the less, UN peacekeepers, although they may on occasion have the capacity, opportunity, or need to pass the Chapter VII threshold, would normally be expected to operate in the absence of a Chapter VII authorisation.[64]

Defining UN peacekeeping in intra-state conflicts

The nature and characteristics of UN peacekeeping, then, cannot be taken as a given. In the post-Cold War period we have seen clear-cut Chapter VII operations, which were in practice neither authorised nor designed to carry out enforcement (for instance, the UN Transitional Administration (UNTAES) in Croatia). Some commentators have actually argued that with this last category of operations we have seen the birth of Chapter VII peacekeeping as opposed to Chapter VII peace enforcement.[65] By the same token, it has been observed that the Hammarskjöldian 'norms of peacekeeping' have sometimes been abandoned in this period.[66] Peacekeeping, therefore, is a rather ambiguous category. Its ambiguity arises in part from the absence of any explicit reference to it in the Charter. More important perhaps is the lack of clarity as to the criteria by which this generic activity is to be distinguished from associated notions (especially peace enforcement), or broken down into specific types. Take the examples of 'wider',[67] 'expanded',[68] 'multi-dimensional'[69] and 'second generation'[70] peacekeeping.[71] There are considerable conceptual overlaps between these and similar categories. Not infrequently they are used synonymously, especially in policy circles.

For our purposes it is particularly useful to recall and underline a long detected fact: *each* UN response is in fact a unique mission combining different types of operational tasks, personnel, methods and instruments.[72] In this study UN peacekeeping is understood in the broader sense of the term, and encompasses therefore quite diverse types of operation. The term is employed in its popular sense – as a catch-all phrase. A distinction between peacekeeping and peace enforcement (or, for that matter, between different 'types' of peacekeeping) is neither relevant nor helpful to our analytical purpose. The potential drawback of any rigid distinction between the two notions for our particular research plan becomes abundantly clear in such cases as Somalia or Bosnia. If we examined the two UN Operations in Somalia (UNOSOM I and UNOSOM II) and the Unified Task Force (UNITAF) in isolation from each other, for example, it would become extremely difficult to form any judgement about the normative implications of the UN's response to the Somalia conflict. Was there a collective normative expectation in the international community that the UN should use force against one or more of the intra-state parties, or, for that matter, against disorganised groups of intra-state 'bandits' in Somalia to achieve a certain objective? If one looks purely at the 'peacekeeping' component of the mission (in the narrow sense), one might be too quick to answer 'no'. But that might not be an entirely fair judgement in the presence of the evolving mandate and associated actions taken by combat forces with the UN's blessing. Since this study sets out to explore international players' normative views on the UN's role, it is more fruitful to ascertain what exactly they expect of 'UN peacekeeping' in its wider sense, and of the UN in general, *vis-à-vis* intra-state conflicts.

UN peacekeeping is defined here in terms of UN-authorised deployment of multinational personnel in situations of potential or actual violent conflict[73] with the express purpose of addressing such violence.[74] In order to qualify as UN peacekeeping such deployment must not only be welcomed, supported or tolerated by the UN, but officially authorised by the UN's competent organs, which in practical terms means either the Security Council or the General Assembly.[75] UN peacekeeping missions must involve deployment of personnel, but not necessarily military personnel. They may involve, or consist exclusively of, civilian, police, or para-military personnel. But it would be a safe assumption – in the light of past UN experience – that the express purpose of addressing a conflict by way of a field presence would usually require the fulfilment of some military tasks. As a consequence, the use of military personnel would normally be part of UN peacekeeping, although the size and operational capabilities of the deployed units would vary considerably from one operation to the next, and at different times in the course of the same operation.

UN peacekeeping as we define it addresses violent conflicts, but these need not be exclusively or primarily inter-state in character. Indeed, this study concentrates on those peacekeeping environments where the UN addresses intra-state conflicts. For analytical convenience we regard any violent conflict that is not unambiguously/predominantly inter-state in nature as coming under the 'intra-state' category. Our notion of intra-state conflicts corresponds roughly to what international lawyers prefer to designate as 'non-international conflicts'.[76] This term refers to conflicts which are primarily internal to a state, without, however, labelling them as such.[77] On the other hand, the term leaves open the option that a violent conflict may have intra-state, inter-state and trans-state dimensions.

Two other terms have been suggested to designate what we call 'intra-state' conflicts: 'intermestic conflicts' and 'international social conflicts'. Pugh observes that distinctions between inter- and intra-state conflicts are exaggerated, and maintains that the majority of contemporary conflicts fall between the two.[78] He cites the examples of Bosnia and the Democratic Republic of Congo, where 'interests of states and rebels intermingle freely across borders'. Hence the term 'inter(national)-(do)mestic'. Woodhouse and Ramsbotham, whose concept of 'international social conflict' is also referred to by Pugh, are in agreement.[79] Their emphasis, however, is on the humanitarian implications of such conflicts, hence the reference to international 'social' conflicts. We do prefer the designation 'intra-state' over 'non-international', 'intermestic' and 'international social' conflict, because it serves as a constant reminder of the main problem at hand, namely the UN's active efforts *within* states' boundaries. Our emphasis in this study is clearly on the UN's response to the intra-state dimensions of conflicts.[80]

Normative significance of 'peacekeeping environments'

Peacekeeping is an activity where the UN becomes clearly 'visible' in its capacity as an actor.[81] This observation, coupled with the uncertain nature of the very practice of peacekeeping, whether in inter-state or in intra-state conflicts, leads to several questions. What exactly are the objectives of UN peacekeeping missions? What is the scope of the UN's authority during its 'intervention'? What are the functions which are thought to serve its pursuit of objectives and its exercise of authority? And how do crucial Charter principles relate to the objectives, functions and authority prescribed for the UN in its capacity as peacekeeper?

The interpretation of the Charter in the context of peacekeeping becomes particularly instructive in those conflicts which are commonly believed to be intra-state in nature.[82] The fact that peacekeeping activities are conducted *within* the 'sovereign' domain of member-states poses prima facie a major problem for the UN so far as its Charter is concerned. On the one hand, the UN has to reconcile its involvement in internal conflicts with the related principles of sovereignty, non-intervention, territorial integrity, and political independence. On the other hand, it has to give effect to equally valid principles implicit in notions of human rights and humanitarianism – and perhaps socio-economic development – particularly when such principles are fundamental to those internal conflicts and their resolution. What is at stake here is not merely the presence of disparate sets of principles, but the potential tension, indeed irreconcilability, between them. What appears as an interesting question, then, is whether such a normative tension is handled uniformly over time.

The questions we have thus far elaborated cannot be adequately dealt with if one overestimates the importance of the fine and contested dividing line between different types of UN activity, such as peacekeeping, peacemaking, peacebuilding and peace enforcement.[83] The reason is the complex interconnectedness between various types of simultaneous and overlapping activity on the one hand,[84] and the dynamism of field operations (i.e. the change in the nature of a mission in the course of time) on the other.

To illustrate, the dividing line between peacekeeping and peacemaking is not as clear-cut as might be assumed. There are several peacekeeping operations where the chief of mission has been the primary peacemaker.[85] The two roles have not been mechanically separable. In any case, negotiation and mediation, that is the main operational methods of peacemaking, have long been placed within the job description of peacekeepers.[86] The criticisms levelled against Boutros-Ghali for placing peace enforcement within the notion of peacemaking are perhaps a little misplaced,[87] given that the two have often gone hand in hand. Similarly, when the military contingents in Bosnia were building or restoring roads, schools and hospitals, it is a moot point whether they were acting as peacekeepers or as peacebuilders. How useful would it be to classify the 1960s UN mission to the Congo (ONUC) as peacekeeping or peace enforcement, when the UN-authorised actions on the ground undeniably constituted what is nowadays generally referred to as a 'grey area'?[88]

Especially important in this regard is whether any connection is created by the UN between several distinct operations and instruments addressing the same intra-state conflict. Since the UN's response to intra-state conflicts involves the use of a great many methods and instruments, actors' collective expectations of the UN may not be discernible simply by examining only one of the UN's activities, even if that activity (in this case peacekeeping) proves to be the centerpiece of the UN's response to that conflict. For this reason this study prefers to concentrate on peacekeeping 'environments', which necessarily comprise, but are not limited to, theatre peacekeeping operations. 'Peacekeeping environment' encompasses not only the geographical or territorial space in which UN peacekeeping takes place alongside other UN and non-UN operations, but also, and perhaps more importantly, the political space within which normative views are expressed in relation to the conflict in question.

If a conceptual and/or legal 'connection' is established by a UN resolution between a predominantly military operation and a simultaneous humanitarian or developmental operation, our focus on the peacekeeping environment would help to detect the wider normative implications of such extensive engagement. A particularly important connection in this context is that between the relatively peaceful UN military presence in the field and accompanying coercive measures, ranging from limited sanctions to massive military strikes.

There is, of course, more to the dynamism of UN operations than the simultaneity of diverse operations or the role of coercion. How can we capture the UN's evolving response to the Haiti crisis, if we insist on focusing on the four successive UN operations as separate entities with quite separate rationales? The same question may be asked in the context of several other missions. How can we make sense of the successive operations in Croatia without taking into account the evolving response of the United Nations to it? Our decision to focus on the environment rather than the operations *per se*, therefore, reflects our theoretical concern that we should not miss the forest by concentrating on a single tree as is sometimes done in the peacekeeping literature.

Objectives, functions, and authority as detected in peacekeeping environments

Our concentration on peacekeeping environments is intended to uncover any changes to the normative connection between the UN and intra-state conflicts. In this context we have already made reference to the 'normative basis' of UN peacekeeping, alluding to its connection with three crucial concepts that we use in this study, namely, objectives, functions and authority. At this stage, we will clarify our conceptualisation of these three terms.

The objectives of the UN, as understood here, do not refer to the political or psycho-social motivations of member states, which inform their support for UN action or non-action. Rather, they pertain to the normative, that is value-based, standard-setting and expectation-creating, rationale underlying the UN's active involvement in intra-state conflicts and authorisation of peace-keeping missions. What are the ends which should be achieved? In other words, what are desirable outcomes of action?

Given the uncontested value of 'peace and security', the first reasonable question would revolve around the way this value manifests itself in the objectives of intra-state peacekeeping. Is the UN supposed to intervene in intra-state conflicts in the first place? Hypothetically, at least, it could be argued that the UN is mandated to address only the *international* dimensions of intra-state conflicts. In other words, the UN may well be expected to conduct 'inter-state' peacekeeping even when deployed in an 'intra-state' conflict. For instance, it may be called upon simply to monitor any possible cross-border infiltrations and nothing else. More importantly, regardless of what exactly peacekeepers are required to do on the ground, the international community may be concerned solely with the maintenance of international peace and security. UN deployment may be predominantly an expression – in rhetoric as well as in practice – of an almost exclusive preoccupation with 'international' peace and security, which, at least from a state-centric perspective, would be relatively less problematic.

The other three crucial principles in the Charter are equally relevant to the question of objectives. State sovereignty, human rights and socio-economic development may all influence collective expectations of the UN in intra-state conflict environments. Admittedly, the specified norms are not easily comparable. In a sense, they may be seen as apples and pears. Nevertheless, given the obvious importance assigned to these principles in the Charter, and their prima facie relevance to intra-state peacekeeping, it is possible to discern what kinds of normative 'objectives' may be inherent in these three values. To put it simply, protection and/or promotion of state sovereignty, protection and/or promotion of human rights, and promotion of socio-economic development readily suggest themselves as potential Charter-based objectives of UN peacekeeping in intra-state conflicts.

Not only are state sovereignty, human rights and socio-economic development not easily comparable, but they are not even easily definable, and we will not attempt to 'define' them in any formal sense. After all, our study necessarily involves, at least indirectly, an enquiry into 'notions' of state sovereignty, human rights and socio-economic development as they were understood at different moments in the international realm and as they manifested themselves in peacekeeping environments. On the other hand, given that *our* description, interpretation and evaluation of international normative preferences will take place within the confines of *our own* framework, we propose to make clear, without elaboration, which 'standard characterisations' of these three principles inform our analysis.

In this study, actors' normative expectations of the UN *vis-à-vis* state sovereignty will be discussed in reference to the 'external' and 'internal' aspects of sovereignty.[89] Understood as a principle of exclusion, state sovereignty may be taken to imply, at one level, independence from any authority *outside of* the state, with obvious implications for the principle of non-intervention (external sovereignty). At another level, it may be said to connote supremacy *within* the state, indicating that there cannot be two or more authorities vying for sovereignty at the same time and in the same space (internal sovereignty).[90] As for human rights and socio-economic development, both principles will be used here in an inclusive sense. To illustrate, human rights, whether in peacekeeping or other contexts, may be invoked with respect to 'individual' or 'collective' rights, to 'first', 'second' or 'third' generation rights, to 'civil and political' rights or 'social, economic and cultural' rights. Similarly, development may be considered in relation to the wide spectrum of functions in the 'economic' or 'social' fields, including income, employment, production, trade, health and education.

Functions, as applied in this study, pertain primarily to the operational tasks the UN is entrusted with in a peacekeeping environment, and can be conveniently visualised with the benefit of what Ratner calls the *breadth* and *depth* of responsibility.[91] The *breadth* of responsibility relates to the range of policy areas which the UN addresses in a peacekeeping theatre. According to Ratner, the major functions of UN peacekeeping involve military matters, elections, human rights, national reconciliation, law and order, refugees, humanitarian relief, governmental administration, economic reconstruction and relationships with outside actors. He also details each of these functions in terms of their major components. For instance, military functions encompass more specific tasks related to cease-fires, withdrawal of foreign forces, termination of foreign military assistance, cantonment of forces, disarmament of forces, demobilisation of forces, custody of weapons, transition to civilian jobs and creation of armed forces. While we are aware that the potential problem of 'apples and pears' is equally visible here,[92] this listing of operational tasks is perfectly adequate for our purposes in that it helps us to clarify and visualise what we mean by 'functions'.

The *depth* of responsibility, on the other hand, concerns the intensity of the UN's involvement in a policy area. 'Monitoring' and 'education' indicate the least depth. The former refers to investigation, observation and verification without a mandate to influence directly the actors involved, while the latter involves technical assistance and public information.[93] 'Supervision', on the other hand, implies oversight over situations with a mandate to request changes in the behaviour of actors, but not to order those actors directly to correct their behaviour. 'Control' signifies a deeper level of involvement, and implies competence to take certain binding decisions. Finally, 'conduct' means ability to perform certain tasks directly, with or without the assistance of local authorities and notwithstanding their views on those matters.

Although 'functions' is a key analytical concept used in this study, we propose to focus on prescribed functions precisely *because* – and *to the extent* that – they relate to the more significant questions of 'objectives' and 'authority', both of which are more abstract and less easily manageable concepts, yet critical to the task of illuminating actors' normative attitudes. Objectives are translated into action by way of prescribed functions. Different operational tasks may serve different objectives. Methodologically, 'hidden' objectives are sometimes most easily discernible by examining the prescribed functions. For instance, a key actor's reluctant support for the incorporation of a human rights component into a peacekeeping mission would have implications for the objectives it assigns to the UN. In relation to authority, too, prescribed functions are of significance, since they may be legitimately considered as constituting one crucial aspect of the authority envisaged for the UN. At this stage, it is appropriate to turn to our concept of authority.

Authority is an especially difficult category to grapple with. It is nevertheless a particularly useful concept for an enquiry that sets out to explore the role of the UN as envisaged by international actors. For our purposes, authority can be operationalised in a four-dimensional way. First, authority involves functions. In other words, 'who performs which function with what degree of involvement' is inevitably a question of authority. After all, one aspect of 'governmental' authority relates to the functions that are attributed to a government, both in terms of breadth and depth. Secondly, authority concerns the issue of consent. Whether the UN is expected to act with or without the consent of the parties to a conflict is highly relevant to the exercise of its authority. Thirdly, authority involves the issue of judgement or 'verdict' along the good/bad–right/wrong spectra. Whether or not the UN is expected and encouraged to render judgements on a given issue is a sign of the authority assigned to it. Finally, authority manifests itself in the implementation of judgements. The critical question here is whether, and to what degree, the UN is expected to enforce its 'verdicts'. As the last three dimensions make clear, the question of authority is inextricably linked to the notions of consent, neutrality/impartiality and non-use of force, that is, to the classical UN peacekeeping doctrine. It has, equally visibly, overarching implications for several state-centric Charter principles, especially non-intervention.

A closer analysis of objectives, functions and authority – as they emerge in peacekeeping environments – should prove highly revealing of the normative basis of UN peacekeeping missions and any changes it may have undergone over time. While all three concepts are crucial for this study, 'functions', rather than be discussed separately in the ensuing chapters, will, for reasons already mentioned, be incorporated into our examination of 'objectives' and 'authority'.

Specifying peacekeeping environments: rationale of time periods and cases

While we concentrate on two periods in this study, the early 1960s (1960–65) and the early 1990s (1990–95), it goes without saying that there can be no strict cut-off date for an analysis of the kind we envisage here, and we will not hesitate to draw from time to time on the events which took place in the one or two years that immediately follow or precede these periods and which warrant mention. Our choice of these periods is not a random one. It is based on two main considerations. Firstly, both periods witnessed ambitious UN peacekeeping. What is even more distinctive about them is that both emerged in quite a 'revolutionary' way, in the sense that UN peacekeeping was not as visible and topical in the years that immediately preceded these periods. As such, an examination of these periods, with plenty of views expressed about UN peacekeeping, promises a rich contribution to our understanding of its normative basis.

Moreover, it would be a relatively safe assumption that the relevant actors were spontaneous in reacting to the fast-changing peacekeeping environments, given that events in peacekeeping theatres unfolded quite rapidly in both periods. The actors in question were in a sense caught by a number of 'surprises' in the course of peacekeeping processes, especially during and after deployment. Their normative preferences in relation to UN peacekeeping were probably not as carefully and deliberately thought through as would be the case post facto. This would enable us, in all probability, to discern relevant actors' normative preferences and accompanying interests that were already solidly in place when entering each period. It would make it possible to detect the norms that were more deeply embedded in actors' value systems. In other words, the likelihood of discerning actors' interests and normative attitudes increases by concentrating on the peacekeeping environments of the specified two periods. Even mere 'justifications' used by the actors in these two periods are likely to illuminate the underlying normative positions.

Our detailed case studies are chosen from among that cluster of intra-state conflicts where the UN's response included authorisation of multifunctional and large-scale UN peacekeeping operations.[94] This enables us to compare and contrast various normative views, the resolution of which gave rise to ambitious UN peacekeeping operations in both periods. Particularly important in this respect is the relevance of such missions to the issue of governance, especially as it impinges on the principles of sovereignty, human rights and socio-economic development. For the early 1960s the two selected cases involve the two most ambitious operations at the time: the Congo and Cyprus. These two operations are the two important exceptions in the Cold War period, when UN peacekeeping was generally characterised by military tasks, with the role of civilians often limited to administration.[95] Similarly, for the 1990s the two case studies involve UN operations of considerable scale and complexity: Angola and Cambodia.

A particular subcategory of missions, that is, the so-called 'humanitarian interventions', though taken into account in our overview (see Chapter 4), have been deliberately excluded from our case studies.[96] The rationale behind the UN's intervention in those cases revolved around a substantial concern about gross human suffering. Even if humanitarianism were just a pretext for intervention, this rhetoric in itself nevertheless alludes to significant change so far as the UN's objectives are concerned. Furthermore, the means and *modus operandi* of humanitarian interventions involved active use of physical force under UN authorisation, which points to greater UN authority *vis-à-vis* intra-state conflicts. On both counts, therefore, choosing cases from this subcategory would diminish the explanatory utility of our study.

Normative 'difference' and 'change': what do peacekeeping environments tell us?

Changes in the normative basis of intra-state peacekeeping may have been explicit (as demonstrated in relevant actors' public statements) or implicit (as demonstrated in their actions), both of which are interesting from our perspective. The primary method used here is to compare the normative discourses of relevant actors. We concentrate on actors' rhetoric and, to a lesser extent, on their practice. As far as the former is concerned, we observe and critically evaluate actors' normative statements before, during and after key decisions that connect the UN to the specified intra-state conflicts. Our methodology rests on a qualitative rather than quantitative evaluation of texts. As for the latter, our focus is on actors' implementation and institutional 'body language'.

Our enquiry into normative attitudes, especially in case studies, proceeds in two mental steps which may not always be easily separable. As a first step we attempt to establish whether questions pertaining to objectives, functions and authority are addressed by the relevant actors in any direct or obvious sense. In other words, have actors tackled these questions in the first place;

and are their answers clearly discernible?[97] If explicit answers are not offered, can we identify the 'implied' answers by way of interpretation, that is, by examining the actor's overall statements and behaviour? The aim here is to identify the normative positions that seem to have particularly influenced the UN's course of action. To give a hypothetical example, if a Third World member of the Security Council expresses and advocates a view as to what should be the UN's objectives in an intra-state conflict, and if that view should then find its way to the operationalisation of a peacekeeping mandate, it would certainly be useful to identify and characterise that view. Similarly, should an NGO's view on, say, what the UN's authority should be in a given conflict was able to initiate intense discussions at the General Assembly, that view would need to be identified.

As a second step, we try to juxtapose significant clusters of normative views in relation to peacekeeping environments. Of particular interest is the extent to which 'differences' of opinion and perception between crucial actors have a bearing on the UN's response to intra-state conflicts in the different periods. Whether clearly expressed or merely implied, are the answers consensual; or are different answers offered by different actors? Might these answers stand in opposition to each other? Can one detect patterns of agreement and disagreement? If so, can certain answers be considered dominant (which further raises the question: What is the basis of their dominance, or for that matter, of their legitimacy)? The answers to these questions should shed useful light on how possible normative tensions are resolved by international actors in different periods.

Identification of differences is only a first move towards exploring 'change' in the normative basis of UN involvement in intra-state conflicts. Change is necessarily a function of time. It alludes to observed differences in a specified attribute over a specified timespan. The postulated change has two dimensions. In the first place, we set out to discern any possible change in the influence exerted by this or that Charter principle on the UN's response to intra-state conflicts. To illustrate, if actors' concern over state sovereignty had a greater impact on the UN's active involvement in intra-state conflicts in the 1960s than human rights, and the situation was reversed in the 1990s, this would certainly qualify as significant change in the normative basis of intra-state peacekeeping. Secondly, and perhaps more importantly, we are interested to establish whether the interaction between the specified Charter values – i.e. the relationship that the international community establishes between them in peacekeeping environments – has changed. Is there, for instance, a 'permanent' duality between state sovereignty and human rights? Have peace and security always related to sovereignty, human rights and socio-economic development the same way?

Discerning changes in the influence of the specified principles and in their content or interpretation requires comparisons between significant normative views across time. Those normative views which were most widely held in the 1960s, as articulated and advocated by certain crucial actors, may have diminished in influence or altogether disappeared in the 1990s and been replaced, or at least complemented, by alternative views as expressed by other relevant actors. What is more, the normative gap, that is, the divergence between the views of different actors, may have disappeared, narrowed or widened over time. Careful qualitative comparison and juxtaposition of normative trends as they manifested themselves in the early 1960s and 1990s will be a useful tool in our analysis of normative change in relation to the UN's intra-state peacekeeping.

We have already suggested that historical structural insights are helpful in situating and exploring the interest-norm complexes that may have influenced the evolution of the UN's role. For an interpretation of the significance of the early 1960s and 1990s from this perspective, we now turn to a brief historical sketch of the post-World War II history. Our aim is to introduce the 'historical structural' element more firmly into our normative enquiry. Once we do that, we will proceed to a more focused discussion of the UN's intra-state peacekeeping and will address more closely the evolving normative connection between the UN and intra-state conflicts in the specified period.

NOTES

1 Keohane notes, for instance, that 'the conclusions of formal models of cooperation are often highly dependent on the assumptions with which the investigations begin': see R. O. Keohane, 'International institutions: two approaches', *International Studies Quarterly*, 32 (1988), 388.

2 One such dilemma is the failure to understand how interests change as a result of changes in belief systems: see Keohane, 'International institutions', 391.

3 See Keohane, 'International institutions', 386–9.

4 See Keohane, 'International institutions', 389–93.

5 Knight, *A Changing United Nations*.

6 Knight, *A Changing United Nations*, p. 181.

7 Knight, *A Changing United Nations*, pp. 110, 191.

8 Knight, *A Changing United Nations*, p. 6.

9 For Knight, 'organisational change' is distinct from but related to 'evolution of multilateralism' (and its institutions): see Knight, *A Changing United Nations*, pp. 38–9.

10 See Knight, *A Changing United Nations*, especially pp. 82–129.

11 R. W. Cox with T. J. Sinclair, *Approaches to World Order* (Cambridge: Cambridge University Press, 1996), p. 97.

12 Cox with Sinclair, *Approaches to World Order*, pp. 97–8.

13 He defines institutions as 'the broadly understood and accepted ways of organizing particular spheres of social action': see Cox with Sinclair, *Approaches to World Order*, p. 149.

14 See Keohane, 'International institutions', 383.

15 Historical structures, according to Cox, can be depicted both 'synchronically' and

'diachronically': see Cox with Sinclair, *Approaches to World Order*, pp. 8, 78. Historical structures, therefore, are conceived of as detached from or independent of other (co-existing, preceding or following) historical structures.

16 Cox with Sinclair, *Approaches to World Order*, pp. 103–4.

17 T. Risse and K. Sikkink, 'The socialization of international human rights norms into domestic practices: introduction', in T. Risse, S. C. Ropp and K. Sikkink (eds), *The Power of Human Rights: International Norms and Domestic Change* (Cambridge: Cambridge University Press, 1999), p. 7. Elsewhere Sikkink notes that political scientists are arriving at a consensus definition of norms as 'standards of appropriate behaviour for actors with a given identity': see K. Sikkink, 'Transnational politics, international relations theory, and human rights', *Political Science & Politics*, 31:3 (September 1998), 518.

18 In fact, in international relations theory there has always been some space to refer to collective expectations of more singular actors. Implicit in the hegemonic stability theory (as advanced by Kindleberger and Gilpin), for instance, are expectations of a global 'hegemon'.

19 Such expectations of the UN would, of course, draw, at least to a certain degree, on actors' (most notably states') expectations of each other. To give but one example, the expectation that the UN should uphold the principle of non-intervention necessarily draws on an established international prescription that states should not intervene in each other's domestic affairs. Nevertheless, it may be the case that international actors are increasingly expecting, indeed encouraging, the UN to intervene in states' internal affairs, whereas states themselves may still be required to apply far more strictly the principle of non-intervention.

20 For an elaboration of these levels, see Government of Canada, *Towards A Rapid Reaction Capability for the United Nations* (Ottawa: September 1995).

21 Economic and Social Council (ECOSOC) Resolution 1296 of 23 May 1968 defines an NGO as any organisation not created by inter-governmental agreement. Depending on the nature and scope of its activities, a non-governmental organisation can be granted 'general' or 'special' consultative status with ECOSOC, or can be included on a list known as the 'roster': see www.ishr.ch/about%20ISHR/Advisory/consultative_status.htm (27 March 2001). Apart from the NGOs in consultative status with the ECOSOC, several NGOs have been associated with the UN Department of Public Information (DPI) pursuant to Resolution 1296. As of early 1999, there were over 1,500 NGOs who had consultative status with the United Nations.

22 One of the UN's special funds/programmes.

23 One of the UN's specialised technical agencies.

24 One of the NGOs in 'general' consultative status with the ECOSOC. This organisation is one of the eight major families or federations of NGOs each of which control about US$500 million in the US$8 billion relief 'market': see P. J. Simmons, 'Learning to live with NGOs', *Foreign Policy*, 112 (Fall 1998), 92.

25 For an account, see J. Mermin, *Debating War and Peace: Media Coverage of U.S. Intervention in the post-Vietnam Era* (Princeton, NJ: Princeton University Press, 1999), pp. 120–42.

26 See Frost, *Toward a Normative Theory of International Relations*, pp. 120–8.

27 As such the starting point of this study may be said to fit in the declaratory tradition of international ethics: see D. V. Jones, 'The declaratory tradition in modern international law', in T. Nardin and D. R. Mapel (eds), *Traditions of International Ethics* (Cambridge: Cambridge University Press, 1992), pp. 42–61.

28 So far, there have been three amendments to the original Charter. By General Assembly Resolution 1991 A and B (XVIII) of 17 December 1963, the number of members in the

Security Council and ECOSOC was increased from 11 to 15 and from 18 to 27 respectively. This resolution entered into force on 30 August 1965. At first, the alteration of Article 109 Paragraph 1 was overlooked. This paragraph was later amended by General Assembly Resolution 201 (XX) of 20 December 1965, which came into force on 12 June 1968. The number of ECOSOC members was further increased to 54 by General Assembly Resolution 2846 (XXVI) of 20 December 1971, which entered into effect on 24 September 1973.

29 In our opinion, one of the Charter's normative strengths is its *explicitness* in terms of both 'commitment' and 'expression'; see F. V. Kratochwil, *Rules, Norms and Decisions: On the Conditions of Practical and Legal Reasoning in International Relations and Domestic Affairs* (Cambridge: Cambridge University Press, 1989), p. 55.

30 Keohane, 'International institutions', 383.

31 Article 1.1. mentions the maintenance of *international* peace and security, Article 1.2. refers to the strengthening of *universal* peace and security. Either way, the express devotion of the UN to 'peace and security' is clear.

32 Most of these principles are encapsulated in four crucial Charter provisions: Articles 1, 2, 55 and 56.

33 It is well known that a number of regional organisations (e.g. the Organization of American States (OAS), the Organization of African Unity (OAU), the Organization for Security and Cooperation in Europe (OSCE), the Association of South East Asian Nations (ASEAN) and the Economic Community of West African States (ECOWAS)) and states have acted, or claimed to have acted, as peacekeepers on a number of occasions. The US troops that invaded Grenada were called the 'Caribbean Peacekeeping Forces': see P. F. Diehl, *International Peacekeeping* (Baltimore, MD: Johns Hopkins University Press, 1993), p. 4.

34 For a very broad understanding of peacekeeping, which includes even the Monroe and Brezhnev Doctrines, see J. Galtung, 'Three realistic approaches to peace: peacekeeping, peacemaking, peacebuilding', *Impact of Science on Society*, 26:1/2 (1976), 103–5.

35 I. J. Rikhye, *The Theory and Practice of Peacekeeping* (London: C. Hurst & Co., 1984), pp. 1–2.

36 The taxonomy of 'actual and potential' peacekeeping missions developed by Diehl, Druckman and Wall is indicative of the broad range of operations that are referred to as peacekeeping; see P. F. Diehl, 'Forks in the road: theoretical and policy concerns for 21st century peacekeeping', *Global Society*, 14:3 (July 2000), 351, 358–60.

37 The first United Nations Emergency Force (UNEF I) was deployed in the Sinai Peninsula after the Suez War.

38 Also known as 'the Committee of 33'; see R. C. R. Siekmann, *Basic Documents on United Nations and Related Peace-keeping Forces*, 2nd edn (Dordrecht: Martinus Nijhoff, 1989), p. vii.

39 Rikhye, *The Theory and Practice of Peacekeeping*, p. 1.

40 Though there have been serious attempts to place peacekeeping in the framework of the Charter: see, Rikhye, *The Theory and Practice of Peacekeeping*, p. 180.

41 UK Foreign and Commonwealth Office, *Western Sahara: Moving The Peace Process Forward* (London: December 2000), p. 8.

42 See United Nations, *The Blue Helmets: A Review of United Nations Peace-keeping*, 3rd edn (New York: UNDPI, 1996), p. 652.

43 Roberts and Kingsbury, *Presiding over A Divided World*, p. 40.

44 See A. B. Fetherston, *Towards A Theory of United Nations Peacekeeping* (London: Macmillan, 1994), p. 13. The proposal to create UNEF I in Sinai came from Lester Pearson in close consultation with Hammarskjöld; see G. Abi-Saab, 'United Nations

peacekeeping old and new: an overview of the issues' in D. Warner (ed.), *New Dimensions of Peacekeeping* (Dordrecht: Martinus Nijhoff Publishers, 1995), p. 2.

45 Hammarskjöld's two reports during the Suez crisis are especially important in the formulation of UN peacekeeping doctrine; see W. R. Frye, *A United Nations Peace Force* (New York: Oceana Publications, 1957), pp. 11–17. The initial formulation of Hammarskjöld principles can be found in A/3943 of 9 October 1958.

46 Fetherston, *Towards A Theory of United Nations Peacekeeping*, p. 13.

47 Neutrality and impartiality are usually taken to be synonymous. However, neutrality, according to Weller, implies that a third party must not undertake or possibly permit activities which would assist the war effort of any party to a conflict. Impartiality, on the other hand, implies that the third party develops certain standards which it applies *equally* to all parties. We should also add that Weller's definitions refer to the application of these concepts to humanitarian action. In fact his overall point is that neutrality and impartiality need redefinition depending on the context in which they are applied: see M. Weller, 'The relativity of humanitarian neutrality and impartiality', *Journal of Humanitarian Assistance*, available online at www-jha.sps.cam.ac.uk/a/a528.htm (10 February 1998).

48 See Raymond, 'Problems and prospects in the study of international norms', 214.

49 See, for example, D. M. Snow, *Uncivil Wars: International Security and the New Internal Conflicts* (Boulder, CO: Lynne Rienner, 1996). Also Tom Farer seems to think along the same line: see 'A paradigm of legitimate intervention' in Damrosch (ed.), *Enforcing Restraint*, p. 329.

50 Take the examples of Mission of the Representative of the Secretary-General in the Dominican Republic (DOMREP, 1965–66), United Nations Good Offices Mission in Afghanistan and Pakistan (UNGOMAP, 1988–90), United Nations Iraq–Kuwait Observation Mission (UNIKOM, 1991–present), United Nations Observer Mission in South Africa (UNOMSA, 1992–94), and United Nations Protection Force (UNPROFOR, 1992–95) in the former Yugoslavia. Each of these missions has been included, by some authority or other, for some reason or other, within the sphere of UN peacekeeping. Such inclusion has given rise to much disagreement, which is perhaps not surprising given that UN peacekeeping does not even have a clear-cut constitutional basis. Compare, for instance, United Nations, *The Blue Helmets*, 3rd edn; Fetherston, *Towards A Theory of United Nations Peacekeeping*; W. J. Durch (ed.), *The Evolution of UN Peacekeeping: Case Studies and Comparative Analysis* (London: Macmillan, 1994); and S. R. Ratner, *The New Peacekeeping: Building Peace in Lands of Conflict After the Cold War* (New York: St. Martin's Press, 1995).

51 See United Nations, *The Blue Helmets: A Review of United Nations Peace-keeping* (New York: UNDPI, 1985), p. 8. This is a commonplace distinction widely shared by other sources as well. See, for instance, N. D. White, *The United Nations and The Maintenance of International Peace and Security* (Manchester: Manchester University Press, 1990), pp. 169–80, and Siekmann, *Basic Documents*, p. vii.

52 See, for example, Durch (ed.), *The Evolution of UN Peacekeeping*, pp. 7–8.

53 See United Nations, *The Blue Helmets*, 3rd edn, pp. 7–8.

54 The main exceptions are the two 'collective security actions' taken during the Korean and Iraq–Kuwait crises.

55 'Wider peacekeeping' is an attempt to reconcile the classical UN peacekeeping doctrine with the 1990s actual UN experiences on the ground. In practical terms, wider peace-keeping endeavours to reconcile casual use of force with the traditional requirement of consent: see J. G. Ruggie, 'The UN and the collective use of force: whither or whether?', *International Peacekeeping*, 3:4 (Winter 1996), 9–10.

56 In Bosnia, for instance, NATO enforcement backed UNPROFOR. In Somalia, the US-led UNITAF supported UNOSOM. In Rwanda, the French conducted *Operation Turquoise* in support of the UN Assistance Mission for Rwanda (UNAMIR). In Haiti, a US-led multinational force intervened alongside the UN Mission in Haiti (UNMIH).

57 Durch reduces peace operations to four basic types, suggesting that 'humanitarian interventions' should be distinguished not only from 'traditional peacekeeping' and 'multidimensional peace operations', but also from 'peace enforcement': see W. J. Durch, 'Keeping the peace: politics and lessons of the 1990s', in W. J. Durch (ed.), *UN Peacekeeping, American Politics, and the Uncivil Wars of the 1990s* (New York: St. Martin's Press, 1996), p. 3.

58 Former Norwegian Foreign Minister, Johan Jorgen Holst, for example, seems to follow this approach: see his 'Keeping a fractured peace', in Heiberg (ed.), *Subduing Sovereignty*, p. 142. While Chapter VI deals with 'pacific settlement of disputes', Chapter VII is the only chapter in the UN Charter, which points to coercive measures. As Ratner reminds us, however, not all provisions of Chapter VII are about enforcement. 'Resort to Chapter VII provisions' is generally taken to mean application of Articles 41 and 42. Article 40, which is also located in Chapter VII, on the other hand, does not amount to enforcement: see Ratner, *The New Peacekeeping*, p. 57.

59 See Ramsbotham, 'Humanitarian intervention 1990–5', 454.

60 See, for example, Durch (ed.), *The Evolution of UN Peacekeeping*, pp. 7–8.

61 Drawing on UN peacekeeping during the Cold War, Greindl suggests that peacekeeping operations (in the narrow sense) may be grouped into three categories: those which are launched as part of a politically negotiated and agreed solution to a conflict (e.g. the UN Temporary Executive Authority (UNTEA)/UN Security Force (UNSF) in West Irian); those which are deployed after a cease-fire agreement has been negotiated and signed between the conflicting parties (e.g. the UN Disengagement Observer Force (UNDOF) in the Golan Heights); and those which are interposed with only a broad definition of their missions, but with the consent of the conflicting parties, in order to bring hostilities to an end (e.g. the UN Peacekeeping Force in Cyprus (UNFICYP)): see G. G. Greindl, 'Peacekeeping and peacemaking: the need for patience', in I. J. Rikhye and K. Skjelsbaek, *The United Nations and Peacekeeping: Results, Limitations and Prospects: The Lessons of 40 Years of Experience* (London: Macmillan / International Peace Academy, 1990), p. 69.

62 Admittedly, however, the importance of a UN presence lies not so much in its numerical strength or military capacity as the international political will which it represents: see B. E. Urquhart, 'United Nations peace-keeping in the Middle East', *The World Today*, 36:3 (March 1980), 93.

63 Edward Luck considers peacekeeping under Chapter VI and not under Chapter VII; see E. C. Luck, 'The case for engagement: American interests in UN peace operations' in D. C. F. Daniel and B. C. Hayes, *Beyond Traditional Peacekeeping* (New York: St. Martin's Press, 1995), pp. 68–9. Gareth Evans, on the other hand, includes the operations in Bosnia and Somalia (each involving Chapter VII) within the domain of UN peacekeeping only for budgetary and administrative purposes: see his *Cooperating for Peace: The Global Agenda for the 1990s and Beyond* (St. Leonards: Allen & Unwin, 1993).

64 While the application of Chapter VII may not always indicate that the UN action concerned must be enforcement, the non-application of Chapter VII always indicates (i.e. legally guarantees) that the UN action concerned *must not* be enforcement. Hence the authorisation of UN missions under Chapter VII sometimes leads to extensive discussions about how their mandate should be interpreted. Authorisation of a UN mission

under Chapter VII always implies that there are legitimate grounds for discussing whether that mission may have been intended to take enforcement measures.

65 See Bratt, 'Peace over justice', 64.

66 For a problematisation of the 'abandonment' of peacekeeping principles, see H. Smith, 'Prospects for peacekeeping' in H. Smith (ed.), *International Peacekeeping: Building on the Cambodian Experience* (Canberra: Australian Defence Studies Centre, 1994), pp. 201–13.

67 HMSO, *The Army Field Manual* (London: HMSO, 1994).

68 See Evans, *Cooperating for Peace*, pp. 11–12.

69 See the UN Webpage at www.un.org/Depts/dpko/pkeep.htm (23 February 1999).

70 See Smith, 'Prospects for peacekeeping', p. 203; Ratner, *The New UN Peacekeeping.*

71 The British and US Armies have adopted 'peace support operations' and 'peace operations' as their generic terms respectively: see Collins and Weiss, *An Overview and Assessment*, p. 3. Another expression that is in circulation is 'operations other than war'.

72 Lt. Gen. Sanderson, commander of the UN Transitional Authority in Cambodia (UNTAC), once stated: 'I am not keen to draw comparisons between UNTAC and other United Nations missions, since every operation is unique': see J. M. Sanderson, 'Reflections on the Cambodia experience', in Community Aid Abroad, *Learning the Lessons: United Nations Interventions in Conflict Situations* (Melbourne: Community Aid Abroad, December 1994), p. 23.

73 The UN mission in Macedonia – the Preventive Deployment Force (UNPREDEP) – exemplifies deployment in a potential conflict situation as opposed to an actual one.

74 The designated personnel must be deployed specifically to address that violent conflict. Not *any* field presence would qualify as a peacekeeping mission.

75 Hereafter, resolutions adopted by the Security Council and by the General Assembly will be referred to as 'SC resolution' and 'GA resolution' respectively.

76 McCoubrey and White use 'non-international' conflicts as the centrepiece of their study on civil wars: see H. McCoubrey and N. D. White, *International Organizations and Civil Wars* (Aldershot: Dartmouth, 1995), pp. viii, 19–22, 65–7.

77 The term was coined to overcome political difficulties especially during the codification of international humanitarian law. Given that several victims of violence around the world suffer from violence which does not stem from 'wars' in the classic sense of the term, it was necessary to find a way to bring them under the protection of codified humanitarian laws. Yet what is not clearly international cannot be easily labelled 'internal' or 'intra-state', for doing so would in practice attract opposition from a great number of governments which, jealous of their 'sovereignty', would invoke the principle of non-intervention.

78 M. Pugh, 'Post-conflict rehabilitation: the humanitarian dimension'; available online at www.isn.ethz.ch/securityforum/Online_Publications (14 August 2000).

79 T. Woodhouse and O. Ramsbotham, 'Terra incognita: here be dragons: peacekeeping and conflict resolution in contemporary conflict; some relationships considered' (Paper presented at the INCORE Conference on Training and Preparation of Military and Civilian Peacekeepers, University of Ulster, 13–15 June 1996): see www.incore.ulst.ac.uk/publications/research/peacekeeping/terra.html (17 June 2000).

80 It is, however, crucial to acknowledge in advance that almost *any* contemporary conflict has intra-state, inter-state and trans-state dimensions, though, depending on the case, one or two may prove more critical than the other(s). Furthermore, it is more or less self-evident that by becoming involved in an internal conflict, the UN helps to internationalise that conflict to some degree.

81 Implications of UN peacekeeping may go even deeper than is usually realised. US

Senator Robert Byrd once reacted to US involvement in Somalia in following terms: 'I do not see in the front of this chamber the UN flag. I have never saluted the UN flag. I salute Old Glory, the American flag'; cited in Rosenau and Durfee, *Thinking Theory Thoroughly*, p. 117.

82 We use the term 'believed to be', because the international dimensions of intra-state conflicts may prove so dominant that to describe them as intra-state may be seriously misleading.

83 For standard definitions of these and related terms, see B. Boutros-Ghali, *An Agenda for Peace: Preventive Diplomacy, Peacemaking and Peace-keeping* (New York: United Nations, 1992). While alluding to the need of removing the 'conceptual' and 'practical' confusion between these different types of activity, in particular peacekeeping and peacemaking, Bertrand usefully demonstrates how tightly knit these activities actually are: see M. Bertrand, 'The confusion between peacemaking and peacekeeping', in Warner (ed.), *New Dimensions of Peacekeeping*, pp. 163–71.

84 See T. Findlay, *The New Peacekeepers and the New Peacekeeping* (Canberra: The ANU, Department of International Relations, Working Paper No. 1996/2, May 1996), p. 18.

85 Usually a Special Representative of the Secretary-General – as in Cyprus.

86 International Peace Academy, *The Peacekeeper's Handbook* (New York: Pergamon Press, 1984).

87 See Boutros-Ghali, *An Agenda for Peace*, paras 44–5.

88 A term used by the French military and NATO planners to express the need that peace-keepers should be equipped to take active enforcement measures when necessary: see Stedman, *International Actors and Internal Conflicts*, p. 21.

89 The idea is elaborated on by Bull, Giddens, Hinsley, Hoffmann, Morgenthau, Ruggie and Wight: see H. Malmvig, 'The false dilemma? Between two sovereign foundations during legitimizations of interventions' (Paper presented at the ISA Convention, Los Angeles, CA, 14–19 March 2000), p. 5.

90 It may be argued that the external rather than internal aspect of sovereignty has captured the public imagination and dominated recent academic discourse: see J. A. Camilleri and J. Falk, *The End of Sovereignty?: The Politics of A Shrinking and Fragmenting World* (Aldershot: Edward Elgar, 1992), p. 139.

91 See Ratner, *The New Peacekeeping*, pp. 42–3. The same notions are found also in Smith, 'Prospects for peacekeeping', p. 205.

92 For instance, 'national reconciliation' is much more abstract than 'elections', and in any case, the two inevitably overlap.

93 Although Ratner maintains that 'education' is actually not included in the hierarchy of involvement, it cannot be taken to indicate a deeper involvement than 'control' and 'conduct', or for that matter 'supervision'.

94 In the context of UN peacekeeping, 'large-scale' may be taken to mean basically the size of a small division or a large brigade, that is, around 7–8,000 troops. For names and strengths of the basic elements in modern armies, see J. R. Brinkerhoff, 'Organization, army' in *Brassey's Encyclopedia of Land Forces and Warfare* (Washington, DC: Brassey's, 1996), pp. 807–17.

95 C. Heye, ' United Nations peacekeeping – an introduction', in E. Moxon-Brown (ed.), *A Future for Peacekeeping?* (Houndmills: Macmillan, 1998), p. 11.

96 The main examples are 'Operation Provide Comfort' in Iraq, and the operations in Somalia, Bosnia, Rwanda and Haiti: see Durch, 'Keeping the peace', p. 5; R. Väyrynen, 'Enforcement and humanitarian intervention: two faces of collective action by the United Nations', in C. F. Alger (ed.), *The Future of the United Nations System: Potential for the Twenty-first Century* (Tokyo: United Nations University, 1998), p. 64; and R.

Diethelm, *Das Friedenssicherungssystem der Vereinten Nationen in der Mitte der 90er Jahre* (St. Gallen: ETH Forschungsstelle fur Internationale Beziehungen, Beitrag Nr.7, Juni 1996), p. 21.

97 Whether or not questions relating to the normative basis of UN peacekeeping are clearly addressed by international actors has normative significance in its own right. The notorious ambiguity of several peacekeeping mandates is a case in point. Not infrequently we find in those mandates a striking silence on important aspects of objectives, functions and authority.

3

The UN's role in historical context: impact of structural tensions and thresholds

THE UN'S RESPONSE to intra-state conflicts did not take shape in a vacuum. International normative preferences which had an impact on active UN involvement in intra-state conflicts drew their inspiration from and interacted with the international political milieu. No doubt the wider historical context in which the UN had to operate underwent constant change, as did the UN itself. The present chapter reviews, with the benefit of historical structural insights, the evolving international context in the aftermath of World War II. The purpose of recalling this well known historical record here is to discern the most significant 'material' and 'ideational' configurations that evolved in connection with the UN as an 'institution' and impacted on the behaviour of and prescriptions for the UN as an actor. This chapter does not *directly* address UN involvement in intra-state conflicts the way subsequent chapters do, but it seeks to perform an equally critical task. It situates, that is, it gives meaning to, our detailed and more specific explorations in the following chapters. Above all, it establishes that the early 1960s and the early 1990s were critical junctures in post-1945 world politics, each reflecting different power and value configurations.

A quick examination of the period since World War II suggests that two patterns of global conflict were especially significant for the UN's evolution. The first, situated along the East–West divide, is commonly known as the Cold War. The second involves the confrontation between North and South, which is less easily captured by any single phrase. While the East–West divide rested on strategic and ideological bipolarity, the precise nature of the North–South divide was less clear. What is designated as the 'North' comprises mainly industrialised liberal/capitalist countries (geographically located for the most part in the northern hemisphere), many of which had an imperial past. The 'South', on the other hand, refers to a large number of poorer countries, most of which had experienced colonial occupation. As with the East–West tension, the North–South confrontation would decisively impact on the UN's evolving role in world politics.

Neither the East–West nor the North–South confrontation is easy to depict in a few paragraphs, especially if they are to illuminate such a complex phenomenon as the UN's relationship to intra-state conflicts. At the risk of oversimplification, we will provide no more than a cursory account of the post-1945 period, with the emphasis on how the two global conflicts manifested themselves as part of the structural evolution of the international system, which both constrained and facilitated the relationship between international actors and the UN.

Towards double 'peaks': superpower rivalry and decolonisation/non-alignment

In the immediate aftermath of World War II, the arrangements for a new world order reflected a multipolar power configuration, the embodiment of which can be found in the Security Council. In economic terms, the United States was clearly the dominant source of power.[1] Yet politically, the colonial powers, the Soviet Union and China had to be reckoned with. The main preoccupation of war-wary actors was maintenance of international peace and security. Protection of and respect for state sovereignty, and prevention of acts of aggression signified the most important ideational aspect of the new world order. The holocaust did no doubt preoccupy the minds of many, but the German and Japanese aggression in Europe and elsewhere was arguably more important for the major powers, which had been directly subjected to aggression and not to holocaust. The Charter, then, inescapably reflected a particular blend of value preferences which corresponded to the material and ideational characteristics of the international context. Before long, profound changes would impact on the political landscape.

Emergence and escalation of the East–West conflict (1945–62)

The 'Cold War'[2] was a conflict prosecuted by the United States and the Soviet Union, whose spheres of influence were separated by an imaginary 'Iron Curtain'.[3] The emergence of the Cold War was a landmark event in several respects: first and most obvious was the beginning of the transition from a multipolar to a bipolar world. Secondly, for the first time in history, an ordering principle encompassed the *entire* world. There was virtually no corner of the world that did not define itself with reference to the Cold War. Thirdly, the two poles of the new system were not merely 'great' powers. They were 'superpowers' with nuclear capabilities and a truly global reach. As we shall see, all three characteristics would constrain the role envisaged for the UN in world politics.

44

The period between 1945 and 1962 saw the emergence and step-by-step escalation of the worldwide ideological and strategic confrontation between the two superpowers. The expansion of their spheres of influence and the formation of their respective power 'blocs' became distinguishing characteristics of the period. Immediately after the war, a number of significant events signalled the onset of tension. In 1947, the Truman Doctrine, the domino theory, the rise of McCarthyism and the Marshall Plan paved the way for the first major geopolitical confrontation: the 1948 Berlin crisis. Although a war was barely averted, the crisis added to the intensification of the Cold War. The following year, NATO would be created to counter the perceived Soviet threat.[4]

The end of the Chinese civil war, coupled with NATO's creation, would gradually contribute to the process of escalation. The scope of East–West tension had now extended beyond European borders. Although, strategically, Sino-Soviet relations would drastically deteriorate in due course,[5] western perception of the 'communist threat' had no doubt considerably increased following Mao's take-over. Soon after came the formation of the Council for Mutual Economic Assistance (COMECON).[6] The communist powers, already reasonably unified ideologically, were also beginning to organise themselves economically if not yet militarily. Before long, however, would come signs of increasing Soviet military strength – the first Soviet atomic bomb was detonated on 29 August 1949.

Given Stalin's prominence in the development of the Cold War, his death in 1953 might have been expected to slow down the escalation of East–West tension. This did not turn out to be the case. By then, the Cold War had developed its own logic and dynamic. In 1954, the Soviet Union tested its hydrogen bomb. The same year, the United States coerced the members of the OAS to adopt the Caracas Declaration, condemning communist efforts to gain control in any American state.[7] Between 1954 and 1955 the two blocs further expanded. The Southeast Asia Treaty Organization (SEATO)[8] and the Central Treaty Organization (CENTO)[9] joined NATO to form a western security umbrella.[10] This 'capitalist encirclement' (to quote the Soviet view) was finally counterbalanced by the formation of the Warsaw Pact in 1955.[11] After Khrushchev's rise to power, the Soviet Union launched, in August–October 1957, the world's first inter-continental ballistic missile (ICBM) and the first earth satellite, *Sputnik*.[12] By November 1959, Khrushchev would declare that the Soviet Union had stockpiled enough rockets to wipe all its probable enemies from the face of the earth.[13]

In 1958 the establishment of the European Economic Community (EEC) represented a major advance on the European Coal and Steel Community (ECSC). The idea of European integration was becoming ever more concrete. Adoption of a 'capitalist' model of development and political integration in

Western Europe was certainly of vital concern to the Soviet bloc. It concerned the United States as well, since an integrated Europe might increasingly distance itself from its trans-Atlantic ally, especially given that the driving force behind such integration was the former enemy, Germany, and de Gaulle's uncooperative France.[14]

In the early 1960s the Cold War reached its climax. Formal relations were established in 1960 between Castro's revolutionary Cuba (just a few miles from Florida) and the Soviet Union. The same year an American U–2 spy plane was shot down in the Soviet territory. Meanwhile, in 1961 the Berlin Wall was built. A concrete embodiment of the imaginary Iron Curtain was now in place. The same year, the US attempt to overthrow Castro in the famous Bay of Pigs expedition ended in failure. In 1962, the East–West confrontation had virtually reached its peak with the Cuban missile crisis, which brought the world within a whisker of a full-scale nuclear war.

Emergence of the contemporary North–South conflict (1955–64)

The struggle between rich and poor countries, to put it crudely, has deep historical roots. The North–South conflict is in this sense much older than the East–West conflict. A politically organised 'South', however, did not emerge until after World War II. The 1950s witnessed a conceptual breakthrough in policy and academic circles alike, whereby the multi-dimensional divide between rich and poor countries began to be considered a worldwide phenomenon.[15] The precise nature of the relationship between these two loosely identified groups of countries or coalitions was the subject of intense debate, but there was little doubt that North and South stood in opposition to each other.[16]

The contemporary North–South conflict, as we use the term, came into being in the mid-1950s when the South began to organise itself politically. In its initial period, the conflict had two major manifestations: decolonisation and non-alignment. The significant point in relation to both is that during this early phase the South defined itself *vis-à-vis* the North primarily in 'negative' terms. In other words, the southern countries stipulated what they were *not* and what they were *against*, rather than what they *were* and what they were *for*.[17] Yet they asserted their position with such strength and venom that their messages carried almost the same weight on the world political stage as those of the Cold War protagonists. In the transition from multipolarity to bipolarity, the South took its place alongside the western and socialist camps as a third, yet looser, 'bloc'.

Politics of decolonisation

Although decolonisation was not a recent phenomenon, the largest 'waves' of decolonisation were seen in the twentieth century, following World Wars I

and II. 1955–65 was by far the most active period in the history of decolonisation, with forty-seven new states emerging during this 'decolonisation
decade'.[18] The impact of the radical transition from colonialism to post-colonialism was twofold: it changed the way the (neo)colonial powers exercised
influence over (ex-)colonies; but equally importantly, it provided the South
with a unifying concept during the period of decolonisation.

The first dimension of the transition to post-colonialism involved the
continued ambitions of great powers and business interests in relation to
(ex-)colonies. Britain and France particularly, but also the other colonial
powers, were intent on maintaining their influence over their former colonies.
From their perspective, the rapidly evolving post-1945 environment posed an
enormous challenge. Economically devastated, they were not in a position to
maintain physical control of the territories they once ruled. Yet they still
needed relatively easy access to the cheap resources they used to extract from
those same colonies. Just as importantly perhaps, Britain and France in particular were anxious to retain, in the face of the emerging bipolar system, their
national pride and the vestiges of their glorious past.[19] In a sense, the old
multipolar system was struggling to survive.

In the late 1950s, the former colonial powers were yet to find new ways of
pursuing their old colonial ambitions. Should they try to retain physical
control of remote territories, or should they attempt to establish alternative,
less costly, but equally effective methods of control? They understood perfectly
well that the choice would not always be theirs, that the decolonisation
process had its own accelerating dynamic. Still, should they at least attempt to
maintain a physical presence backed by military capabilities? They attempted
to do precisely this during the 1956 Suez crisis.[20] A choice in favour of arms-
based classical colonialism, whether realistic or not, would imply the
persistence of the military mode of rivalry between great powers.

The answers to these questions varied with each individual case. In some
cases, these powers remained devoted to classical colonialism.[21] In others,
they gradually transformed into 'neo'colonisers – a transformation which
greatly benefited from the carefully established colonial structures they had
bequeathed to the newly independent states. Former colonial powers had
established powerful administrative, economic, social and cultural links with
these countries over several years of colonial exploitation.[22] Traditional colonialism was primarily, if not exclusively, based on military means. The pursuit
of neocolonial ambitions, on the other hand, required alternative sources of
influence. In any case, the emerging political trend in Western Europe was
working against the continuation of an intra-European rivalry based on
massive military investments. The transition from military-based classical
colonialism to influence-based neocolonialism was not an easy one. In the
process, the colonial powers held strongly to the principle of state sovereignty,

arguing that the colonies and protectorates were part of their 'sovereign domain'.

The second dimension of the transition from colonialism to post-colonialism involved the search for identity by the former colonies. There were multiple influences over popular self-perceptions, with religion, race, nation, ethno-linguistic affinity, ideology and colonial heritage all playing a part.[23] The most important common denominator of these self-perceptions was the scepticism, indeed hostility, towards the North – in particular the former colonial powers. Hence, Nasser's Arab nationalism and Nkrumah's Africanism were able to converge in their oppositional attitude towards colonial powers, especially Britain and France.[24] In addition, the fast crystallising Third World mindset was able to establish cross-continental links. Decolonisation served as a pivotal concept around which the colonised world gained consciousness of their collective identity.[25]

Another aspect of the search for identity was the influence exerted by the two superpowers. Leaders in several former colonies were convinced that their escape from subordination could not be accomplished without the help of either or both superpowers. It would be wrong to disregard the role played by the capitalism–communism debate in the decolonisation movement of the late 1950s, but it would also be a mistake to try and explain the fashion of the day, as is sometimes done, merely in terms of 'ideology' along the East–West axis. In certain cases political pragmatism played at least as important a role as commitment to ideology.

Nasser's appeal to the Soviet Union cannot be adequately explained in terms of ideology, especially given the potency of religious and traditional sentiment in Egypt, which has always been antithetical to the atheistic and anti-feudal worldview attached to communism. In the Congo (one of our case studies) ideological appeals were sometimes made quite pragmatically, and perhaps even unconsciously. In December 1959, when Joseph Kasavubu told the socialist newspaper *Le Peuple* that political parties were 'being manufactured by the dozen at the drop of a bank-note', he was echoing the communist press of the day.[26] However, as we shall see in Chapter 5, in retrospect it is difficult to argue that Kasavubu had communist tendencies. In any case, the search for identity in the South coincided with, contributed to and benefited from the escalation of geopolitical bipolarity.

Politics of non-alignment

A second dimension of the North–South conflict manifested itself in the non-aligned movement (NAM), which began to take shape at the Bandung conference held on 18–25 April 1955. The conference was convened at the initiative of a loose association of five states, known as the 'Colombo powers': Burma (Myanmar), Ceylon (Sri Lanka), India, Indonesia and Pakistan.

Although there were only two criteria for participation (independence and being an Afro-Asian state), neither criterion was applied in a straightforward fashion. On the one hand, two colonies (Sudan and Ghana) were included among the invitees. On the other hand, such geographically eligible countries as Israel, South Africa, South Korea, North Korea and Taiwan were not. The Arab states would not tolerate Israeli participation. South Africa was considered an outcast. Participation of the two Koreas might create political problems for the organisers. And Taiwan could not be invited in China's presence.[27]

The gathering of 29 relatively less developed states at a time when the UN had only 59 members marked a turning point for the Third World.[28] The major, perhaps the only, achievement of this conference was that it brought together several underdeveloped countries for the first time to discuss their worldviews. Significantly, the final *communiqué* stressed the importance of decolonisation and economic development for the South. After a number of significant follow-up meetings,[29] in September 1961, at the invitation of Egypt, India and Yugoslavia, the first NAM summit (Belgrade) took place with the participation of 25 states.[30]

Reportedly, there were three competing analyses as to the critical issues at stake. One group, led by Sukarno and Nkrumah, put the emphasis on colonialism and continuing great power intervention in the Third World.[31] Another, led by Nehru, saw the growing nuclear threat and superpower rivalry as the overriding problem.[32] Nasser and Tito, on the other hand, preferred to take the middle ground,[33] not in the sense that their position was lukewarm and moderate, but in the sense that they put the emphasis on both the North–South and East–West conflicts. The final resolution reflected this last view. The organised South had established itself in terms of a powerful opposition to both colonialism and the Cold War.[34]

The early 1960s: locating the UN at a critical juncture

Both in its structure and in its self-understanding, the UN was born in ambiguity. In one sense, the organisation had some of the characteristics of an alliance[35] – a feature still reflected in the composition of the Security Council. Originally, 'United Nations' was a term that the Allied Powers had used to describe themselves.[36] In 1945, at the San Fransisco conference, this name would be given to a new organisation entrusted with the future maintenance of international peace and security. Considered from this vantage point, the UN was intended to serve the whole international community; it was to lay the groundwork of a future world where disputes would be resolved in a collective manner. From the outset, the smooth functioning of the world body was premised upon the peaceful coexistence of different actors and opposing worldviews, among them the two superpowers and their respective ideologies.

The escalation of the Cold War influenced UN actions, including involvement in intra-state conflicts, in two significant respects. In the first place, as a logical extension of their geopolitical strategies, the two superpowers sought to counterbalance each other everywhere in the world. Their aim was not only to increase their own military and economic capabilities, but also to create new allies or client states. At the same time, they were intent on gaining access to the resources of former colonies. The Cold War was after all a costly struggle. Rhetoric aside, the superpowers were increasingly disposed to taking their place alongside the traditional colonial powers in what soon emerged as a neocolonial competition for Third World resources.[37] In the process, many, if not most, intra-state conflicts were viewed as capable of altering, directly or indirectly, the balance of power between the two blocs. Whether a government was 'friendly' or 'hostile' mattered greatly to both superpowers. The mode and degree of UN responses to conflicts depended in part on how crucial a conflict was to the global strategic balance. The UN would be 'allowed' to become actively involved only at the margins of this balance.[38]

Secondly, almost all conflicts in the world came to be seen by the superpowers as 'international' conflicts. *Each* conflict, whether intra-state, inter-state, or trans-state, assumed a global, geostrategic dimension so far as the two poles were concerned. In addition, and related with the transition from a multipolar to a bipolar world, the attitudes of the two superpowers to several conflicts contrasted sharply with those of the former colonial powers. What seemed 'internal' conflicts to the old colonialists (meaning internal to their colonial empires, as in Algeria or Rhodesia) were considered 'international' by the superpowers (meaning that the other superpower might intrude into that conflict at any moment). In this sense, the UN's response to intra-state conflicts could not but reflect an overwhelming preoccupation with *international* peace and security, in a way that was not perhaps incompatible with the original intent of the Charter.

For several years, the Cold War prevented the increase of UN membership.[39] Membership increased from the original 51 to 76 in the first decade, and then to 118 in the second decade. All of the new members between 1945 and 1955 were from either the Asia-Pacific region or Europe. In the mid-1950s the decolonisation process accelerated considerably, especially in Africa. Under mounting Third World pressure, the veto barrier to membership was eventually sidestepped. Out of the 42 new members between 1955 and 1965, all but 10 were African.[40] By the early 1960s, the majority of the UN's members were under the strong influence of the transition from colonialism to post-colonialism, with the Cold War cutting across that influence.

The interaction between the UN and non-state actors was at best embryonic in the first twenty years of the organisation's history. Social movements and forces, which would be increasingly influential in shaping collective expectations of the UN in the years to come, had not yet fully developed. Several major IGOs, whether multipurpose or functional, were almost as new and inexperienced as the UN itself, with many of them established between the late 1940s and the early 1960s.[41] Non-governmental organisations had been present at the San Fransisco Conference as consultants of national delegations, with American NGOs, in particular, instrumental in defining Article 71 of the UN Charter.[42] The earliest ECOSOC–NGO consultative arrangements were set forth in ECOSOC Resolutions 2/3 in 1946 and 288 B (X) in 1950. In the first twenty years, ECOSOC's standing NGO committee was dominated by western states.[43] By 1968, there were no more than 377 NGOs in consultative status with ECOSOC, with only 12 of them in the most influential 'general' category.[44]

Almost from the outset, certainly from the Berlin crisis on, the Cold War had rendered the Security Council largely ineffectual, the first strong manifestation of which was the adoption of the 'Uniting for Peace' Resolution[45] by the General Assembly during the 1950 Korean crisis – the first major outbreak of hostilities in which the UN played an active role. This was perhaps the first indicator of the General Assembly's 'rise in power', a trend that would continue until the early 1960s.[46] The Korean 'War' was indeed a direct byproduct of strategic and ideological rivalry, in which the two superpowers as well as the emerging communist power, China, figured prominently.

Led by the United States, a group of pro-western states contributed to a military force under the UN flag, and waged war in an intra-Korean conflict which had clear international, even geostrategic, dimensions.[47] This was perhaps the first blow to the UN's 'credibility', at least in the eyes of the socialist powers. Thereafter, the Soviet Union tried to play its cards more carefully. The UN, it seemed, *could* become an effective actor in the hands of whichever power was best able to manipulate it. With hindsight, it appears as if Moscow was less well placed than Washington to influence or mobilise the UN in support of its interests, which is not to say that the Soviet Union did not successfully neutralise the UN on several occasions.[48]

With the controversy over the Korean intervention the Cold War barriers to the UN's peace and security function became fully apparent. The UN was rendered virtually impotent during the US intervention in Guatemala in 1954 and the Soviet intervention in Hungary in 1956.[49] Strategic bipolarity would make it practically impossible for the UN to intervene in conflicts, be they inter- or intra-state, if they were located within the US and Soviet spheres of influence, or in some way cut across the interests and priorities of either Washington or Moscow. The idea of UN peacekeeping matured almost at the same time as the Guatemala and Hungary crises. It is noteworthy that this mechanism was developed in response to the Suez crisis rather than to events in Guatemala or Hungary.[50] The Suez dispute had more to do with decolonisation than with the Cold War. In the aftermath of World War II, decolonisation was a dominant worldwide political project, enjoying the support of a significant coalition of international actors, including the superpowers.

In the early 1960s, the General Assembly would reaffirm its commitment to a key Charter principle, namely state sovereignty. In 1962, a resolution was adopted on states' Permanent Sovereignty over Natural Resources.[51] In 1965, a declaration was adopted on the Inadmissibility of Intervention in the Domestic Affairs of States and the Protection of Their Independence and Sovereignty.[52] These instruments showed the Third World's insistence on the primacy of state sovereignty.[53] Despite their occasional reservations,[54] the colonial powers, too, held strongly to this UN principle which was best suited to protect their colonial interests. Colonies and protectorates were within the 'sovereign domain' of the colonial powers. No one else, including the UN, could be allowed to penetrate it. As a consequence, the questions of Algeria and Northern Ireland, to cite just two examples, were not even inscribed to the agenda of the Security Council, while the Rhodesian question was consistently referred to Britain for it to take appropriate action in its capacity as the 'sovereign' authority.[55]

Primarily as a result of resistance by the South, the General Assembly began to elaborate a number of principles during this period. It emphasised, tentatively at first, various aspects of the human rights as well as socioeconomic or development agendas.[56] A landmark initiative was the adoption of the Declaration on the Granting of Independence to Colonial Countries and Peoples,[57] which may be described as a concrete embodiment of the decolonisation project. Adopted by 89 votes in favour and none against, the resolution was clearly Wilsonian in orientation, though the United States was among the nine abstaining countries,[58] reflecting its support for its major allies. Other examples include the Convention on the Elimination of All Forms of Racial Discrimination[59] and the inauguration of the (first) Development Decade.[60]

In its first twenty years, the UN was ever more constrained by escalating superpower rivalry, while the organised South sought active UN action for the purposes of, and in contexts of, decolonisation. By the early 1960s, geopolitical bipolarity had become strong enough to outweigh the legacy of an earlier multipolar power configuration. With the decolonisation project speedily accomplished, the South began to lose its strength. The difficulty of maintaining unity among a fast growing Third World membership was no doubt an important factor. World politics entered a phase which, though it reflected a new power configuration, was nevertheless compatible with the ideational attributes of the immediate post-War international order, namely preoccupation with the maintenance of international peace and security and protection of sovereignty.

The aftermath of double peaks

In the early 1960s, the multipolar power configuration was largely replaced by Cold War bipolarity. This, as we shall see, did not mean the complete disappearance of other important sources of influence. Nor did it mean a lack of 'variety' in the configuration of material capabilities. France in the western camp and China in the socialist camp, for instance, developed their relatively independent political attitudes. None the less, superpower rivalry was strong enough to be the primary influence in world politics. The rapidly unfolding decolonisation project and increasing ambiguities in the non-aligned spectrum added to this influence in the context of UN politics to the extent that the organised South lost two important unifying concepts that had facilitated UN action in the field of peace and security.

Consolidation of the East–West conflict (1962–85)

What we call the 'consolidation' of the East–West conflict corresponds roughly to the long rule of Brezhnev (1964–82) and to the successive US presidencies of Johnson (1963–69), Nixon (1969–74), Ford (1974–77) and Carter (1977–81). This period of more than twenty years was so rich in political drama and the evolution of the Cold War so exquisitely nuanced that it may seem inappropriate not to break it down into shorter periods. While we do not intend to do violence to the intricate nature of the Cold War, our seemingly oversimplistic presentation has a purpose. The point is that, once the Cold War matured and reached its peak (with the 'blocs' and nuclear arsenals firmly in place), it was consolidated at that peak level for over twenty years, with only relatively minor swings of the pendulum.[61]

East–West relations were continuously tense throughout this period, though this tension did not always manifest itself in outright crises. There was a constant oscillation between overt crises and covert rivalry. The intensity of the bipolar struggle, however, would not substantially moderate, except in a cosmetic sense, until the mid-1980s. The so-called periods of *détente* did not indicate a genuine soothing of the bipolar struggle, but a covert full-speed continuation of rivalry by other means. After the climax of confrontation in the early 1960s, both the United States and the Soviet Union felt that the probability of 'hot' conflict should be reduced. To do otherwise could prove costly for both sides, given the fast expanding strategic arsenals available to both parties. With the doctrine of Mutual Assured Destruction (MAD) coming to full maturity during this period, the Cold War would remain in full swing for more than twenty years, but with each party prudent enough not to provoke the other to a full-scale confrontation.

The oscillating pattern of relations between the two blocs was clearly visible in the 1960s. In 1963 confidence-building agreements were signed between the superpowers, including the Nuclear Test Ban Treaty. In 1964, the United States entered the war in Vietnam. In 1967, President Johnson met with Soviet Prime Minister Kosygin in Glassboro. The following year came the Warsaw Pact intervention in Czechoslovakia. In 1969 the Americans landed on the moon, a 'giant leap for mankind' with serious implications for future development of strategic weaponry. Negotiations between the superpowers resulted in summit meetings and the signing of strategic arms limitation treaties in the early 1970s. SALT I (the first series of Strategic Arms Limitation Talks) was concluded in 1972. Meanwhile, Brezhnev proclaimed that peaceful coexistence was the normal, permanent, and irreversible state of relations between imperialist and communist countries.[62] He warned, though, that conflict might continue in the Third World. The Cold War had now stabilised at its 'centre', but instability resulting from fierce superpower competition was tolerated at the periphery.

Another significant development in the 1960s was China's emerging 'two front' policy. Between 1963 and 1969, Beijing chose to confront both Washington and Moscow. Although no separate 'bloc' was formed around Beijing, the China factor emerged as another dimension in Cold War calculations. In 1969, in connection with heightening border conflicts, the Soviet Union threatened to launch a military strike against Chinese nuclear weapon installations,[63] prompting China to move further away from the Soviet bloc, making the Sino-American *rapprochement* of the early 1970s possible.[64]

In 1972, in the wake of the escalating Vietnam crisis, the superpowers signed a document setting out twelve basic principles governing their relations.[65] The agreement had three main provisions.[66] The first held that in the nuclear age there was no alternative to conducting mutual relations on the basis of peaceful coexistence and on the principles of sovereignty, equality and non-interference in internal affairs. Secondly, both superpowers recognised the 'importance of preventing the development of situations capable of causing a dangerous exacerbation of their relations'. Thirdly, both accepted a 'special responsibility to do everything in their power so that conflicts or situations will not arise which would serve to increase international tensions'.

This document is instructive in that it points to the intermeshing of Cold War political calculations with two germane normative principles: state sovereignty and non-intervention. In other words, the new phase of the post-

1945 history was based on a new power configuration but reflected (was compatible with) the old value preferences. Violation of these principles would have the inevitable consequence of escalating tension, perhaps to the point of armed conflict. The principles were invoked with their geopolitical dimension in mind. Their main implication was that, if peace was to be maintained, the two superpowers had to stay clear of each other's sphere of influence. The 'internal' affairs of Czechoslovakia, to give an example, should be of no concern to the United States. By the same token, 'domestic' politics in Chile should not overly concern the Soviet Union. The principles of sovereignty and non-intervention, then, served the purposes of both superpowers. Not in the sense that the superpowers would necessarily and absolutely keep away from each other's backyards, but that they knew the boundaries of their respective spheres of influence. These principles would be inevitably reflected in the prescriptions which the two superpowers would seek to impose on the UN.

It is plausible to argue that the rhetorical superpower adherence to the principle of state sovereignty was in fact contradictory. The United States had justified its violations of other states' sovereignty with reference to democracy and the 'free world'. By the same token, Brezhnev had defended the Warsaw Pact operation in Czechoslovakia in the following terms:

> We cannot ignore the assertions, held in some places, that the actions of the five socialist countries run counter to the Marxist-Leninist principle of sovereignty and the rights of nations to self-determination. The groundlessness of such reasoning consists primarily in that it is based on an abstract, non-class approach to the question of sovereignty ... The sovereignty of each socialist country cannot be opposed to the interests of the world of socialism, of the world revolutionary movement.[67]

This superpower attitude may be seen as the beginning of the erosion of the principle of state sovereignty both in rhetoric and in practice. On the one hand, state sovereignty was frequently invoked by the superpowers as the key value in the prevailing world order. On the other hand, it was frequently violated in practice, but also endowed with multiple, even inconsistent, meanings.[68] Implicit in the superpower mentality was the normative support for the idea that other states should sacrifice their sovereignty for a 'greater common good'. This normative attitude may be seen as paving the way for the 'interventionist' normative prescriptions of the post-Cold War period. The Cold War had systematised and, to a degree, 'legitimised' such contradiction as was inherent in superpower thinking.[69]

In July 1975, the American–Soviet joint 'Apollo Soyuz Test Project' matured. During the mid-1970s, the Conference on Security and Cooperation in Europe (CSCE) process was set in train. The two blocs were now in search of an acceptable pattern of coexistence. The ensuing *Helsinki Final Act* of 1 August 1975 is perhaps best known for its 'third basket' which dealt with humanitarian issues.[70] This instrument may be considered as the first serious attempt on the part of the western camp to address the western and socialist audiences in order to 'corner' the Soviet bloc on the grounds of human rights abuses. In 1977, Jimmy Carter became US President, with an express commitment to the promotion of human rights as a key objective of foreign policy. Despite his adoption of the human rights discourse, however, Carter himself signalled early in the piece that this normative 'commitment' would be applied quite selectively.[71]

In 1979 came SALT II, as did the Soviet invasion of Afghanistan, which quickly opened up a new phase of renewed confrontation. The invasion of Afghanistan coincided with Reagan's election to the US Presidency. He came to power with the express intention of defeating what he called the 'Evil Empire', that is the Soviet Union. His most notable strategic policy, the Strategic Defense Initiative (SDI), would intensify the Cold War. Meanwhile, Brezhnev's death and the ensuing search for a new leader weakened the Soviet end of the geopolitical balance. The Soviet Union experienced a leadership crisis, not unlike, in some respects, the three-year power struggle after Stalin's demise. Following the short-lived reigns of Andropov (1982–84) and Chernenko (1984–85), Gorbachev rose to power. His unexpectedly radical reformist policies paved the way for a *rapprochement* between the superpowers, and the Cold War entered its last phase in 1985.

Ascent and descent: dual trends in the South (1964–82)

By the time the second non-aligned summit took place (Cairo, 1964), the organised South had already become an influential, though somewhat loose, 'bloc' in world politics. The strong opposition to colonialism was coupled with the search for political and strategic non-alignment. Furthermore, the relatively independent moves of such important state actors as France in the western camp and China in the socialist camp provided further impetus and greater political or geopolitical space for several Third World leaders intent on carving out a non-aligned posture.[72] Nevertheless, in the 1960s, the Cold War overshadowed the North–South divide in its structural impact on the UN's peace and security function. Ironically, the period of *détente* made it more and more difficult for Third World countries to play the superpowers against each other.

It is arguable that the Cold War was all along present within the NAM. Nasser had received Soviet aid during the Suez crisis in 1956. The participants of the Cairo Conference of December 1957 had included socialist delegations. From the late 1950s onwards, superpower confrontation managed to penetrate the movement at a greater pace. One manifestation of this penetration was the establishment of military regimes with the active support of the superpowers. To cite but a few examples, the coercive regime changes in Cuba and Iraq were backed by the Soviet Union, while that in the Congo enjoyed US support. Perhaps a striking case, which vividly demonstrates the point, is that of Indonesia, a leading non-aligned country, where a Soviet-backed *coup* attempt was countered by an American-backed counter-*coup* which installed the Suharto regime in 1965.

The Third World's endeavours to eradicate colonialism, bypass strategic bipolarity, and achieve socio-economic development led to a number of multi-lateral initiatives which would coexist with Cold War alliances. Several major IGOs had been established in the South, adding further weight to Third World responses to the East–West and North–South conflicts. The League of Arab States (Arab League) and the Organization of American States (OAS),[73] founded in 1945 and 1948 respectively, were joined by the Organization of African Unity (OAU) in 1963 and the Association of South-East Asian Nations (ASEAN) in 1967. Although the Cold War inescapably influenced the formation and policies of these organisations, they added a different dimension to the institutionalisation of governance. As our subsequent chapters will demonstrate, these organisations would not necessarily or always 'compete' with the UN in dealing with intra-state conflicts in their respective regions. Unable to deal with those conflicts single-handedly – unable not only because they lacked the necessary means and capacity, but also because they were not well placed to reconcile the local, regional and global interests at stake – they would seek ways of introducing the UN into those conflict environments.

From the mid-1960s, non-aligned politics was increasingly connected to and reinforced by the development-oriented activities of less developed countries whose efforts led to the first UN Conference on Trade and Development (UNCTAD) in 1964.[74] Finding partial shelter under the umbrella of NAM and UNCTAD, Third World states, whose number grew with each passing year, were now questioning the legitimacy of the post-1945 order. The third NAM conference, held in Lusaka in 1970, would be followed by conferences in Algiers (1973), Colombo (1976), Havana (1979) and New Delhi (1983). The NAM was unambiguously opposed to colonialism, an attitude which the movement had maintained since its inception and which carried with it a particular normative position, best described as defence of state sovereignty writ large. Attempts to prevent the Cold War from penetrating into the domestic affairs of Third World states strengthened the consolidation of this normative position. In this sense at least, 'solidarity' was an inherent quality of non-alignment, in that it had contributed significantly to the ascent of the Third World as a political force with its own normative baggage.

On the socio-economic front, the international monetary crisis of 1971 was perhaps the first blow to the socio-economic aspirations of the Third World.[75] Following the Six-Day War and the oil crisis precipitated by the

Organization of the Petroleum Exporting Countries (OPEC) in 1973, the United States attempted to break up the conjunctural unity of the South. Secretary of State Kissinger invited the 'most seriously affected' states (the 'Fourth World'), that is the poorest oil-importing states, to participate in the Western Energy Coordinating Group. Algeria countered by proposing a New International Economic Order (NIEO). Under OPEC pressure, a Conference on International Economic Cooperation (CIEC) was convened between 1975 and 1977.[76] It soon became apparent, however, that the South was unable to act as a unified group, although the general emphasis on a broadly stated normative objective, namely the need to press ahead with the socio-economic development of Third World countries, assumed increasing legitimacy.[77]

The 1980s was the decade of debt crises. Beginning with Mexico in August 1982, a number of southern countries, including Argentina, Brazil and Venezuela, experienced serious and at times crippling financial difficulties. This left them in a highly ambiguous position. On the one hand, they became ever more critical of the existing global economic system, but on the other, they had to be on good terms with the North just to survive. This may be seen both as an early sign of – and a contributing factor to – the western dominance that would mature in the following decade.

The UN after double peaks: towards ideational changes

The second twenty years of the UN were marked by the ineffectiveness of the Security Council for obvious reasons related to the Cold War. In 1971, as a result of the Sino-American *rapprochement* China replaced Taiwan in the Security Council. This, in effect, rendered the Security Council even more idle. The Council's ineffectiveness was coupled with the 'stagnation' of the General Assembly,[78] notwithstanding the proliferation of UN standard-setting activities, especially with respect to human rights. In 1966, the General Assembly had adopted the International Covenant on Civil and Political Rights and the International Covenant on Economic, Social and Cultural Rights.[79] From 22 April to 13 May 1968, the first International Conference on Human Rights was held in Tehran. The increasing pace of UN norm-setting in human rights resulted, in part, from the fact that the principles of state sovereignty and non-intervention were already firmly endorsed as the primary rules of the game in international relations. In other words, the necessary space had been created to deal more flexibly with relatively 'secondary' social issues, which were nevertheless institutionalised in the Charter.

The superpowers had endorsed the primacy of state sovereignty as a requirement of their coexistence. The (neo)colonial powers had given their utmost support to the principle, for intervention in their 'internal' affairs might hasten the break-up of their empires. Third World states had jealously embraced state sovereignty, simply because it embodied their political independence and territorial integrity. If this consensus of state actors was a permissive factor for the increasing norm-setting in human rights under UN auspices – permissive in the sense that the 'house' was in order, or so it seemed – the influence of transnational social forces was a proactive factor. The proliferation and empowerment of non-state actors was but one manifestation of this influence. Perhaps more important was the increasing maturity of national and transnational 'audiences'[80] in response to which state and non-state actors positioned themselves. Finding encouragement, at least in rhetoric, from such developments as the CSCE process and the Carter Presidency, human rights organisations made their voices more widely heard in UN corridors in the 1970s.

In May 1968, ECOSOC established new consultative arrangements for NGOs at the UN. In accordance with Resolution 1296 two major reviews were conducted on ECOSOC–NGO relations, in 1968–69 and in 1978 respectively.[81] The former was initiated by Tanzania, while the latter was called for by Argentina in the face of mounting criticism from NGOs.[82] In August 1977, a draft decision sponsored by Argentina, and supported by the Soviet Union and Yugoslavia,[83] was adopted by ECOSOC, which requested the Secretary-General 'to invite interested Member States to provide any relevant information concerning compliance by non-governmental organizations with the principles governing consultative status'.[84] Only eight governments responded to the invitation, four of which (Britain, Sweden, the Netherlands and West Germany) defended and praised the role of NGOs, while two (Argentina and Syria) were bitterly critical.[85]

The creation of the Working Group on Forced or Involuntary Disappearances was largely motivated by the detailed NGO reports in relation to Chile and Argentina.[86] Amnesty International's fact-finding mission to Argentina in 1977 would be described by an observer as 'one of the most significant human rights missions ever undertaken by a non-governmental organisation'.[87] When discussions in the Commission of Human Rights were blocked by governments, it was again NGOs which mobilised media and diplomatic pressure and managed, eventually, to systematise the so-called 'thematic' human rights mechanisms.[88]

These developments contributed to increasing legitimacy of non-governmental human rights activism under the UN umbrella. Furthermore, beginning with the late 1970s, the number and field activities of non-governmental development and humanitarian agencies increased, leading to growing NGO–UN interaction.[89] Yet, the Cold War did not easily allow for UN and non-UN humanitarian action. As Donini puts it, 'cross border humanitarian assistance was basically taboo for the UN since it was tantamount to a violation of sovereignty'.[90] In other words, the dominant interpretations of institutionalised values (Charter principles) tended to resist the ideational changes slowly taking place as a result of strengthening social movements that had to operate within Cold War structural constraints.

The period between 1967 and 1978 saw the assumption of responsibility by the UN Commission on Human Rights, which would gradually evolve 'towards an effective response' from 1979 onwards.[91] In the process, two significant UN procedures were developed by the adoption of ECOSOC Resolutions 1235 and 1503. The former stated that violations could be examined and responded to in a public debate at the Commission. The latter called for consistent patterns of gross human rights violations to be pursued with governments in private.[92] On the other hand, in its instruments and decisions, UNESCO increasingly linked 'human rights' and 'peace'.[93]

In two exceptional cases, the strengthening human rights agenda made its presence felt in the field of peace and security. In 1966, in a series of resolutions, the Security Council imposed, reaffirmed and intensified sanctions on Southern Rhodesia.[94] Each resolution made explicit reference either to Chapter VII in general or to Articles 39 and 41 in particular. As legally binding instruments, these resolutions were 'decisions' rather than 'calls upon' member states. The Security Council decision on the interception of tankers carrying oil to Southern Rhodesia in 1966[95] was the only instance in the UN's history – after Korea, but before Iraq – in which member states were authorised to use military force on behalf of the UN.[96] Then, in November 1977, the Security Council adopted, expressly under Chapter VII, its first and only binding decision to impose mandatory sanctions on South Africa[97] which remained, after the lifting of sanctions against Rhodesia,[98] the only country to be subjected to UN sanctions. The Security Council's subsequent resolutions merely 'recommended' rather than 'decided' that sanctions be imposed.[99] More importantly, three proposed resolutions providing for mandatory sanctions were vetoed by Britain and the United States.[100] The limited and selective nature of the UN's response to Rhodesia and South Africa notwithstanding, common to the UN's response in both cases was a growing preoccupation with the human rights dimensions of the conflict.[101]

If human rights were one emerging international concern that began to be voiced more vigorously under UN auspices, another was socio-economic development. Advocacy of this second concern was most obviously associated with the Third World whose impact on the UN in the field of peace and security (such exceptional cases as South Africa and Southern Rhodesia notwithstanding) became increasingly marginalised. UNCTAD I saw the formation of the so-called 'Group of 77' – a coalition based primarily on a shared criticism of the post-War liberal economic order, best symbolised by the General Agreement on Tariffs and Trade (GATT) regime. Under enormous pressure from the South, the industrialised countries did participate in

UNCTAD, albeit reluctantly. In the course of discussions they proposed that UNCTAD be placed under the authority of ECOSOC rather than be created as an autonomous specialised agency. Another proposal, which envisaged equal representation of developed and developing countries on the standing committee, was subsequently revised to allow substantive decisions to be taken by the approval of the twelve major trading countries. As these terms were unacceptable to the South, a compromise formula was eventually crafted, whereby UNCTAD became a subsidiary organ of the General Assembly, and an elaborate voting procedure was devised to allow for decisions by consensus.[102]

In November 1965, the UNDP was established. In the lead-up to UNCTAD II (New Delhi, 1968), the Group of 77 adopted the Algiers Charter, which may be considered the South's first major declaration on socio-economic development. It called for action in a number of sectors which the South deemed critical to its development prospects.[103] In the aftermath of UNCTAD III (Santiago, 1972), Algeria's NIEO proposal would be translated at the General Assembly in December 1974 into the Charter of Economic Rights and Duties of States. These moves contributed to changes in the international context, especially in its ideational dimension. Subsequent UN Conferences on Trade and Development would be held in Nairobi (1976), Manila (1979) and Belgrade (1983). Yet, partly as a consequence of successive international economic crises and the steady deterioration of the relative position of the developing economies – with the exception of the newly industrialised countries, particularly in East Asia – the impetus which the UNCTAD process had generated would lose steam with each passing conference.

Despite the structural constraints on the UN's peace and security function, the UN as actor increasingly entered into the orbit of ideational change characteristic of this period. The rising importance of human rights and socio-economic development would crystallise even more after the Cold War. Human rights and, to a lesser degree, socio-economic development, would find their way into the collective expectations which international actors now had of the UN in relation to peacekeeping environments.

When North equals West: 'unipolar' configuration and rising hegemony

In the mid-1980s came the early signals of yet another critical juncture in world history. In 1985, Gorbachev engaged in his dual policies of *perestroika* (reconstruction) and *glasnost* (openness). If the former implied the search for breaking the economic stagnation of the Soviet Union, the latter was in part a response to mounting international and domestic pressure for human rights and democratisation. The Cold War had entered its last phase.

The social potential for reform had already gathered momentum in several Soviet client states as exemplified by the Hungarian (1956) and Czechoslovak (1968) crises and the Solidarity movement in Poland (1980). In 1989 the Berlin Wall was dismantled. Liberal revolutions took place one by one in Eastern European countries. In 1990, West and East Germany unified. This was a significant indicator not only of the end of the Cold War, but also of the re-birth of another world power. Germany, with its restored self-confidence, would gain ever more status, prestige and influence within what would soon become the European 'Union'.

With these events unfolding, a 'unipolar moment',[104] which had been gradually emerging since the global debt crisis on the economic front and Gorbachev's rise to power on the political front, reached its maturity. At this particular moment, geopolitical bipolarity was seemingly replaced by unipolarity. Perhaps the best visual representation of this unipolarity, strategically, was the ascendancy of NATO.[105] The increasing sway of a particular phase of the capitalist/liberal doctrine, with a stronger than usual emphasis on 'free market' and democracy, embodied the ideological dimension.[106] By 1992, the Soviet bloc had ceased to exist.[107] At this particular moment, the United States epitomised strategic and ideological unipolarity in international politics. In 1993, Clinton took over from Bush, putting 'assertive multilateralism' in the forefront of US foreign policy, implying increased US participation in multilateral peace and security operations.

With the elimination of the Second World, the 'North' became a synonym for the 'West'. The four-decade old East–West and North–South conflicts were replaced by a more ambiguous pattern of global conflict between the West and the South, in which the increasing homogeneity of the former was juxtaposed with the increasing heterogeneity of the latter. The historical/cultural/political traditions of the states comprising the western alliance system were, it seemed, sufficiently similar to sustain an emerging western 'hegemony',[108] whereas the South now encompassed (with the inclusion of the former Soviet bloc) an even broader spectrum of historical/cultural/political traditions and orientations, less able to rely on such unifying concepts as 'decolonisation' or 'non-alignment'. The NAM summits in Harare (1986), Belgrade (1989), Jakarta (1992), Cartagena (1995) and the UNCTAD conferences in Geneva (1987) and Cartagena (1992) failed to produce coherent alternatives to the West's dominant ideology. The influence that the South had exercised in the early 1960s in defining the normative basis of the UN's peace and security function had for the time being markedly diminished.[109]

At the same time, the fusion of the two previous axes of global conflict enhanced the widespread perception of a rapidly 'globalising' world[110] in that the territorial and conceptual 'boundaries' along the East–West and North–South axes were increasingly irrelevant to the global mosaic of peace and security problems.[111] More concretely, the European Union was not immune to the challenges posed by the break-up of Yugoslavia. Nor was the United States immune to drug trafficking through Central America, nor Russia or China immune to ethnic and religious tensions in their vicinity.

What is more, the West and the South, while standing in opposition, penetrated each other at an accelerating rate in the absence of any central ordering principles of the kind provided by the Cold War. In the first place, the 'ungovernable' states in the South caused regional political instability, most obviously in their immediate neighbourhood.[112] Such regional instability, while important in its own right, also created new obstacles to western exploitation of the material resources and commercial, financial, and labour markets in the regions adjacent to conflict.[113] Moreover, several of these conflicts posed new security threats for the West, including cross-continent refugee flows, political terrorism, transnational crime and environmental degradation.

The West's response was to export comprehensive recipes for 'governability'. On one side, 'liberal' recipes for political governance – whether through bilateral arrangements or through such organisations as the EU and the CSCE (now OSCE)[114] – were offered to, often imposed on, the South.[115] On the other side, 'capitalist' recipes for economic governance were exported – whether through bilateral programmes or through such organisations as the OECD, the Bretton Woods Institutions or the GATT (since 1995 the World Trade Organization (WTO)). Furthermore, the recipes for 'economic' governance were increasingly tied to political 'good governance'.

Western penetration of the South, however, was not merely the result of government policies. The influence of global mass media, civil society networks, and transnational companies was far from negligible.[116] Several of the most influential non-state actors flourished within the West,[117] and necessarily reflected as well as contributed to western power configurations, be they material or ideational.[118] Equally important was the growing inter-action,[119] indeed interconnectedness, between western governmental, semi-governmental and non-governmental actors.[120] None of this, of course, is to argue that the West was a homogeneous entity. Significant tensions now existed among western states as well as between state and non-state actors.[121]

The early 1990s: the UN at another critical juncture

With a unipolar power configuration at its peak, both the West and the South increasingly turned to the UN for action – though for different reasons. The West, now the dominant source of influence, would gain wider 'legitimacy' by acting through UN channels. The South, on the other hand, could still exert a degree of influence over the actions of this globally multilateral institution which had relative transparency, accountability and sensitivity to public scrutiny. The UN had also long endorsed the principle of 'sovereign equality', and established mechanisms through which each and every member state could present its case and make its voice 'heard' by the great powers.[122] Furthermore, under the emerging hegemony, there was now an audience inside as well as outside of the West, which shared ever more of the western 'image' of an ideal world order, revolving around capitalist/liberal recipes, with its corresponding human rights and democracy discourse.

With the erosion of the Cold War, the Security Council gradually assumed its original functions, while the General Assembly entered a phase of 'decline' from the mid-1980s,[123] becoming increasingly irrelevant to the UN's peace and security function. On the one hand, the South, dissatisfied with the non-amelioration of its global condition, had lost the influence of earlier decades. On the other, the West – the United States in particular – was not disposed to using the General Assembly for vital policy choices, for it knew that it might no longer be able to mobilise the necessary two-thirds majority. At the same time, however, the General Assembly continued to build on the ideational advances that had begun to take shape in the earlier period. It organised land-mark conferences such as the World Conference on Human Rights held in Vienna in June 1993,[124] with the participation of 171 governments and 1,529 NGOs.[125] There were now 978 NGOs in consultative status with ECOSOC, with 42 of them in the 'general' category.[126] On 20 December 1993, the General Assembly adopted Resolution 48/141 and established the post of the UN High Commissioner for Human Rights (UNHCHR). Now the UN as an organisation was increasingly coming under the influence of a re-assessment of the Charter, in which the human rights and socio-economic concerns were given higher priority than before *vis-à-vis* state sovereignty.

The years following 1988 represented by far the UN's most active period so far as its peace and security function is concerned. The revival of UN peace-keeping after two decades of stagnation came with the end of the two arguably most important international conflicts of the 1980s. Following the with-drawal of the Soviet troops from Afghanistan, UNGOMAP was established to report possible violations of the Agreement on the Settlement of the Situation Relating to Afghanistan, while the UN Iran–Iraq Military Observer Group (UNIIMOG) was given the task of verifying compliance with the cease-fire agreement reached between Iran and Iraq after the first Gulf War.

The following year, the UN introduced peacekeeping forces into the complex southern African crises. The First UN Angola Verification Mission (UNAVEM I) was deployed in Angola and the UN Transition Assistance Group (UNTAG) in Namibia. The same year, the UN Observer Group in Central America (ONUCA) was called upon to verify observance of the Central American security agreement, *Esquipulas II*, between Costa Rica, El Salvador,

Guatemala, Honduras and Nicaragua. Although Central America had always been a region of severe conflicts, this was the first time a UN peacekeeping mission would be deployed in this exclusively American sphere of influence.[127] In 1989, two other operations were authorised in Central America, in Nicaragua (ONUVEN) and in Haiti (ONUVEH).

Following the Iraqi invasion of Kuwait in August 1990, the Security Council imposed 'previously unimaginable sanctions'[128] on Iraq.[129] Upon the alleged failure of these sanctions, the early days of 1991 witnessed the second UN collective security action after Korea: Operation Desert Storm.[130] Thirty-eight countries participated directly in the Gulf War coalition, and four others provided major financial and logistic support.[131] A wide range of other military and civilian missions soon followed.[132] The aftermath of the Gulf War saw a rapid proliferation of UN peacekeeping efforts in general,[133] including the 'humanitarian interventions' where the discourse on human rights and democracy achieved striking prominence.

Concluding observations

The East–West and North–South conflicts may be said to have structurally constrained, and at times shaped, not only the UN's evolving role in world politics, but also the normative preferences of international actors, which in turn influenced the agenda and the functioning of the world body. The two active periods of intra-state peacekeeping largely coincided with two critical junctures of the post-1945 period: the early 1960s and the early 1990s. This coincidence is instructive not because it helps us to 'explain' in causal terms why the two periods witnessed a proliferation of intra-state peacekeeping operations (though there is a strong correlation), but because international expectations as to how the UN should act *vis-à-vis* intra-state conflicts were strikingly influenced by the material and ideational characteristics of the prevailing environment.

The Cold War reached its peak in the early 1960s. The decolonisation project and the South's ambitious experiment with non-alignment had made equal strides by then. The almost 'organic' links between the two axes of conflict became particularly visible and influential at this critical juncture. In the first place, the major Cold War allies of the United States (the colonial powers) were direct parties to the 'political' North–South conflict. Secondly, the two superpowers had in a sense become participants in an emerging 'neo'-colonial rivalry over Third World resources. Thirdly, the newly decolonised territories of Asia and Africa had become part of the global superpower contest for strategic and ideological influence. A policy of aligning with or leaning towards one superpower was almost invariably treated as intolerable by the other.

The West, the East and the South were not, of course, at any stage mono-lithic entities. Nevertheless, reasonably 'uniform' western, eastern and southern political positions were discernible by the early 1960s. In this sense, it could be argued that a short-lived 'tripolar' power configuration heavily impacted on the UN's peace and security function. The ideational component of this particular historical moment reflected an ambiguous but significant consensus between these three sources of influence. That consensus – one that was still compatible with the normative preferences that prevailed at the close of World War II – centred on the relative primacy of two Charter princi-ples: maintenance of international peace and security, and state sovereignty (understood largely in its external dimension). This consensus would, as we shall see in subsequent chapters, greatly influence the UN's 'objectives'. The acute tension between the three main sources of geopolitical influence, on the other hand, would impact on the definition of the UN's 'authority' in intra-state peacekeeping environments.

The 1970s and 1980s witnessed the increasing irrelevance of the UN in the field of peace and security, partly epitomised, as we shall see in the next chapter, by the relative absence and low profile of peacekeeping missions. The weakening southern voice in the political domain, coupled with an intense bipolarity, rendered the UN relatively ineffectual. The normative texture of the international community, however, underwent considerable change in these two decades, paving the way for the ideational attributes of the post-Cold War period. While, in a sense, the UN's objectives and author-ity in peace and security were 'frozen' in time, its activities in the fields of human rights and socio-economic development laid the groundwork for ideational changes in the international realm. In other words, usually considered nothing more than a 'talk shop' in realpolitik terms, the UN as a forum nevertheless slowly yet steadily helped to redefine the normative pref-erences of the international community. This redefinition would, in turn, help to reformulate, over time, the international community's normative expectations of the UN.

In the mid- to late 1980s, with the erosion of the Cold War and the impact of financial and debt crises, the interaction of the East–West and North–South conflicts entered a new phase. The prevailing power configuration at this 'strategically unipolar' moment was even more difficult to identify than in previous periods, be it in its material, ideational or institutional dimension. The ascending northern/western 'hegemony' reflected the economic, politi-cal, cultural and ideological influences exerted by both state and non-state actors. Not only the United States, but Britain, France, Germany and Japan were no doubt part of the emerging liberal/capitalist hegemony. So were inter-governmental organisations/arrangements (e.g. the EU, OECD, G7, NAFTA) and a host of non-governmental agencies, formally and informally organised (e.g. business, media, human rights, humanitarian, developmentalist, environmentalist and feminist groups), all of which in varying degrees contributed to, mirrored, yet also challenged the West-centred hegemony. In other words, the prevailing hegemony had to contend with its own internal contradictions. It carried, in other words, the seeds for possible future change.

Not surprisingly, then, the early 1990s would mark another critical juncture in the evolution of the UN. Not only did the international community have higher expectations of the UN than before, but the influences bearing upon international normative prescriptions for the UN would become more diverse and less easily identifiable than in the earlier periods. In countless ways, the United States and other leading members comprising the loose western coalition were the 'most' influential actors defining the normative basis of UN action in this period, yet underlying the 'western hegemony' were more subtle but stronger structural constraints. No single actor or group of actors could be equated with the exercise of structural influence. The rising profile of human rights and socio-economic development was not easily attributable to any one source of power, whether expressed in material, ideational or institutional terms. In the early 1990s, the UN's objectives and authority as manifested in peacekeeping environments would, as subsequent chapters will demonstrate, increasingly reflect a normative shift of quasi-paradigmatic proportions.

NOTES

1 From a political economy viewpoint, Cox considers the 1945–65 period as a hegemonic historical structure: see Cox with Sinclair, *Approaches to World Order* (Cambridge: Cambridge University Press, 1996), pp. 135–6.

2 A phrase first used by Bernard Baruch in 1947 and subsequently popularised by Walter Lippman.

3 A term first coined by Winston Churchill in 1946.

4 The Treaty of Washington (the North Atlantic Treaty) was signed on 4 April 1949, by Belgium, Britain, Canada, Denmark, France, Iceland, Italy, Luxembourg, the Netherlands, Norway, Portugal and the United States. Greece (1952), Turkey (1952) and West Germany (1955) would later accede to the Treaty. Spain would join NATO as late as 1982.

5 Key factors included the nuclear issue, Taiwan, and border disputes: see S. J. Ball, *The Cold War: An International History, 1947–1991* (London: Arnold, 1998), p. 85.

6 COMECON was founded in January 1949 by a joint *communiqué* of Bulgaria, Czechoslovakia, Hungary, Poland, Romania and the Soviet Union. Its Charter would be adopted in 1959. COMECON's members were Bulgaria, Cuba, Czechoslovakia, East Germany, Hungary, Mongolia, Poland, Romania, the Soviet Union and Vietnam.

7 See C. L. Robertson, *International Politics since World War II: A Short History* (Armonk, NY: M. E. Sharpe, 1997), p. 122.

8 The Southeast Asia Collective Defense Treaty (the Manila Pact) was signed on 8 September 1954 by Australia, Britain, France, New Zealand, Pakistan, the Philippines, Thailand and the United States.

9 The Pact of Mutual Cooperation between Britain, Iran, Iraq, Pakistan and Turkey (the Baghdad Pact) was signed on 24 February 1955.

10 The Security Treaty between Australia, New Zealand and the United States (ANZUS) was already signed on 1 September 1951.

11 The Warsaw Treaty of Friendship, Cooperation, and Mutual Assistance was signed on 14 May 1955 by Albania, Bulgaria, Czechoslovakia, East Germany, Hungary, Poland, Romania and the Soviet Union.

12 Ball, *The Cold War*, p. 84.

13 Ball, *The Cold War*, p. 72.

14 In a few years' time, France would sign a Treaty of Friendship and Cooperation with Germany; announce the withdrawal of its fleet from the Atlantic Allied Command; recognise the People's Republic of China; withdraw from the NATO Integrated Military Command in protest over what de Gaulle portrayed as US domination of the Alliance; and would force NATO to move its headquarters from Paris to Brussels; for a chronology, see www.france.diplomatie.fr/archives/archives.gb/expo/140/index.html (19 June 2000).

15 While this notion was not entirely new – Hobson's and Lenin's views on imperialism, for instance, were already known – its penetration into everyday political thought in virtually all parts of the world was new.

16 While the 1960s would produce more significant studies on what we call the North–South divide, notable studies from the 1950s include P. A. Baran, *The Political Economy of Growth* (New York: Monthly Review Press, 1957), and G. Myrdal, *Development and Underdevelopment: A Note on the Mechanism of National and International Economic Inequality* (Cairo: National Bank of Egypt, 1956).

17 The Group of G-77 would declare that theirs 'is basically a unity of opposition': see K. Iida, 'Third World Solidarity: The Group of 77 in the UN General Assembly', *International Organization*, 32:2 (1988), 375.

18 G. Gleason, 'Independence and decolonization in Central Asia', *Asian Perspective*, 21:2 (Fall 1997), 228.

19 For an account of Britain's and France's experiences with decolonisation, see, respectively, J. Darwin, *Britain and Decolonisation: The Retreat from Empire in the post-Cold War World* (Houndmills: Macmillan, 1988) and R. F. Betts, *France and Decolonisation 1900–1960* (Houndmills: Macmillan, 1991).

20 The lingering attempts of certain states to preserve multipolarity in the face of crystallising bipolarity was especially evident in this episode. The United Sates strongly disapproved of the joint Anglo-French policy that was devised and implemented in the absence of any consultation with Washington: see Frye, *A United Nations Peace Force*, p. 10.

21 Lusophone Africa, for instance, remained under direct Portuguese control until the mid-1970s.

22 The *Commonwealth* and the *Francophonie*, with 54 and 51 members respectively, are illuminating examples of how deep-rooted and important those links can be.

23 For instance, on 15 December 1960 the Heads of State of Francophone Africa held a conference in Brazzaville. Not only 'being African' or 'fighting for independence', but also 'speaking French' was part of the emerging collective identity of these states.

24 See, for instance, A. A. Mazrui, *Africa's International Relations: The Diplomacy of Dependency and Change* (Boulder, CO: Westview Press, 1977), especially pp. 41–67, 134–6.

25 This, of course, is not to argue that the Third World was strongly 'united'.

26 T. Kanza, *Conflict in the Congo: The Rise and Fall of Lumumba* (Middlesex: Penguin Books, 1972), p. 76.

27 See R. A. Mortimer, *The Third World Coalition in International Politics* (New York: Praeger, 1980), pp. 8–9.

28 Five roughly defined groups attended the conference: the Arab countries (Egypt, Iraq, Jordan, Lebanon, Libya, Saudi Arabia, Sudan, Syria and Yemen); Southeast Asia (Burma, Cambodia, Indonesia, Laos, North Vietnam, South Vietnam, Thailand and the Philippines); South Asia (Afghanistan, Ceylon, India, Iran, Nepal and Pakistan); Black Africa (Ethiopia, Ghana and Liberia); and special cases (China, Japan and Turkey): see Mortimer, *The Third World Coalition* (New York: Praeger, 1980), pp. 8–9.

29 In July 1956, Nasser, Nehru and Tito met at Brioni to exchange their ideas on non-alignment. In December 1957, the Afro-Asia Peoples' Solidarity Organisation (AAPSO) conference in Cairo was attended by forty-four delegations. In June 1961, again in Cairo, a preparatory meeting took place, which paved the way for the first NAM summit. A non-aligned state was now defined as one that 'pursued a foreign policy of national independence based on peaceful coexistence, supported national liberation movements, and eschewed the multilateral military alliances . . . and bilateral alliances with the great powers': see Mortimer, *The Third World Coalition*, p. 12. This definition would lead to a conference whose composition was radically different from Bandung, where almost half of the participants would have failed the test set by these criteria.

30 Afghanistan, Algeria (the only non-independent state to be invited, which was represented by its provisional government-in-exile), Ceylon, the Congo (Léopoldville), Cuba, Cyprus, Ethiopia, Ghana, Guinea, India, Indonesia, Iraq, Kampuchea (Cambodia), Kuwait, Lebanon, Mali, Morocco, Nepal, Saudi Arabia, Somalia, Sudan, Tunisia, Yemen, the United Arab Republic (established in February 1958, the UAR would represent both Egypt and Syria until its dissolution in October 1961) and Yugoslavia.

31 Sukarno's Indonesia was a crucial actor in bringing about the UN peacekeeping mission in West Irian; and Nkrumah's Ghana would be a major troop contributor in the Congo operation: see Chapters 4 and 5 respectively.

32 While bitterly critical of the pro-western policies of the UN mission in the Congo, Nehru's India would refuse to strengthen the hand of the Soviet Union: see Chapter 5.

33 Nasser's Egypt had not obstructed UN peacekeeping in the Suez and Lebanon, and would not object to the Yemen operation. In all three cases Egypt was a party to the conflict: see Chapter 4. When the Security Council was blocked during the Suez crisis, on the other hand, it was Tito's Yugoslavia who proposed that the matter be transferred to the General Assembly for action: see United Nations, *The Blue Helmets*, 3rd edn, p. 36.

34 Yet important differences would be detected in due course between the views of such leading figures as Castro and Gaddafi: see P. Braillard and M-R. Djalili, *The Third World and International Relations* (London: Frances Pinter, 1986), pp. 134–7.

35 As of 2000, Switzerland was not a member of the UN on the grounds of its commitment to neutrality.

36 The *Declaration by the United Nations* was signed by 26 states on 1 January 1942.

37 For US economic 'national interests' in Africa, for instance, see V. McKay, *Africa in World Politics* (Westport, CT: Greenwood Press, 1974), pp. 278–82; and for Soviet economic policy toward Africa, especially between 1965 and 1974, see E. K. Valkenier, 'Great power economic competition in Africa: Soviet progress and problems', *Journal of International Affairs*, 34:2 (Fall/Winter 1980/81), 259–68.

38 See M. Tamkoç, *The Turkish Cypriot State: The Embodiment of the Right of Self-Determination* (London: K. Rustem & Brother, 1988), p. 87.

39 For a list of Soviet vetoes of membership between 1946 and 1961, see A. V. Patil, *The UN Veto in World Affairs, 1946–1990* (Sarasota, FL: UNIFO, 1992), pp. 471–8.

40 For a good visual presentation of the geographic breakdown of the increase in the UN membership, see S. Morphet, 'States groups at the United Nations and growth of member states at the United Nations', in P. Taylor and A. J. R. Groom (eds), *The United Nations at the Millennium: The Principal Organs* (London: Continuum, 2000), pp. 262–5.

41 See A. L. Bennett, *International Organizations: Principles and Issues*, 6th edn (Englewood Cliffs, NJ: Prentice Hall, 1995), pp. 237–8.

42 C. S. Stephenson, 'NGOs and the principal organs of the United Nations', in Taylor and Groom (eds), *The United Nations at the Millennium*, p. 274.

43 In 1955, the only non-western member of the NGO committee was the Soviet Union. By 1968, the West still retained its majority, though by a decreasing margin. The West would not lose its majority until 1969; see Liskofsky, *The UN Reviews its NGO System*, cited in C. Pei-heng, *Non-Governmental Organizations at the United Nations: Identity, Role, and Function* (New York: Praeger, 1981), pp. 112–13.

44 Stephenson, 'NGOs and the principal organs of the United Nations', p. 283.

45 GA resolution 377 (V) of 3 November 1950 was adopted by 52 votes to 5, with 2 abstentions. Byelorussia, Czechoslovakia, Poland, the Soviet Union, and Ukraine voted against; Argentina and India abstained.

46 See M-C. Smouts, 'The General Assembly: grandeur and decadence', in Taylor and Groom (eds), *The United Nations at the Millennium*, pp. 39–44.

47 At the time, because of a major disagreement over whether China or Taiwan should be seated in the UN, the Soviet Union was boycotting the Security Council. When the Soviet Union returned to its seat in the Security Council, however, it was too late to reverse the course of UN action. In the light of a previous Security Council decision, and given the re-appearing stagnation in the Security Council, the General Assembly had actively become seized of the Korea question.

48 Out of the 111 vetoes cast until the discussions about Southern Rhodesia in 1963, all but 7 belonged to the Soviet Union. Between 1946 and 1990, the veto was cast 124 times by the Soviet Union, 82 by the United States, 33 by Britain, 18 by France and 22 by China: see Patil, *The UN Veto in World Affairs*, pp. 471–86.

49 India, a leading non-aligned state, abstained on a US-sponsored resolution calling for Soviet withdrawal from Hungary, and voted against a resolution calling for free elections: see R. H. Donaldson, 'The Soviet Union in South Asia: a friend to rely on?', *Journal of International Affairs*, 34:2 (Fall/Winter 1980/81), 248.

50 The UN's Suez operation was authorised by GA Resolution 1000 (ES-I) of 5 November 1956, by 57 votes to 0, with 19 abstentions, including the parties to the conflict (Egypt, Israel, Britain and France) and the Soviet bloc.

51 GA Resolution 1803 (XVII) of 14 December 1962, adopted by 87 votes to 2, with 12 abstentions.

52 GA Resolution 2131 (XX) of 21 December 1965, adopted by 109 to 0, with 1 abstention.

53 Consider also the five key principles enunciated by Nehru in April 1954 (known as the Panch Shila) which were adopted as the basis of relations among Afro-Asian states as early as the Bandung Conference.

54 France had voted against GA Resolution 1803, and Britain had abstained in the voting of GA Resolution 2131.

55 See S. D. Bailey, 'The Security Council', in P. Alston (ed.), *The United Nations and Human Rights: A Critical Appraisal* (Oxford: Clarendon Press, 1995), pp. 306, 309.

56 For instance, the UN High Commissioner for Refugees (UNHCR) was established pursuant to GA Resolutions 319 (IV) of 3 December 1949 and 428 (V) of 14 December 1950. The Universal Declaration of Human Rights of 1948, although of considerable significance, expressed relatively vague ideas. This instrument would gain ever more normative status in the course of time.

57 GA Resolution 1514 (XV) of 14 December 1960.

58 The others were Australia, Belgium, Britain, the Dominican Republic, France, Portugal, South Africa and Spain.

59 GA Resolution 2106 A (XX) of 21 December 1965, adopted by 106 to 0, with 1 abstention.

60 GA Resolution 1710 (XVI) of 19 December 1961, adopted unanimously.

61 Reportedly, even as late as 1989, the addition of new strategic options did not alter the basic nuclear war scenario of the 1960s; for a brief account, see the 'American Memory' website: http://memory.loc.gov/cgi-bin/query/r?frd/cstdy:@field(DOCID+su0441 (26 March 2001).

62 See www.ibiblio.org/expo/soviet.exhibit/coldwar.html (27 February 2001).

63 See S. S. Kaplan *et al.*, *Diplomacy of Power: Soviet Armed Forces as A Political Instrument* (Washington, DC: Brookings Institution, 1981), pp. 270–88.

64 S. J. Morris, *Why Vietnam Invaded Cambodia: Political Culture and the Causes of War* (Stanford, CA: Stanford University Press, 1999), p. 87.

65 *Basic Principles of Relations Between the United States of America and the Union of Soviet Socialist Republics* (29 May 1972), available online at www.ioc.u-tokyo.ac.jp/~worldjpn/documents/texts/docs/19720529.O1E.html (25 March 2001).

66 Ball, *The Cold War*, p. 146.

67 See *Pravda*, 25 September 1968; reprinted in L. S. Stavrianos, *The Epic of Man* (Englewood Cliffs, NJ: Prentice-Hall, 1971), pp. 465–6, available online at www.fordham.edu/halsall/mod/1968brezhnev.html (31 May 2001).

68 This observation on superpower behaviour reflects not only our third party/academic judgement, but also the view of a great number of international actors, hence hinting at their notion of state sovereignty. To give but one example, in 1968 Albania would harshly criticise the Warsaw Pact intervention in Czechoslovakia, and leave the alliance.

69 Yet perhaps we should not overestimate the significance of this factor, since the principle of state sovereignty was beset by inconsistencies and contradictions, both in rhetoric and in practice, long before the Cold War was in sight. One only needs to recall the Monroe doctrine.

70 It is, however, frequently ignored that the 'first basket' (on security) ranked the principles that would guide relations between the participating states in the following order: 1. Sovereign equality, respect for their rights inherent in sovereignty; 2. Refraining from the threat or use of force; 3. Inviolability of frontiers; 4. Territorial integrity of States; 5. Peaceful settlement of disputes; 6. Non-intervention in internal affairs; 7. Respect for human rights and fundamental freedoms, including the freedom of thought, conscience, religion or belief; 8. Equal rights and self-determination of peoples; 9. Cooperation among States; 10. Fulfilment in good faith of obligations under international law.

71 His following statement is a case in point: 'We have reaffirmed America's commitment to human rights as a fundamental tenet of our foreign policy ... This does not mean that we can conduct our foreign policy by rigid moral maxims. We live in a world

that is imperfect and which will always be imperfect – a world that is complex and confused and which will always be complex and confused.' See *Public Papers of the Presidents of the United States: Jimmy Carter*, 1 (1977), 954, available online at www.civnet.org/resources/teach/basic/part8/55.htm (22 May 2001).

72 A typical case was Sihanouk in Cambodia.

73 Admittedly, the OAS was a US-driven organisation, but several Latin American voices in the OAS would periodically oppose the US policy. The case of the Dominican Republic (1965–66) is a good example: see Chapter 4.

74 See Mortimer, *The Third World Coalition*, pp. 24–42.

75 The crisis was prompted by Nixon's *Address to the Nation Outlining a New Economic Policy: 'The Challenge of Peace'* (15 August 1971). The convertibility of US dollar into gold and other reserve assets was suspended; an additional tax of 10 per cent was levied on goods imported into the US; and the US foreign economic aid was cut by 10 per cent: see P. Marshall, 'The North–South dialogue: Britain at odds', in E. Jensen and T. Fisher (eds), *The United Kingdom – The United Nations* (Houndmills: Macmillan, 1990), p. 201.

76 Almost simultaneously, the wealthy 'Group of 7' was beginning to take shape at the Rambouillet (1975), San Juan (1976) and London (1977) summits.

77 Meanwhile, with the conclusion of the first Lomé Convention in February 1975, the European Community created what is known today as the 'African, Caribbean, and Pacific (ACP) states of the EU', including some 70 southern states. The convention established a close link of development aid between the EU and a great many underdeveloped countries, explicitly responding to the demands by UNCTAD, yet implicitly weakening the non-aligned ideology to which many of these countries were devoted.

78 See Smouts, 'The General Assembly', pp. 44–6.

79 GA Resolution 2200 A (XXI) of 16 December 1966.

80 This is what Rosenau calls 'publics': see J. N. Rosenau, *Along the Domestic–Foreign Frontier: Exploring Governance in a Turbulent World* (Cambridge: Cambridge University Press, 1997), pp. 299–310.

81 Pei-heng, *Non-Governmental Organizations at the United Nations*, p. 171.

82 Pei-heng, *Non-Governmental Organizations at the United Nations*, p. 187.

83 At about the same time, especially the Soviet Union was highly critical of human rights NGOs, among them Amnesty International, the International League for Human Rights, and the Anti-Slavery Society; Pei-heng, *Non-Governmental Organizations at the United Nations*, p. 189.

84 See E/AC.24/SR.627 of 2 August 1977; E/AC.24/SR.628 of 3 August 1977; and ECOSOC Official Records 63rd session, 2085th meeting, 4 August 1977 cited in Pei-heng, *Non-Governmental Organizations at the United Nations*, p. 190.

85 Pei-heng, *Non-Governmental Organizations at the United Nations*, p. 191.

86 This was the first mechanism that could take action globally on individual cases on an emergency basis: see F. D. Gaer, 'Reality check: human rights NGOs confront governments at the UN', in T. G. Weiss and L. Gordenker (eds), *NGOs, the UN, and Global Governance* (Boulder, CO: Lynne Rienner, 1996), p. 54.

87 Gaer, 'Reality check', p. 54.

88 Gaer, 'Reality check', pp. 54–5.

89 A. Donini, 'The bureaucracy and the free spirits: stagnation and innovation in the relationship between the UN and NGOs', in Weiss and Gordenker (eds), *NGOs, the UN, and Global Governance*, pp. 92–3.

90 Donini, 'The bureaucracy and the free spirits', p. 93.

91 See P. Alston, 'The Commission on Human Rights', in Alston (ed.), *The United Nations and Human Rights*, pp. 139–45.

92 Peck, *Sustainable Peace*, p. 81.

93 The best examples were the 'Declaration of the Principles of International Cultural Cooperation' of 4 November 1966, and the 'Recommendation concerning Education for International Understanding, Cooperation and Peace and Education relating to Human Rights and Fundamental Freedoms', adopted by the General Conference of UNESCO in 1974: see United Nations, *United Nations Action in the Field of Human Rights* (New York: United Nations, 1980), p. 251.

94 See U. Beyerlin, 'Sanctions', in R. Wolfrum and C. Philipp (eds), *United Nations: Law, Policies and Practice*, vol. 2 (Dordrecht: Martinus Nijhoff Publishers, 1995), p. 1116.

95 SC Resolution 221 of 9 April 1966 (adopted by 10 votes to none, with Bulgaria, France, Mali, the Soviet Union and Uruguay abstaining) called upon Britain to 'prevent, by the use of force if necessary, the arrival at Beira of vessels reasonably believed to be carrying oil destined for Southern Rhodesia': see operative para. 5.

96 See Boutros-Ghali's statement in United Nations, *The United Nations and Rwanda, 1993–1996* (New York: UNDPI, 1996), p. 54.

97 SC Resolution 418 of 4 November 1977 imposed an arms embargo on South Africa. SC Resolution 421 of 9 December 1977 set up a Security Council sanctions committee. The sanctions on South Africa would continue until the adoption of SC Resolution 919 of 25 May 1994.

98 SC Resolution 460 of 21 December 1979.

99 For instance, SC Resolution 569 dated 26 July 1985.

100 See Beyerlin, 'Sanctions', p. 1117.

101 For the gradual formation of an anti-Apartheid coalition, with a particular emphasis on the 'change of identity' which it implied, see A. Klotz, *Norms in International Relations: The Struggle against Apartheid* (Ithaca: Cornell University Press, 1995).

102 See Mortimer, *The Third World Coalition*, p. 17.

103 These included trade in raw materials, trade in manufactured and semi-finished products, development finance, maritime transport and some special measures for the least developed countries.

104 Borrowed from C. Krauthammer, 'The Unipolar Moment', *Foreign Affairs*, 70:1 (1990/91), 23–33.

105 Three former Warsaw Pact members (the Czech Republic, Hungary and Poland) would become NATO members as of 1999.

106 Our task here is to offer an analysis and not a moral judgement. Nevertheless, given our remarks about the impact of a researcher's normative convictions on his research (see Chapter 1), it should be noted in passing that we find the 'liberal' political recipes, including especially the insistence on human rights and democracy, as beneficial, but the 'capitalist' economic recipes as biased and ill-informed. Furthermore, in our view, the argument that liberalism and capitalism are inseparable twin-concepts lacks credibility.

107 In July 1991, the Warsaw Treaty Organisation dissolved. On 8 December 1991, the Minsk Declaration recognised the official dissolution of the Soviet Union.

108 Although rightly criticised by several commentators, Huntington's 'clash of civilisations' thesis does illuminate this aspect of the 'West': see S. P. Huntington, *The Clash of Civilizations and The Remaking of World Order* (New York: Simon & Schuster, 1996).

109 By the time the ninth NAM conference was held in Belgrade, the movement's political effectiveness had largely weakened. Castro had not even attended the summit; see Robertson, *International Politics since World War II*, pp. 283–4.

110 'Perception of globalisation' rather than 'globalisation', because – as pointed out by several observers – the phenomenon itself was not new.

111 Although 'globalisation' is a buzzword which means different things to different people, common to most interpretations of globalisation is the notion that 'boundaries' (both territorial and conceptual) are fluid and increasingly less relevant. For a useful discussion of globalisation with particular emphasis on its multiple facets and on its impact on boundaries in international politics, see Camilleri and Falk, *The End of Sovereignty?*.

112 The immediate neighbours were sometimes the western states themselves as in the cases of Haiti and Bosnia.

113 Good examples include the regional instabilities caused by the conflicts in Angola, Liberia and Central America. The stakes in the Sierra Leone conflict, for instance, were 'high not only for the warring factions but also for the mining companies and their military counterparts.'; see C. de Jonge Oudraat, *Intervention in Internal Conflicts: Legal and Political Conundrums* (Washington, DC: Carnegie Endowment for International Peace, Working Paper No. 15, August 2000), p. 17.

114 The *Document of the Moscow Meeting of the Conference on the Human Dimension of the CSCE*, adopted on 3 October 1991 would present a sharp contrast with the normative texture of the *Helsinki Final Act* we have noted above: 'The participating States empha-size that issues relating to human rights, fundamental freedoms, democracy and the rule of law are of international concern, as respect for these rights and freedoms consti-tutes one of the foundations of the international order. They categorically and irrevocably declare that the commitments undertaken in the field of the human dimen-sion of the CSCE are matters of direct and legitimate concern to all participating States and *do not belong exclusively to the internal affairs* of the State concerned'; emphasis added.

115 For instance, under the US leadership, the OAS formalised a 'democracy protection doctrine' by adopting the Santiago Declaration on 5 June 1991. Soon after its adop-tion, the Haiti crisis would fall within the scope of this Declaration.

116 As Urquhart aptly puts it, 'The truth is that governments do not control the major forces which are shaping the future – if they ever did.' See B. Urquhart, 'The United Nations in 1992: problems and opportunities', *International Affairs*, 68:2 (April 1992), 313.

117 See the concise depiction of these factors in Carnegie Commission, *Final Report*, pp. 111–27.

118 For a 'semi-official' acknowledgment of the growing impact of non-governmental actors on US foreign policy, see US Department of State, *US Foreign Policy Agenda*, 5:1 (March 2000) [special issue on the making of US foreign policy].

119 Murphy aptly reminds us that NGOs are increasingly funded by major donor govern-ments and IGOs; see C. N. Murphy, 'Global governance: poorly done and poorly understood', *International Affairs*, 76:4 (2000), 795.

120 This interconnectedness is well encapsulated in Shaw's term 'the Western state': see M. Shaw, 'Global voices: civil society and the media in global crises', in T. Dunne and N. J. Wheeler (eds.), *Human Rights in Global Politics* (Cambridge: Cambridge University Press, 1999), pp. 214–18.

121 For example, Falk uses 'West', 'North' and 'South' as analytical categories, but makes it amply clear throughout his study that while these are not monolithic entities, they are sufficiently homogeneous to be analytically useful; see R. A. Falk, *On Humane Governance: Toward A New Global Politics* (University Park, PA: The Pennsylvania State University Press, 1995).

122 For instance, during deliberations about the Angola case, as we shall see in Chapter 7, a great number of small African states participated in the Security Council deliberations.

123 Smouts, 'The General Assembly', pp. 46–8.

124 Pursuant to GA Resolution 45/155 of 18 December 1990. Other significant conferences include the World Summit for Children (September 1990, New York), the United Nations Conference on Environment and Development (June 1992, Rio de Janeiro), the International Conference on Population and Development (September 1994, Cairo), and the World Summit for Social Development (March 1995, Copenhagen).

125 For details of participation, see Gaer, 'Reality check', p. 58.

126 Stephenson, 'NGOs and the principal organs of the United Nations', p. 283.

127 DOMREP (1965–66), the only previous experience, consisted of no more than a few military observers.

128 Ratner, *The New Peacekeeping*, p. 15.

129 The initial resolution, which imposed economic sanctions on Iraq, was SC Resolution 661 of 6 August 1990.

130 This operation was authorised by SC Resolution 678 dated 29 November 1990, adopted by 12 votes in favour, Cuba and Yemen against, and China abstaining.

131 Evans, *Cooperating for Peace*, p. 148.

132 UNIKOM was an observer mission created to monitor the demilitarised zone along the Iraq/Kuwait border. UNSCOM was set up by SC Resolution 687 of 3 April 1991 to dismantle Iraqi capabilities in weapons of mass destruction. The UN Consolidated Inter-Agency Humanitarian Programme, deriving its mandate from SC Resolution 688 of 5 April 1991, involved the establishment of UN humanitarian centres to assist in the repatriation of the Iraqi Kurds. Between August 1992 and March 1993, the UN would resort to another important enforcement operation in Iraq (Operation Southern Watch) which was intended to impose a 'no-fly' zone in southern Iraq below the 32nd parallel, and was based on SC Resolution 688 of 5 April 1991: see J. E. Stromseth, 'Iraq's repression of its civilian population: collective responses and continuing challenges' in Damrosch (ed.), *Enforcing Restraint*, pp. 94–5. For a non-critical account of events, see United Nations, *The United Nations and the Iraq–Kuwait Conflict, 1990–1996* (New York: UNDPI, 1996).

133 Between 1991 and 1995 the UN authorised peacekeeping operations in Angola (UNAVEM II and III), Bosnia and Hercegovina (UNPROFOR II, UNMIBH), Cambodia (UNAMIC, UNTAC), Chad (UNASOG), Croatia (UNPROFOR, UNCRO), El Salvador (ONUSAL), Eritrea (UNOVER), Georgia (UNOMIG), Haiti (MICIVIH, UNMIH), Liberia (UNOMIL), Macedonia (UNPREDEP), Mozambique (ONUMOZ), Rwanda (UNAMIR I, Operation Turquoise, UNAMIR II), Rwanda/Uganda (UNOMUR), Somalia (UNOSOM I, UNITAF and UNOSOM II), South Africa (UNOMSA), Tajikistan (UNMOT), and Western Sahara (MINURSO). Several of these operations were also supported by sanctions. Moreover, in relation to Libya's involvement in the Lockerbie disaster, the Security Council for the first time authorised measures against state-backed international terrorism; see SC Resolution 748 of 31 March 1992.

4

UN peacekeeping in intra-state conflicts: evolution of the normative basis

THE CHANGING MACROPOLITICAL landscape brought in its wake both continuities and discontinuities in the normative basis of intra-state peacekeeping, which we will closely examine in the context of four detailed case studies. Each case study in the following chapters will of necessity be handled in its 'own' time, in seemingly static fashion. This chapter will reinforce the change dimension that we introduced in the preceding chapter in which we tried to account for the historical trends impacting on the UN's peace and security function and on the evolution of international norm-setting understood as the gradual fleshing out and re-interpretation of the Charter's relatively vague provisions.

This chapter will not only situate the four case studies in the overall context of intra-state peacekeeping, but also further develop an important element of our argument, namely that the two periods under scrutiny (i.e. the early 1960s and the early 1990s) constituted critical thresholds in intra-state peacekeeping, each with its own particular normative resolution as to the UN's objectives and authority. We will demonstrate how the interests and normative preferences of key actors interacted in intra-state peacekeeping environments in the early 1960s, and juxtapose the ensuing normative synthesis with the ideational attributes of the 1990s, which took shape in a different historical structural setting.

Emerging normative basis on the eve of double 'peaks'

The emergence of UN peacekeeping missions can be traced almost as far back as the creation of the UN itself. The UN's first peacekeeping mission (UNSCOB) was authorised in response to the Greek civil war in 1947. Missions to Palestine,[1] Indonesia,[2] Kashmir,[3] and Korea[4] soon followed. All of these cases involved intra-state conflicts with strong inter-state dimensions. This early intra-state involvement by the UN should perhaps be considered normal given that, contrary to conventional wisdom, the 'shift in the balance between civil and interstate wars ... is a post-World War II, not a post-Cold War phenomenon'.[5] In any case, the UN's peacekeeping efforts in the 1940s and 1950s were embryonic.

The very notion of peacekeeping did not fully emerge until the Suez crisis, when the Canadians proposed the establishment of a neutral inter-positionary force under UN command and control. Pearson's proposal, developed in close consultation with Hammarskjöld, was heartily embraced by the United States, which had not been consulted by the Anglo-French coalition on the one hand, and had to confront Soviet threats of retaliatory action on the other. Within two years from Suez came the Lebanon operation which was the UN's first notable intra-state peacekeeping effort.

In Lebanon, a constitutional amendment pushed by the pro-American President Chamoun to permit a second term in office led to the formation of the United Front – a joint opposition by Arab nationalists in Lebanon – which received support from Nasser's pan-Arab movement. On 22 May 1958 Chamoun brought the issue to the Security Council, charging the UAR with intervention in Lebanon's domestic affairs. Eventually, a Swedish draft was adopted by 10 votes to none, with the Soviet Union abstaining, which, taking into account the positions of both Lebanon and the UAR, authorised the dispatch of an observer group to 'ensure that there is no illegal infiltration of personnel or supply' into Lebanese territory.[6] The mission, UNOGIL, continued for seven months until December 1958.

Building on the UN's experience, especially in Suez and Lebanon, the most visible examples of UN peacekeeping came into being in the first half of the 1960s – the first ambitious period of UN peacekeeping. In addition to the three missions already under way (Palestine, Kashmir and Suez), six new missions were authorised: the Congo, West Irian, Yemen, Cyprus, the Dominican Republic, and India–Pakistan.[7] All but the last had strong intra-state dimensions. Between 1960 and 1965 the world witnessed thirty-seven violent intra-state conflicts.[8] A quick survey of the UN's agenda between 1960 and 1965 reveals that out of forty-two conflicts brought before the competent organs of the UN, nineteen had clear-cut intra-state dimensions, which is almost half of the cases considered.[9] However, only in five intra-state conflicts did the UN go so far as to introduce peacekeeping forces.

Three of the UN's pre-1960 operations – Korea, Suez and Lebanon – are relevant to our argument, but only to the extent that they show a conceptual transformation in the UN's approach to its peace and security function. These missions provide useful insight into the crystallisation of the normative basis of intra-state peacekeeping in the 1960s. While we do not intend to dwell on these cases at length, the point needs to be made, at least in passing, that one key notion which had dominated the original development of the Charter, namely 'collective security', informed the post-1945 approach to 'maintenance of international peace and security', and subsequently found its way to the normative basis of intra-state peacekeeping in the early 1960s.

Korea was the first and only embodiment of the consensual 'collective security' idea in the Cold War period. That the Soviet bloc strongly opposed the American-led UN action, while of significance politically and of explanatory value for subsequent UN inaction in several instances, is normatively speaking largely irrelevant. The dispute between the superpowers was not about 'how the UN should respond to threats to international peace', but about whether or not the Korean case constituted a threat to international peace, indeed an act of aggression. The Soviet Union held that it did not, whereas the United States and its allies argued otherwise. Eventually the United States managed to mobilise the General Assembly, and the UN's first collective security exercise came into being.

The Suez crisis was perhaps the first step in the conceptual transformation of the UN's response to security crises. Unable to resort to collective security measures in the presence of bipolarity, the UN (in the person of its Secretary-General) and sympathetic middle powers found a way to get the UN involved in the crisis – largely with the encouragement and blessing of the United States. This was the first attempt to introduce a conceptual distinction between collective security and 'peacekeeping', and implied a change in the normative basis of the UN's security role, which related more to its authority than to its objectives.

Maintenance of international peace and security was still the main objective, with the utmost emphasis placed on protecting the sovereignty of state parties to the conflict. At the same time, the UN was required to respect fully state sovereignty, that is, uphold the principle of non-intervention. The notion of UN authority inherent in Hammarskjöld's peacekeeping doctrine, however, contrasted sharply with that implicit in collective security thinking. Almost by definition, collective security envisaged that the UN would pronounce judgement on 'threats to peace' or 'acts of aggression', and would, if necessary, enforce its decision by force. It goes without saying that consent was considered irrelevant. Peacekeeping, on the other hand, was introduced with exactly opposite notions in mind, with the emphasis on government consent, neutrality, and non-use of force. While this distinction was introduced by Hammarskjöld, and found support from the United States and a group of middle powers which sought a speedy settlement to the conflict, it was nevertheless the collective security approach that shaped the normative attitude of a considerable number of actors, among them the Soviet Union and Egypt, which insisted that the UN punish the 'aggressors'. In other words, the idea of 'peacekeeping' and the normative preferences which accompanied it were not necessarily embraced by all key actors.

The Lebanon crisis, two years after Suez, was yet another step in the conceptual transformation of the UN's peace and security function, since this was the first time that the UN became involved – to be more precise, the first time the UN emphatically admitted that it became involved – in a conflict in which the external and internal dimensions were highly prominent and closely connected.[10] This time, the UN, again in the person of its Secretary-General, tried to introduce a distinction between what might be labelled crudely 'inter-state' and 'intra-state' peacekeeping. This second shift, too, had normative baggage attached to it. Again, the UN's main objectives remained unchanged. Maintenance of international peace and security was the dominant international preoccupation. The importance of protecting and respecting state sovereignty was not open to question. The authority of the UN, on the other hand, rested on ambiguities, reflecting both the notion of 'collective security' and that of 'inter-state peacekeeping' and yet in need of a normative basis distinct from both these notions.

Where the parties to a conflict were not governments, government consent lost its relevance, whether the UN chose to seek it (as in inter-state peacekeeping) or not to seek it (as in collective security). Where the threat to peace and security (or act of aggression) was not 'external' to a state, the UN's pronouncement of 'judgement' would violate the principle of neutrality (as in collective security). Its strict adherence to neutrality between parties (as required by the doctrine of inter-state peacekeeping), on the other hand, would contradict protection of and respect for sovereignty as symbolised and exercised by the government. Resort to coercive measures (especially the use of force) against any internal party would bring into question the validity and solidity of the non-intervention principle.

By 1960, as the following chapter will demonstrate, Hammarskjöld himself was less than clear as to the exact nature of the UN's authority *vis-à-vis* intra-state conflicts, and the manner in which that authority might be reconciled with the UN's overarching objectives, that is maintenance of *international* peace and security, and protection of and respect for state sovereignty. He was at pains to reconcile, conceptually, the demanding situation on the ground with the interests of key actors and with his own guidelines which he had devised in the light of the Suez and Lebanon experiences. Despite the ambiguities surrounding the idea of intra-state peacekeeping, as it prematurely emerged in the 1950s, the crucial point is that by the 1960s an international consensus had emerged on UN objectives in intra-state peacekeeping environments. However, a variety of views surrounded the question of the UN's authority. Vestiges of 'collective security' thinking would soon be detected in the socialist and, to some extent, Third World responses to the Congo and Cyprus crises.

Consensus on objectives: sovereignty writ large

In the 1960s, at the height of the Cold War, there was little space for UN peacekeeping in intra-state conflicts, for the simple reason that the two super-powers strongly discouraged multilateral interventions in their respective spheres of influence. In one exceptional case, the United States 'tolerated' a tiny and largely ineffective UN presence in the Dominican Republic just to avoid harsh criticism from the Soviet bloc and the Third World against its overt intervention.[11] Even the OAS, known for its overall pro-American stance, had only marginally supported US intervention. While both super-powers were more willing to tolerate UN peacekeeping outside of their spheres of influence, the Soviet Union in particular insisted that, when deployed, UN peacekeeping should aim to protect the host state's sovereignty and not inter-vene in its domestic affairs.

In this period, what created space for active UN involvement (but minu-scule UN governance) in intra-state conflicts was, in the first instance, strong Third World demands for UN action.[12] While several Third World govern-ments were ideologically and strategically aligned with either the West or the East, a majority of them tried to pursue a more independent foreign policy. Whether aligned or 'non-aligned', the entire Third World shared strong anti-colonial sentiments. Having suffered at the hands of colonial powers, the new states wanted an end to colonialism. Significantly, the decolonisation project enjoyed support from both superpowers. In search of a mechanism capable of taming the former colonial powers, perhaps the 'natural' tendency of the Third World was to turn to the UN – an option not altogether disagreeable to the superpowers which were reluctant to engage in an unnecessary confrontation. The North–South conflict, which gave meaning and content to the decolonisation agenda, was perhaps the most crucial factor making possi-ble the few intra-state peacekeeping missions.

The second contributing factor had to do with the efforts of 'non-aligned' states which were preoccupied with their own development programmes and the need to keep the two blocs from intruding into their internal affairs. In the early 1960s, the Third World's insistence that no actor – especially the two blocs, but also the UN itself – should intervene in a state's domestic affairs did certainly influence collective expectations as to what UN peacekeeping could or could not do. The presence and support of such developed neutralist states as Finland and Sweden contributed to non-aligned efforts. A third factor was the declaratory post-1945 consensus on the need to put an end to inter-state aggression. Although the Cold War had rendered the Security Council largely ineffectual in collective security, the Charter principle that the UN should prevent external attacks on its members remained a primary collective expectation.[13]

The strong desire to keep the colonial powers, the superpowers and the external powers generally at bay found its expression in a particular normative resolution of Charter principles in the early 1960s. To put it differently, the prevalent interests and values at this particular juncture were structurally reflected in the UN's role as actor. In this context, maintenance of *international* peace and security emerged as the UN's main objective, even in intra-state peacekeeping environments. As a consequence, whenever the UN became actively involved in an intra-state conflict, it would be expected to address, first and foremost, the international dimensions of the conflict. Even in the most controversial case of the 1960s, the Congo, the shifting emphasis of international diplomacy, as we will observe, could not completely obscure the prior preoccupation with the protection of the Congo's sovereignty against 'externally manipulated' secessionist activities.

In keeping with the normative emphasis on international peace and security, a vertical relationship was created between the Chapter principles of state sovereignty and human rights, with the former largely dominating acceptable prescriptions for UN involvement in intra-state conflicts. Socio-economic development, meanwhile, was almost entirely left out of the scope of UN peacekeeping. Protection of and respect for state sovereignty, defined largely in terms of political independence and territorial integrity *vis-à-vis* external threats, was given priority over protection and promotion of human rights. Even the right to self-determination, arguably a 'collective' human right that necessarily accompanied the political project of decolonisation, was perceived more in relation to its external dimension, implying a people's right to own and defend its 'equally sovereign' state.

Two points need to be underlined here. First, self-determination was, at best, a tangential issue for UN peacekeeping in the 1960s. When it was addressed at all, this was done in relation to its external dimension. Secondly, when addressed in the peacekeeping context, the principle of self-determination tended to clash with the principle of state sovereignty, and the clash of the two principles was resolved – both at the normative and practical level – in favour of the latter.[14] In the Congo, Katanga's claim to self-determination was suppressed. In Cyprus, the embryonic Turkish claim was ignored. In West Irian, Papuan aspirations for self-determination were not incorporated into the peacekeeping mandate, but later reduced to an 'Act of Free Choice' – a well orchestrated and largely cosmetic exercise designed to buttress Indonesian sovereignty.

In the Congo and Cyprus cases, as we will see, the issue of decolonisation was critical. The West Irian operation, too, addressed a peace and security problem arising out of the colonial context.[15] Although the UN had, for the first time, established a 'transitional authority' in West Irian, and set a precedent for its future operations in Namibia, Cambodia, Eastern Slavonia and

East Timor, its intervention was carefully designed, in line with prevailing expectations, not to prejudice the sovereign rights over the territory first of the Netherlands and then of Indonesia. Yet there is no denying that UNTEA represented the UN's first excursion into territorial governance,[16] and in so doing had created a new political space for the organisation.

During the transition from the colonial to the post-colonial era, international actors were, as we will see in the Congo and Cyprus cases, particularly sensitive to the need to protect state sovereignty against perceived colonial/imperial threats. While the UN was expected to defend sovereignty, it was, at the same time, required to respect sovereignty, that is, to uphold the principle of 'non-intervention'. In the transition from colonial rule to independence, a certain fuzziness emerged in the interpretation of the principle: who or what exactly was the 'sovereign' in a given territory? For the new states, UN non-intervention in their domestic affairs signified their newly acquired statehood and the sovereignty which was inextricably linked to it. For the colonial powers, it meant that the UN could not be used to dissolve their empires within which they still claimed to exercise sovereign authority. At this critical historical juncture, this principle, precisely because of its ambiguity, was endorsed not only by the former colonies, but also by the colonial powers.

In Lebanon, Yemen and the Dominican Republic, as in the Congo, the main international preoccupation was to prevent foreign intervention, though not necessarily colonial intervention.[17] In all cases, the UN was called upon to protect sovereignty against external interference. In Lebanon and Yemen,[18] too, the international community insisted that the UN itself should not intervene in the domestic affairs of host countries. Its objective was simply to keep foreign powers at bay. When the state parties most directly involved were prepared to settle the dispute, the two superpowers could tolerate small UN peacekeeping operations of short duration, as in Lebanon and Yemen, which would concentrate on the inter-state dimensions of the conflict. Superpower tolerance, however, was predicated on the expectation that the UN would uphold the principle of non-intervention.[19] During the Congo operation, Hammarskjöld would refer to the Lebanon experience as a precedent in this respect.[20] With Cold War rivalries increasingly intruding into these conflicts, the superpowers had an added reason not to allow the UN to intervene in the domestic affairs of host states. In effect, the superpowers' preference for the UN's non-intervention in domestic affairs largely overlapped with the expectations of the former colonies and those of the colonial powers as mentioned above. Maintenance of international peace and security would go hand in hand with protection of and respect for state sovereignty, with the external aspect primarily in mind.

In the 1960s, concern over human rights was largely absent from the conceptual framework of UN peacekeeping. Although international actors sporadically expressed regret about violations of human rights and lack of humanitarian assistance, these considerations were only marginally attached to prescriptions for UN conduct in peacekeeping environments. Even in the case of the Dominican Republic, where, in comparison with other cases, the human rights objective was much more in the forefront of UN deliberations, human rights and humanitarian concerns were not incorporated to the Security Council resolutions, whereas the OAS force was mandated, at least on paper, with 'maintaining the inviolability of human rights'.[21]

Dominant expectation: minimal UN authority

In the 1960s, the dominant view as to what authority the UN should exercise *vis-à-vis* intra-state conflicts came into being as a result of the clash between the normative requirements of collective security thinking and those of peace-keeping as advocated by Hammarskjöld. The Soviet bloc and parts of the Third World perceived, or at least presented, several intra-state conflicts as having their origin in external manipulation and intervention, hence the advocacy of the direct application of collective security measures, as we will see in the Congo and in Cyprus. The West, especially the colonial powers, on the other hand, went along with the Hammarskjöld principles which were, in a sense, carefully 'designed' by the Secretary-General to bypass continuing colonialist reluctance to create space for UN involvement in intra-state conflicts.

In effect, international concern over the UN's possible 'intervention' in domestic affairs, coupled with the jealous insistence on state sovereignty, both of which we have analysed above, led to minimalist expectations of the UN in terms of its authority. The UN performed a limited range of functions (breadth) with limited involvement (depth) in intra-state conflicts. UN peace-keeping was almost fully subjected to the continuing consent of the parties to the conflict, while the UN itself was generally expected not to pronounce on the rights and wrongs of a particular conflict, and not to brand one side as being in the right and another in the wrong. UN use of force beyond self-defence was hardly imaginable.

The UN's functions were generally limited to such military duties as border patrolling, observation of possible points of cross-border infiltration, reconnaissance, and cease-fire maintenance. The level of UN involvement rarely went beyond monitoring and supervision, since control and conduct of administrative or political functions were considered to be within the exclusive purview of governmental authority. The UN's relationship to host governments was generally defined as one of 'assistance', which is perhaps indicative of the lowest level of involvement in the exercise of authority.

Consent emerged as a sensitive issue in the Cold War period. The Third

World insisted on the principle of host government consent, since this was regarded as a fundamental requirement of the logic of 'sovereign statehood' which many Third World countries had only recently assumed. This view was largely supported by the Soviet bloc which sought further allies from within the ranks of the Third World and tried to make the most of the ever-strengthening anti-colonial (hence partly anti-western) sentiment within new states. The overall importance given to the 'government' in the socialist regimes should not be underestimated as a contributing factor.

The West, on the other hand, generally preferred Hammarskjöld's doctrine of consent, whereby the UN was expected to seek the consent of *all* parties whenever it acted. Such consent, furthermore, should be sought on an ongoing basis. In other words, the initial consent to UN deployment would not necessarily mean continuous consent for subsequent UN actions. The western preference reflected the fact that the colonial powers – a significant wing of the western bloc – were now in a weaker position *vis-à-vis* the governments of former colonies: The consent of those intra-state parties, whom the colonial powers sponsored, should be sought at all stages of UN involvement.

The ensuing normative synthesis of these diverging positions reflected America's inclination to accommodate two contrasting sets of demands: those of its allies and those of the Third World. The reluctance to invite unilateral Soviet intervention in peacekeeping environments was yet another factor influencing the US attempt to reconcile these diverging pressures. As a side effect of the delicate Cold War balance, the UN was expected to seek parties' consent when it acted as peacekeeper. Especially important was the degree of cooperation to be extended by the host government. There was no clear answer, however, as to what should happen, were the government to consent and the other intra-state parties to refuse to do so, or vice versa. Even the Soviet bloc, with its clear-cut emphasis on government consent, was not entirely consistent, as reflected in its attitude in the post-Lumumba period in the Congo.

In the 1960s, parties to intra-state conflicts, including the immediate internal parties as well as indirect external parties, were particularly keen to ensure the UN's 'neutrality'. The requirement of consent was one way of achieving that neutrality; another was to make sure that the UN was not accorded a special normative status which would enable it to declare which party was in the right and which was in the wrong. This normative position is perhaps best understood as a compromise between the conflicting interests of the West and the rest of the world. While the Soviet bloc frequently called for UN judgements against 'illegitimate' parties, this was counterbalanced not only by the West but also by the Third World, whose views on 'legitimate' behaviour did not always match the Soviet standpoint.[22] As an outgrowth of this particular normative resolution, the UN was not expected to pronounce its verdict on the rights and wrongs of a particular conflict – indeed it was positively discouraged from doing so. 'Impartiality' was in general taken to mean 'neutrality', and neutrality *vis-à-vis* immediate parties to any conflict implied, at a deeper level, structurally 'imposed' neutrality in the East–West and North–South conflicts. As a corollary, the use of force in UN peacekeeping was considered out of the question.

Yet in the 1960s the UN was expected to exercise a recognisable degree of authority on two occasions, in two different ways. First, the UN was assigned a degree of authority subsequent to the initial phase of the Congo operation. It was called upon to tell 'right' from 'wrong', to suppress the secessionist Katanga movement and brand as 'illegitimate' Stanleyville's claims to governmental power. ONUC was assigned a role in the re-convening of the Parliament, and in re-activating the 'formally' democratic process. The concrete political result of that process, that is, the creation of Adoula's Government of National Unity, was later used by the international community to prescribe a 'referee role' for the UN in judging the actions of intra-state parties to the conflict. In other words, to the extent that the Congolese Government was seen as a product of a democratic process based on a negotiated 'national (re)conciliation', ONUC was given the authority to declare 'illegitimate' any actions that were deemed harmful for the Government's exercise of the Congo's sovereignty. ONUC was also expected to act upon such judgement, and eventually did use force.

Secondly, in West Irian, the UN was given the exclusive authority to perform all administrative functions in the transition period. The performance of this broad range of functions, as we have already emphasised, was not allowed to prejudice first the Dutch and later the Indonesian claims to sovereignty. Nevertheless, the fact remains that the UN was expected to be in charge of a temporary political space which belonged neither to the sovereign Netherlands nor to sovereign Indonesia. Furthermore, UNTEA's discharge of its administrative functions was 'deep' enough to go beyond mere monitoring or supervision. It involved direct control of a variety of tasks, including the opening and closing of the New Guinea Council and appointment of new representatives to the Council.[23]

Re-ordering objectives: from vertical to horizontal relationship

The twenty-year period between 1967 and 1988 was characterised, as far as UN peacekeeping is concerned, by a remarkable UN inertia.[24] During these two decades, only one operation was authorised by the UN in an intra-state conflict: the UN Interim Force in Lebanon (UNIFIL).[25] The mandate of this second UN mission in Lebanon is a good indicator of the normative continuity between the mid-1960s and late 1980s. To cite a key paragraph, the

Security Council 'strongly deplored' any violation of Lebanese sovereignty and territorial integrity, Israel's military intervention into Lebanon, provision of military assistance to the so-called 'de facto forces', and all obstructions of UNIFIL's ability to take measures deemed necessary to ensure the effective restoration of Lebanon's sovereignty.[26]

In the 1970s and 1980s, largely because of Cold War constraints, collective expectations of UN peacekeeping remained unchanged. Maintenance of international peace and security and protection of sovereignty were the main prescriptions for the UN. With the replacement of Taiwan by China in the Security Council in 1971, the principle of UN non-intervention in domestic affairs, if anything, gained added strength. Even massive human rights violations, as in Cambodia (one of our case studies), were in practice ignored by most influential state actors. However, as indicated in the previous chapter, several interlinked trends would gradually find expression in a subtle but nonetheless visible shift in actors' normative preferences, which is not to say that those preferences were necessarily translated into immediate or sustained action.

Several civil society organisations had begun to flourish and campaign for human rights and humanitarianism, especially in the West, but also in a more informal sense in the rest of the world. While the tireless efforts of dissident groups in the Soviet bloc and of religious organisations in Central America and sub-Saharan Africa placed a degree of pressure on governments to address human rights concerns, it was western NGOs and advocacy groups, with increasing access to money, resources, publicity and support, which proved critical in raising the profile of human rights on the international stage.

The development of the CSCE's 'third basket' conveyed perhaps the first serious signals that human rights could be systematically used as political leverage in the international arena. In 1977, Carter's inauguration marked a shift in declaratory US foreign policy, in that human rights were now brought to the fore of international diplomacy. Rhetorical US support for the protection and promotion of human rights found its parallel in the attitudes of other governments as well, albeit on a more selective basis. A classical case is Moscow's determined propaganda effort in the context of Cambodia (see Chapter 8). It was also not uncommon for state parties to a conflict to accuse each other of systematic human rights abuses, as was the case with Kashmir or the Middle East. Governments generally began to pay lip service to human rights. Perhaps the most notable exception in this regard was China which continued to keep human rights as a low profile issue.

Rhetorical governmental support for human rights was embodied in a great number of human rights instruments between the mid-1960s and the early 1990s. Apart from UN-initiated refinement of human rights law, major regional efforts strengthened human rights discourse by devising their respective instruments. The American Convention on Human Rights (22 November 1969) and the African Charter on Human and Peoples' Rights (7 June 1981) are perhaps the best examples. IGOs were thus able to give added impetus to the increasing prominence of human rights, creating their own human rights regimes, making explicit references to UN human rights instruments, and invoking the human rights discourse, slowly but steadily, in relation to several conflicts in their respective regions.

While implicitly treated as a relatively secondary issue, human rights increasingly found their way into UN involvement in intra-state conflicts. Special human rights teams were sent to South Africa (1967), Israel (1968) and Chile (1975).[27] The sanctions imposed on Southern Rhodesia and South Africa were among the first notable signs of the rising importance of human rights on the international agenda. After 1974, the UN became increasingly concerned with the human rights aspects of the Cyprus conflict, with each party levelling accusations of human rights abuses against the other.

Beginning with the late 1980s, the UN's active involvement in intra-state conflicts grew disproportionately.[28] Between 1990 and 1995 the number of intra-state conflicts in the world reached 75, almost twice as many as in the early 1960s.[29] Of the several countries where the UN performed peacekeeping functions between 1988 and 1995, only a few experienced purely 'inter-state peacekeeping',[30] that is, peacekeeping without explicit reference to intra-state conflict.[31]

When the Cold War drew to a close, the international prescriptions for intra-state peacekeeping reflected, in revolutionary fashion (i.e. instantaneously and with considerable strength), the results of a set of evolutionary normative changes that had occurred over the preceding three decades. The new objectives were less easily identifiable than during the 1960s. While the overarching concern with maintenance of *international* peace and security remained intact, the principles of state sovereignty and human rights were frequently and prominently invoked in relation to intra-state peacekeeping, suggesting at least a partial shift in the relative balance between the two norms – from a predominantly vertical to a more horizontal relationship.

A brief examination of the rhetoric of Security Council resolutions on UN peacekeeping in the 1990s reveals that the UN's 'formalised' concern with *international* peace and security had, if anything, increased rather than decreased, contrary to what might have been expected. In the 1960s, SC Resolutions on Lebanon and the Dominican Republic did not even once refer to peace and security. Neither did two of the five resolutions on the Congo. SC Resolution 169 on the Congo made no more than a vague reference to 'world peace',[32] while the resolution on Yemen simply mentioned a 'situation which might threaten the peace of the area'.[33] In the 1990s, by contrast, crucial peacekeeping resolutions put the emphasis squarely on the maintenance of international peace and security. SC Resolutions 770 (on Bosnia) and 794 (on Somalia) explicitly referred to the threats to 'international peace and security',[34] while SC Resolutions 929 (on Rwanda) and 940 (on Haiti) made reference to threats to 'peace and security in the region'.[35]

More significantly, international actors, in their individual capacity, continued to highlight the objective of the maintenance of international peace and security in the context of intra-state peacekeeping.[36] Whether during UN deliberations or in their statements outside of the UN framework, they frequently related the UN peacekeeping mechanism to the achievement of this Charter objective. Yet, whereas maintenance of international peace and security remained the UN's principal normative objective in intra-state conflicts, the perception of what constituted a threat to peace and security would in the space of three decades undergo substantial change. The emphasis on 'external threats', that is, the strong desire to prevent encroachments by colonial powers, superpowers or other foreign powers, was now replaced by an emphasis on a range of less easily identifiable 'threats', many of them attributed to non-governmental actors. The threats in question were usually posed in terms of the possible ramifications – in several cases highly contested[37] – of domestic upheaval, including gross violations of human rights, humanitarian disasters, and breaches of democratic principles.[38]

In the relative absence of perceived external threats to international peace and security, international actors' prescriptions for UN peacekeeping shifted emphasis from 'protection' of sovereignty to 'promotion' of sovereignty.[39] In other words, an implicit distinction between the external and internal dimensions of state sovereignty manifested itself in actors' normative preferences. The external dimension of state sovereignty was gradually set aside, or at least demoted, and the internal dimension taken up with increasing regularity and enthusiasm. In the process, international insistence on the UN's 'respect' for sovereignty, as embodied in the principle of non-intervention, gradually eroded, or perhaps corroded.

Crucially, the normative shift with respect to sovereignty cannot be adequately understood in isolation from the parallel normative shift that took place on another front, namely human rights and humanitarianism. International players, with non-state actors playing a pioneering role in this regard, increasingly charged UN peacekeeping with the task of protecting and promoting human rights (in particular the basic 'right to life'), especially in situations where human suffering had overstepped the bounds of tolerance. For the purposes of analytical clarity, we choose to treat these two normative shifts as distinct: mindful, however, that they are closely connected – indeed intertwined – and that one is almost incomprehensible without reference to the other.

In keeping with the shift in international perceptions, particularly with respect to the meaning and content of international peace and security, human rights and humanitarian objectives gained prominence in the 1990s. So did the objective of promoting internal state sovereignty. This dual trend manifested itself in the advocacy of such concepts as free and fair elections, national reconciliation, transitional administration, maintenance of civil peace, repatriation and rehabilitation, distribution of vital *matériel*, and reconstruction. These concepts have been frequently translated into concrete sets of functions in peacekeeping theatres.[40]

One useful indicator of the two-pronged normative movement in prescribed objectives was the changing notion of self-determination as witnessed in the context of intra-state peacekeeping. Self-determination, which was a tangential issue for UN peacekeeping in the 1960s, was incorporated into the framework of active UN involvement in intra-state conflicts. In the 1990s, the UN set out to complete the painfully slow processes of self-determination in Namibia and Western Sahara, which had been defined largely in classical terms, that is, by reference to its external dimension.[41] The case of the former Yugoslavia, too, partly reflected concerns over self-determination. Equally important was the growing tendency of the international community to define self-determination with reference to its internal aspects. In Cambodia, as we will see in Chapter 8, elections were considered a means for the exercise of the right to self-determination, and UN peacekeeping, through the organisation of elections, a specific instrument for the achievement of that objective.

Security Council resolutions authorising so-called UN 'humanitarian interventions' make it plain that UN peacekeeping in the early 1990s reflected an unambiguous concern with human rights and humanitarian purposes.[42] These UN-authorised enforcement operations either accompanied or paved the way for other, more 'peaceful', UN operations. In August 1992, the Security Council resolved that the situation in Bosnia and Hercegovina constituted a threat to international peace and security, and that the provision of humanitarian assistance was an important element in the Council's effort to restore international peace and security.[43] In Somalia, SC Resolution 794 of 3 December 1992 was the first UN resolution to authorise explicitly a massive military intervention by member states within a country without any invitation from the host-state.[44] Moreover, for the first time the Security Council established a clear link between a humanitarian crisis and the use of force to restore international peace and security,[45] which had only been 'implied' in SC Resolution 688 on Iraq.[46] In Rwanda, *Operation Turquoise* was authorised by the Security Council under Chapter VII[47] and was carried out by French (and Senegalese) troops.[48] This operation was, in the opinion of the French Government, a strictly humanitarian mission intended to save lives until the arrival of the expanded UN force.[49] Human rights and humanitarian concerns, revolving around the basic right to live, and promotion of internal sovereignty were now in a normative sense clearly incorporated into relevant actors' expectations of the UN's role (and of UN peacekeeping) in intra-state conflicts.

An examination of other peacekeeping environments in the 1990s – for instance, in Angola and Cambodia – reveals that 'humanitarian interventions' were not alone in their emphasis on human rights and humanitarianism. The entire emphasis of the peacekeeping mission in El Salvador, at least in its initial stage, was on verifying 'the compliance by the parties with the Agreement on Human Rights signed at San José on 26 July 1990'.[50] On 19 September 1994, the General Assembly established the Guatemala mission for verifying compliance with the Comprehensive Agreement on Human Rights in the country.[51] In relation to Mozambique, Boutros-Ghali made it known to the President of the Security Council that he felt 'strongly that the international community must act quickly and decisively to avert another large-scale humanitarian disaster in Africa'.[52] While UN and non-UN humanitarian agencies had been active in intra-state peacekeeping environments all along since the 1960s, humanitarian and human rights functions were not systematically attached to UN peacekeeping missions until the early 1990s.

At this point, it is worth noting that promotion of internal sovereignty and human rights/humanitarianism often emerged as integrated objectives for UN peacekeeping in the 1990s. On several occasions, the UN was called upon to assist in the implementation of peace agreements between internal parties. Such agreements, as in Angola, Cambodia, El Salvador, Liberia, Mozambique, or Rwanda, typically addressed multiple dimensions of the conflict that needed to be monitored, supervised or controlled. Even in the cases of 'humanitarian intervention', where overwhelming normative emphasis was placed on the prevention of major humanitarian catastrophes, the wider 'political' aspects of a possible peace settlement were not neglected. In Somalia, for instance, one of the Secretary-General's reports to the Security Council indicated the role played by UNOSOM in relation to the re-establishment of police, judicial and penal systems in the country.[53] And in the case of Haiti, the Security Council would authorise a Chapter VII enforcement action, for the first time, with the objective of restoring democratic government in a member state.[54] At the same time, concern over socio-economic development began to be raised in several peacekeeping environments. UN peacekeeping was more and more expected to facilitate, if not to undertake, the implementation of UN and non-UN projects related to aspects of socio-economic development in the host countries.[55]

With the normative emphasis shifting to the promotion of state sovereignty (mainly in its internal aspect) and human rights, the collective expectation that the UN should not intervene in domestic affairs began to change. The standard prescription that the UN should absolutely 'respect' the host state's sovereignty – already weakened during the later stages of the Congo operation – eroded even more. This erosion was evident not only in practice, but also in the diminishing rhetorical insistence on non-intervention. The dilemma then crystallised: in order to promote internal sovereignty, the UN was allowed, indeed expected, to ignore external sovereignty and intervene in a state's internal affairs.

Although this normative expectation appeared to be in the ascendant in the early 1990s (in the sense that the UN's overall behaviour in peacekeeping environments accorded with that expectation and not with another), it was by no means a consensual view. Speaking on behalf of China, Qian Qichen would state before the Security Council that:

> It is the consistent position of the Chinese Government that a country's internal affairs should be handled by the people in that country themselves. According to the relevant provisions of the United Nations Charter, the United Nations, including the Security Council, should refrain from involving itself and interfering in the internal affairs of any member state. This principled position of the Chinese Government remains unchanged.[56]

Whereas China appeared a consistent and heavy-weight opponent of the UN's intervention in domestic affairs, especially when it came to the use of force to 'undo domestic wrongs', other actors tended to support a non-interventionist stance, but on a more selective basis.[57] In the case of Haiti, Brazil and Cuba joined China in drawing attention to Haitian sovereignty.[58] Brazil, New Zealand, Nigeria and Pakistan abstained in the authorisation of the Rwanda operation. At this unipolar moment, however, most influential governmental actors were located in the West/North and their expectations of the UN had largely converged in the face of mounting advocacy by non-governmental actors. Perhaps more importantly, the western hegemony that had been in the making for some time managed to exert its ideational influence on all players.

Re-assigning authority: from timid criticism to undoing 'domestic wrongs'

The UN's groundbreaking Namibia mission signified a radical turn in the authority assigned to the UN. Beginning with UNTAG, relevant actors created ever more space in which the UN was expected to exercise authority in all four dimensions. The increasing depth and breadth of the functions that the UN was expected to perform in intra-state peacekeeping environments are well documented in the relevant literature, and do not need further elaboration.[59]

The synopsis of the literature is that the international community prescribed increasingly broader and deeper functions for the UN in peacekeeping environments. The functions performed ranged from more traditional and limited military tasks (e.g. patrolling a border area) to such complicated arrangements as facilitating 'national reconciliation' or setting up a 'temporary authority'. These latter functions require not only complex networking along the military–civilian and technical–political spectra as detailed in comprehensive peace accords, but also a higher degree of involvement on the UN's part in 'domestic affairs', as exemplified by direct UN responsibility in 'conducting' elections.

The erosion of the requirement of consent was perhaps most obvious in those cases where 'humanitarian interventions' accompanied peacekeeping efforts. Even in such cases as Angola and Cambodia, where the peacekeeping mission was not primarily in response to exceptional humanitarian circumstances, the principle of consent could be seen to be eroding.[60] The erosion of the principle was evident in the international community's increasing expectation that consent should be extracted from the parties to the conflict on a one-time and comprehensive basis, which would then be considered as a binding arrangement for the duration of the UN presence. In several cases, as in Central America and Mozambique, comprehensive peace plans and agreements created a space for the UN in the settlement of disputes and extracted parties' consent not only for the initial UN deployment, but also for subsequent UN activities in the field. By carefully placing the peacekeeping mandate on peace accords, international actors increasingly downplayed the requirement of seeking consent at every stage of the operation. In this regard, the Congo and Cambodia missions, as we will see, stood in sharp contrast to one another.

A closely related development involved the assignment of a 'referee role' to the UN, which was systematised and frequently grounded in comprehensive peace accords endorsing the organisation's authority to render judgements on the domestic affairs of host states. In Bosnia, El Salvador, Liberia, Mozambique, Rwanda, Somalia and others, the UN was to varying degrees accorded this referee role in certain aspects of the settlement. In each case, this expectation was translated into practice differently. In Angola, as Chapter 7 will demonstrate, the UN was able to assume a degree of authority through Beye's chairmanship of the Joint Commission. In Cambodia the UN became a crucial part of the Supreme National Council. Yet in relation to Mozambique, which is ironically a 'success' story for the UN, the Secretary-General would complain that the parties were reluctant to entrust the chairmanship of the Supervisory and Monitoring Commission to the UN as an 'impartial third party'.[61]

The last dimension of authority, that is, enforcement of decisions, was not immune to change either, although UN coercion, especially its use of force, in intra-state peacekeeping remained a subject of controversy. The 'humanitarian interventions' in Haiti and Rwanda were not received with enthusiasm by all actors, most notably China, on the grounds of violation of sovereignty. Bosnia especially illustrates the degree of disagreement between key international actors, among them the United States, Britain and Russia,[62] as to how much coercion should be used, where, at what level (strategic, operational, or tactical), and by whom.[63] Nevertheless, compared to earlier periods, the UN was expected to enforce Security Council decisions to the best of its material ability. Even key state actors which opposed UN coercion – use of force or sanctions – on a selective basis (e.g. China in Cambodia, Russia in Bosnia, or the United States in Angola) did not go so far as to try and block assertive action. While, on certain occasions, the UN as an actor did not attempt to fulfil its enforcement mandate,[64] it did take enforcement measures on other occasions, ranging from imposition of limited-scope sanctions to full-scale military operations.

Concluding observations

Over the years, despite the radical change in international perceptions as to what constitutes a 'threat' to peace and security, the primary international expectation of the UN in intra-state peacekeeping environments has persisted: maintenance of international peace and security. In the early 1960s, this primary objective was complemented by an emphasis on state sovereignty, which manifested itself in two ways. First, the UN was expected to protect and preserve its members' sovereignty – largely defined in its external dimension, with reference to political independence and territorial integrity. Secondly, the UN itself was not allowed to act in ways which were deemed to violate sovereignty. In other words, the UN was especially sensitive to upholding the principle of non-intervention. The UN, when it entered an intra-state conflict as peacekeeper, was neither expected nor entitled to assume governmental duties, to work for national (re)conciliation, to push for promotion and protection of human rights, or to seek socio-economic development.

During the 1970s and 1980s, human rights entered the international agenda as political leverage. Third World activities in the search of socio-economic development continued unabated. These concerns would find their way into 1990s peacekeeping in the formulation of which human rights and, perhaps to a lesser degree, socio-economic development were just as crucial objectives as state sovereignty. In the process, an implicit distinction came into being between the 'external' and 'internal' dimensions of state sovereignty. Protection of external sovereignty was gradually, though never fully, set aside as an objective, while promotion of internal sovereignty was taken up, which inevitably incorporated human rights and socio-economic concerns. Several new functions were ascribed to the UN in intra-state peace-keeping environments in the early 1990s. Most importantly, the UN, through peacekeeping, was expected to be a direct participant in the political processes of the host country. While such participation took different forms in different cases, it frequently involved temporary control or partial takeover of adminis-trative and political functions.

In the 1960s, a substantial number of actors held that the implementation of peacekeeping mandates required the parties' continuous *de facto* consent. This was not only a practical necessity, which it certainly was, but also an emerging, and soon dominant, normative expectation. The consent norm entailed that the parties agree to the initial UN deployment and then continue to evaluate peacekeepers' individual acts and actions on an individual basis. This might lead to an effective withdrawal of consent as circumstances changed. More importantly, this placed great significance on the parties' own interpretation of the UN peacekeeping mandate. That norm was largely rede-fined in the 1990s. It now required the parties to accept the UN mission's overall mandate *as interpreted by the UN*. In this environment, the presence and activities of UN peacekeepers were increasingly linked to one-time, long-term and binding consent extracted from the parties to the conflict through compre-hensive agreements. Although the parties' continuous *de facto* consent was still believed to be essential for the success of UN peacekeeping, their initial formal/legal consent was normatively deemed sufficient to evaluate, indeed 'judge', their subsequent compliance with the envisaged peace process.

UN peacekeeping in the 1960s was based on the principle of 'impartial-ity', largely perceived as strict 'neutrality'. As an outgrowth of this thinking, the UN was not allowed to use coercion except in strict self-defence. In the 1990s, the UN was expected to be more 'impartial' than 'neutral', in the sense that it was expected to develop certain standards which it applied equally to all parties. This application, however, might well violate the UN's 'neutrality', that is, its obligation not to undertake or permit activities which would assist any party to a conflict. In the Angola and Cambodia cases we will see, for instance, the international expectation of impartiality lead to the weakening of strict neutrality. The actions of all parties were judged by the same 'impar-tial' criteria, or at least such was the expectation, and 'neutrality' was eventually set aside in order to punish UNITA and the Khmer Rouge whose actions were repeatedly judged to be in the wrong.[65] In addition, while impar-tiality (and if possible 'neutrality') continued to be an important prescription for UN peacekeepers, the parties to the conflict were increasingly expected to commit themselves in advance to accepting both the peacekeepers' mandate and their future deeds as impartial. According to the emerging consensus, parties to a conflict were expected to accept in advance not only that the UN and its mission were impartial, but also that the UN peacekeepers' future acts and actions *would be* impartial.

The UN was also increasingly deemed competent – in normative terms, not necessarily in terms of actual capability – to take vital decisions with respect to intra-state conflicts at hand and any necessary follow-up. The UN was able, for instance, to render judgements as to how the political processes in a host state should proceed before, during and after elections. It was expected and entitled to supervise political campaigns, run state departments, channel humanitarian aid, and even *enforce* the 'rules of the game' that were agreed upon by the intra-state parties to a conflict. If we adhere to Weber's classical definition of 'state', the UN was virtually expected to take the place of the state in certain countries. There were instances where the UN was designated, albeit temporarily, as the agency that could claim 'a monopoly of legitimate coercive power' in a given territory. A substantial part of this 'legitimate' authority was exercised directly through UN peacekeeping.

NOTES

Note: In the notes to this chapter, and hereafter, documents prefixed A; E/CN; S; SG and S/PV are UN documents.

1 UN Truce Supervision Organization (UNTSO, 1948–).
2 UN Commission for Indonesia (UNCI, 1949–51).
3 UN Commission for India and Pakistan (UNCIP, 1948–50) and UN Military Observer Group in India and Pakistan (UNMOGIP, 1951–).
4 For a brief outline of the three successive UN commissions in Korea (UNTCOK, UNCOK and UNCURK), see A. James, *The Politics of Peace-keeping* (London: Chatto & Windus, 1969), pp. 376–81.
5 Holloway and Stedman's survey of various data sets on violent conflicts concludes further that 'of the 160 or so wars from 1945 to 1995 only 25 or 26 can be counted unequivocally as interstate wars. The rest were internal wars in which non-state groups – defined in ideological, religious, regional, ethnic or other terms – fought against each other or against established states (Sivard, Tilly 1995, Gantzel 1997). According to one report, the preponderance of civil over interstate wars dates back to the 1950s … (Wallensteen and Sollenberg)': see D. Holloway and S. J. Stedman, 'Civil wars and state-building in Africa and Eurasia', available online at www.icgc.umn.edu/Consortium/ Civil%20Wars.html (17 June 2000).
6 SC Resolution 128 of 11 June 1958.
7 ONUC (1960–64); UNTEA/UNSF (1962–63); UNYOM (1963–64); UNFICYP (1964–); DOMREP (1965–66); and UNIPOM (1965–66) respectively.
8 These figures are derived from the data provided by Center for Systemic Peace, *Major Episodes of Political Violence, 1946–1998*, available online at http://members.aol.com/ CSPmgm/warlist6.htm (17 June 2000). One of the strengths of this database is that it draws on twelve respected sources on violent conflicts, including comprehensive studies by Ted Robert Gurr, David Singer, Melvin Small and Peter Wallensteen.
9 Derived from M. Allsebrook, *Prototypes of Peacemaking: The First Forty Years of the United Nations* (Essex: Longman, 1986), pp. 20–40, these cases are as a follows: Algeria

(1955–62); Cameroons (1947–61); the Congo (1960–64); Cyprus (1963–73); the Dominican Republic (1965–66); Malaysia (1963); Nauru (1947–68); Oman (1957–71); Portuguese Territories (1956–65); Ruanda–Urundi (1946–64); Somaliland (1949–60); South Africa [Apartheid] (1952–65); South West Africa [Namibia] (1961–66); South Vietnam (1963); Southern Rhodesia (1962–71); Tibet (1959–65); West Irian (1954–69); Western Samoa (1947–62) and Yemen (1962–65).

10 See Hammarskjöld's statement in SCOR, 13th Year, 827th Meeting (15 July 1958).

11 The internal unrest in the Dominican Republic, which began on 24 April 1965 with the overthrow of Cabral's military junta by the supporters of former President Bosch, led to unilateral US intervention on 28 April 1965. Similar to the Belgian 'humanitarian intervention' in the Congo (see Chapter 5), the United States had justified its action on the grounds of 'protection to hundreds of Americans' who were still in the Dominican Republic. Within three days of its intervention, the United States also mobilised the OAS mechanism, and managed to secure an official OAS intervention in the Dominican Republic, which would provide the legal justification for continued US presence in the country. Following the adoption of SC Resolutions 203 and 205 in May 1965, the Mission of the Representative of the Secretary-General in the Dominican Republic (DOMREP) was authorised, and remained active until October 1966. The mission was terminated after the new elections, imposed and observed by the OAS, and the withdrawal of the OAS force. For an account, see L. B. Miller, *World Order and Local Disorder: The United Nations and Internal Conflicts* (Princeton, NJ: Princeton University Press, 1967), pp. 149–65.

12 Bloomfield notes: 'We do not know the thought processes that led Khrushchev to go along with UN peacekeeping efforts in Suez, Lebanon, the Congo and Cyprus, although undoubtedly one consideration was the generally favorable attitude of the Arab and African states': L. P. Bloomfield, 'Peacekeeping and peacemaking', *Foreign Affairs*, 44:4 (1966), 672.

13 This expectation and the Cold War barriers were both evident in such cases as China's accusation of US aggression (24 August 1950), Yugoslav claims of Soviet threat (9 November 1951) and Sudanese complaint against Egypt (20 February 1958), not to mention the Guatemala and Hungary cases already noted in Chapter 3.

14 It is crucial to note here that while self-determination in the context of *original* decolonisation (that is, original transfer of authority from a colonial power) was highly valued in the early 1960s, peacekeeping missions were confronted with *post*-decolonisation claims of 'further' self-determination. And these kinds of claims were not easily tolerated by the international community, as would be apparent in the Biafra case (1967–70).

15 In 1949, no agreement had been reached between the Netherlands and Indonesia about the future of West Irian. Eventually, on 15 August 1962, an agreement was reached, according to which the UN would take over the administration of the territory from the Netherlands and hand it over to Indonesia. The UN Temporary Executive Authority in West Irian (UNTEA) was established in October 1962. UNTEA would have full authority to administer the territory, and would be given 'teeth' by a supplementary military mission – the UN Security Force (UNSF). UNTEA/UNSF was terminated upon West Irian's transfer to Indonesia on 1 May 1963.

16 See U Thant's message of 1 May 1963 in SG/1477.

17 The Cyprus case, as we will see, reflected a combination of the two.

18 The civil war in Yemen began in September 1962 when the ruling Imam of Yemen was overthrown by a *coup d'état*. Soon the Imam organised a royalist resistance against the new republican regime. The parties received help from Saudi Arabia and the UAR respectively. Yemen, Saudi Arabia and the UAR eventually agreed to a UN observer

force in Yemen. The Security Council endorsed the report of the Secretary-General 'about certain aspects of the situation in Yemen of external origin' and authorised the establishment of an observation operation (SC Resolution 179 of 11 June 1963, adopted by 10 votes to none, with the Soviet Union abstaining). The UN Yemen Observation Mission (UNYOM) was operational between July 1963 and September 1964.

19 US Secretary of State John Foster Dulles opposed the idea of a UN police force instead of observers in Lebanon, and said: 'We do believe that the presence in Lebanon of foreign troops . . . is not as good a solution as for the Lebanese to find a solution themselves.' See *US Department of State Bulletin*, 39 (July 1958), 105–6.

20 See Security Council Official Records (SCOR), 15th Year, Supl. for July, August, and September 1960, S/4417/Add.6, paras 6–8.

21 See Miller, *World Order and Local Disorder*, p. 153.

22 For instance, in the cases of Cyprus and Yemen there was considerable disagreement over the issue of legitimate government.

23 United Nations, *The Blue Helmets*, 3rd edn, p. 646.

24 Three of the previously established missions (UNTSO, UNMOGIP and UNFICYP) continued in this period, but with the consolidation of the Cold War and the emergence of dual trends in the South, only two inter-state missions were established – both were products of the 1973 Arab–Israeli War: UNEF II (1973–79), deployed in Sinai between the Egyptian and Israeli forces, and UNDOF (1974–), deployed in the Golan Heights between the Syrian and Israeli forces. Between 1965 and 1988 no new peacekeeping mission was established outside of the Middle East: see Fetherston, *Towards A Theory of United Nations Peacekeeping*, p. 18.

25 UNIFIL, authorised by SC Resolution 425 of 19 March 1978, continues its mission to this day, but seems largely ineffective and has been described as 'just another player' among many others in Lebanon: see M. C. Hudson, 'The domestic context and perspectives in Lebanon', in M. J. Esman and S. Telhami (eds), *International Organizations and Ethnic Conflict*, p. 142.

26 SC Resolution 467 of 24 April 1980; operative para. 2.

27 Gaer, 'Reality check', p. 53.

28 During the 1990s the UN conducted peacekeeping operations in response to more than 20 intra-state conflicts. For an examination of the 25 UN operations in 19 intra-state conflicts between 1989 and 1998, see M. Peceny and W. Stanley, 'The Promotion of Liberal Norms in United Nations Efforts to Resolve Civil Wars' (Paper prepared for the 95th APSA Annual Meeting, GA, 2–5 September 1999).

29 Derived from the data provided by Center for Systemic Peace, *Major Episodes of Political Violence, 1946–1998*.

30 Kuwait (UNIKOM), Chad and Libya (UNASOG), Eritrea (UNOVER), Macedonia (UNPREDEP) and Uganda (through UNOMUR).

31 This is not to say that *all* individual UN peacekeeping operations in the other countries involved intra-state conflicts. As we will see, in Angola, for instance, UNAVEM I specifically addressed an inter-state situation.

32 Preambular para. 8.

33 SC Resolution 179 of 11 June 1963; preambular para. 1.

34 Preambular paras 5 and 3 respectively.

35 Preambular para. 10 in both cases.

36 See, for instance, the Belgian statement in S/PV.3062 of 24 March 1992, p. 13.

37 In relation to Haiti, for instance, Henry Carey argues that 'there is no conceivable explanation that the UNSC had any inherent interest in a country with comparatively minor human rights problems or threats to international peace except for the fact of US

insistence on Haiti's importance ... No decent person could have argued that Haitian boat people threatened the US, let alone international peace.' See *Book Review of 'Security Council Decision-Making: The Case of Haiti, 1990–1997', by David Malone, Oxford: Clarendon/Oxford University Press, 1998*; circulated by ACUNS discussion group at acuns-io@lists.yale.edu (Tue, 15 June 1999 12:25:18 – 0400).

38 In some cases, where the nature of the conflict was particularly open to debate, both emphases were frequently combined. In the case of the former Yugoslavia, both foreign intervention and humanitarian catastrophe were underlined as causes of threat to international peace and security: see, for example, the statements by Cape Verde and Ecuador in S/PV.3106 of 13 August 1992, pp. 5–7. Also the Chinese statement before the Security Council is worth noting for its 'classical' emphasis, reminiscent of the 1960s debates: 'The sovereignty, territorial integrity and political independence of Bosnia and Hercegovina, a State Member of the United Nations, should be respected by the international community.' See S/PV.3344 of 4 March 1994, p. 11.

39 This is not to argue that the inviolability of external sovereignty, defined largely in terms of territorial integrity and political independence, was not repeatedly endorsed. In 1994, for instance, the Security Council *reaffirmed* 'the sovereignty, territorial integrity and political independence' of Bosnia and Hercegovina and the 'responsibility of the Security Council in this regard': see SC Resolution 913 of 22 April 1994; preambular para. 3.

40 A detailed analysis of the interaction between the UN and civil society, with specific reference to these concepts, appears as a case study of Mozambique in O. T. Juergensen, *Repatriation as Peacebuilding and Reconstruction: The Case of Northern Mozambique, 1992–1995* (Geneva: UNHCR, Working Paper No. 31, October 2000).

41 'In its external dimension, self-determination implies the right to independence and statehood and the consequent ability to freely determine the state's international political orientation. In its internal dimension, self-determination implies the right of the people to choose their government and to freely determine their political, economic, and socio-cultural development without interference from external forces': see N. Sopiee, 'The question of the form of self-determination for Kampuchea and its international guarantees', in D. H. McMillen (ed.), *Conflict Resolution in Kampuchea* (Brisbane: Centre for the Study of Australia–Asia Relations, Griffith University, Working Paper of the Third International Conference on Indochina, August 1989), p. 102.

42 Falk argues that, given structural constraints, 'sufficient' intervention is *always* interest-based and not value-driven. The inadequate humanitarian intervention in Bosnia is attributed to the fact that it was perceived to be principally a matter of values, and only peripherally a strategic goal. This diagnosis supports the argument that although humanitarian interventions may not have reflected a genuine effort on the part of the international community to stop humanitarian catastrophes, they did nevertheless characterise a normative insistence on humanitarianism and human rights; see R. A. Falk, *Human Rights Horizons: The Pursuit of Justice in A Globalizing World* (London: Routledge, 2000), p. 169. In his 'Two concepts of sovereignty', Kofi Annan makes clear that he is also sceptical of 'so-called humanitarian interventions'. Yet on balance he welcomes the idea: see *Economist* (18 September 1999), pp. 49–50.

43 SC Resolution 770 dated 13 August 1992 was adopted by 12 votes to 0, with China, India and Zimbabwe abstaining.

44 Roberts, 'Humanitarian war', 440.

45 SC Resolution 794 of 3 December 1992.

46 Knudsen, 'Humanitarian intervention revisited', p. 155.

47 SC Resolution 929 of 22 June 1994, adopted by 10 votes to none, with Brazil, China, New Zealand, Nigeria and Pakistan abstaining.

48 The Governments of France and Senegal had sought 'as a legal framework for their intervention, a resolution under Chapter VII': see S/1994/734 of 21 June 1994.

49 N. Hopkinson, *Humanitarian Intervention?* (London: HMSO, Wilton Park Paper 110, 1996), p. 51.

50 SC Resolution 693 of 20 May 1991; operative para. 2.

51 On 20 January 1997, SC Resolution 1094 would broaden MINUGUA's mandate.

52 See 'Letter dated 29 September 1992' reproduced in United Nations, *The United Nations and Mozambique, 1992–1995* (New York: UNDPI, 1995), p. 104.

53 See S/26317 of 17 August 1993.

54 *Operation Uphold Democracy* was authorised by SC Resolution 940 of 31 July 1994, adopted by 12 votes to none, with Brazil and China abstaining, and Rwanda not participating; see especially operative para. 4.

55 Boutros-Ghali writes: 'The responsibilities of the United Nations in the field of social and economic development are central to the purposes and principles of the charter: first, because the maintenance of international peace and security is inextricably entwined with economic and social progress and stability.' See his 'Empowering the United Nations: historic opportunities to strengthen world body', *Foreign Affairs*, 72:5 (1992), 96.

56 S/PV.3009 of 25 September 1991, p. 50.

57 Mills quotes the foreign ministers of Myanmar and Indonesia (countries that are considered major human rights abusers), and observes that 'many other countries, including China, Uganda, and India (also violators of human rights to varying degrees) have also voiced opposition to granting the international community as a whole the right to violate state sovereignty in order to protect human rights': see K. Mills, *Human Rights in the Emerging Global Order: A New Sovereignty?* (Houndmills: Macmillan, 1998), p. 48.

58 See H. F. Carey, *Book Review*.

59 See, for instance, Durch (ed.), *The Evolution of UN Peacekeeping*, Fetherston, *Towards A Theory of United Nations Peacekeeping*, and Ratner, *The New Peacekeeping*.

60 Boutros-Ghali would define peacekeeping as 'the deployment of a United Nations presence in the field, *hitherto* with the consent of all the parties concerned . . .' (emphasis added): see *An Agenda for Peace*, para. 20.

61 See 'Letter dated 29 September 1992', p. 102.

62 In Russia, the Government and public opinion alike were highly critical of NATO involvement in Bosnia; see V. Peresada, 'Unprecedented NATO military action in Balkans', *Pravda* (6 April 1993) reproduced in *The Current Digest of the Post-Soviet Press*, 45:14 (5 May 1993), 27.

63 See, for instance, the statement by D. Bennet, Jr., US Assistant Secretary for International Organization Affairs, 'Peace-keeping and multilateral relations in U.S. foreign policy', *US Department of State Dispatch*, 5:49 (5 December 1994), 809; and 'Bosnia: Russia claims it averted NATO bombing' – selected articles from *Izvestia, Pravda* and *Sevodnya* reproduced in *The Current Digest of the Post-Soviet Press*, 46:7 (16 March 1994), 1–6.

64 For instance, in the notorious Rwanda and Šrebrenica (Bosnia) episodes.

65 More recently, the UN's 'Brahimi Report' explicitly spelt out that 'impartiality is not the same as neutrality or equal treatment of all parties in all cases for all time, which can amount to a policy of appeasement. In some cases, local parties consist not of moral equals but of obvious aggressors and victims and peacekeepers may not only be operationally justified in using force but morally compelled to do so.' See A/55/305-S/2000/809 of 21 August 2000, p. 9.

5

The UN in the Congo conflict: ONUC

ETWEEN 1960 AND 1964, the UN conducted one of the most controversial peacekeeping operations in its history. ONUC[1] drew on 93,000
personnel from 34 states.[2] It involved 19,828 personnel at its peak,[3]
and cost US$400,130,793, provoking a serious financial crisis for the UN.[4]
The Congo case is interesting for our purposes not only because it aroused
immense controversy, but also because the UN was 'entrapped' by a complex
web of interlocking crises with obvious inter-state and intra-state dimensions.

In the Congo, the UN was originally expected to respond to an inter-state
conflict that emerged out of the decolonisation process, but soon found itself
in the position of having to redefine the principles of its involvement. Our
examination will in particular focus on the shift from inter-state to intra-state
peacekeeping, with the international response to secessionist attempts acting
as a bridge between the two. Once the internal dimension of the conflict was
made part of the UN's agenda, as the last part of our analysis will demonstrate,
the UN would be given more and more authority to handle the crisis.

Even a preliminary reading of the ONUC experience clearly demonstrates
that it was not 'typical' of its period. The UN's Congo mission was far more
ambitious than any peacekeeping mission hitherto. Nevertheless, it is
precisely the ambitious nature of the mission that makes it instructive for our
purposes. We know, for instance, that the UN used force in the Congo. But
what precisely were the objectives and underlying dynamics of the operation?
What exactly was the extent and scope of the authority assigned to the UN in
this, the 'boldest' intra-state peacekeeping mission of the 1960s? It is primarily to these questions that this chapter will now turn its attention.

Historical background

Colonised by Belgium in the 1880s,[5] the Congo's great attraction was its mineral
wealth. These resources were especially plentiful in the southern provinces of

Katanga (provincial capital: Elisabethville) and Kasai (provincial capital: Luluabourg).[6] In 1906 the Belgian company Union Minière du Haut Catanga was given exclusive mining rights in Katanga until 1999.[7] While the Belgian colonialism was oppressive, local resistance to it did not mature until the second half of the 1950s.[8] In January 1960, to the surprise of Congolese leaders, Belgium agreed to grant independence to the Congo as early as 30 June 1960.[9]

The ensuing elections failed to produce a politically well organised Congolese Parliament.[10] Consisting of some 70 ethnic groups, the Congolese body politique was characterised by strong communal and regional networks and loyalties. Within this complex cultural and political mosaic, personalities played a far more significant role than the embryonic political organisations. Eventually, on 23 June 1960, the two rival dominant Congolese leaders were elected to the two key positions: Joseph Kasavubu became President[11] and Patrice Lumumba Prime Minister.[12] On 30 June 1960, as planned, the Congo became independent.

On 11 July, Katanga proclaimed its own independence under Moise Tshombé's leadership,[13] and Belgium more or less simultaneously strengthened its military bases in the Congo. For obvious economic reasons, Belgium did not want to lose the Congo, especially Katanga. Having granted the Congo its independence, the Belgians, who had hoped to retain their privileges for some time, were surprised to find that the Congolese Government wanted them to pull out of the country immediately. Belgian interests and Belgian expatriates in the Congo were clearly not reconciled to an early departure from the former colony. However, in the midst of independence euphoria, and with violent attacks on local Belgians on the rise, Belgium found the necessary pretext for its 'humanitarian' intervention in the Congo. The North–South conflict was visible from the outset of the crisis.

UN involvement without a 'prelude'

The UN's formal involvement in the Congo crisis began in response to the Belgian presence in the former colony, and came into being quite suddenly. On 17 July 1960, Kasavubu and Lumumba addressed an ultimatum to the Secretary-General, warning that if the Belgian forces were not completely withdrawn within 48 hours, they would request troops from the Soviet Union. From that moment on, the Cold War would make its presence felt in the Congo.

The initiative to prevent the emergence of a crisis came from Hammarskjöld. The situation had already attracted great interest from a number of international actors. For the West the atrocities committed against foreigners (mainly Belgians) were of particular concern. So were the strong financial, political and strategic ties between Belgium and other western countries. For the Soviet bloc, on the other hand, the upheaval in the Congo provided a perfect opportunity to demonstrate the 'imperialist' tendencies of western policies. To this extent at least, the Secretary-General's initiative met with little opposition. The international community was willing to 'do something'.

'Peacekeeping' against foreign intervention

The original authorisation of ONUC[14] came in response to official approaches by Lumumba and Kasavubu[15] who made it clear that their request for aid was to counter external aggression and 'not to restore the internal situation'.[16] The ensuing resolution treated the Congo crisis as an inter-state conflict. Its first operative paragraph called upon Belgium to withdraw its troops from the Congo. It identified the key problem as the unwanted presence of the troops of a member state within the territory of another independent state.[17]

The second operative paragraph would present considerable difficulties during the later stages of the mission:

> The Security Council,
> 2. *Decides* to authorize the Secretary-General to take the necessary steps, in consultation with the Government of the Republic of the Congo, to provide the Government with such military assistance as may be necessary until, through the efforts of the Congolese Government with the technical assistance of the United Nations, the national security forces may be able, in the opinion of the Government, to meet fully their tasks;

First, it should be noted that it was the Secretary-General who, acting on behalf of the Security Council, would determine what those necessary steps were.[18] In the person of the Secretary-General the UN was given a prominent role in managing the ongoing conflict. This would prove a crucial source of discontent in the later phases of the operation. Secondly, the UN declared that it was dealing with the Government of the Congo. Once the intra-state dimension of the conflict came to dominate the crisis, this provision would create a major obstacle. Thirdly, the Security Council ruled out any neutral assessment of the efficiency of the Congolese security forces. Instead, it undertook to provide assistance until such time as the Congolese Government deemed its security forces equal to the task. This formulation was shaped in relation to the external dimension of the Congo crisis. Once the internal dimension came to the forefront, this original formulation would pose a serious handicap. The UN's resources were placed at the disposal of the Congolese Government, which would, however, soon become an 'internal' party to an intra-state crisis, and would use this provision to its own benefit in the civil war.

A strong disagreement soon emerged within the Security Council as to whether the first operative paragraph (i.e. Belgian withdrawal) depended on the second (i.e. UN guarantee of law and order). The Soviet Union, Poland,

Tunisia, Ecuador, and Ceylon argued that an act of aggression had occurred, and pressed for the unconditional withdrawal of Belgian forces. The US representative categorically rejected the charges of aggression,[19] while the United States, Britain, France and Italy emphasised the humanitarian reasons for Belgian intervention, and held that contingency existed between the paragraphs. Unless law and order could be guaranteed, Belgium could not be expected to withdraw. In fact, the West found the first operative paragraph totally unnecessary.[20] This was perhaps the first crucial moment when the strong anti-colonial voices of the Third World had overlapped with the views of the socialist bloc against the colonial powers which were for the time being backed by their strongest ally, the United States.

In the end, the resolution was passed without a clear Security Council position as to the problem of conditionality. The first operative paragraph did remain in the text. Without it, the Soviet Union would have resorted to a veto. From the Soviet perspective, this provision embodied the minimum of what it considered an acceptable resolution. On the other hand, Britain, France, Taiwan and the United States could have vetoed the resolution, had Hammarskjöld pressed for collective sanctions against Belgium. Three Soviet amendments to the Tunisian draft had already been rejected.[21] The Security Council's call to Belgium was therefore a balancing act between two extremes.

Rikhye maintains that Hammarskjöld dominated the decision-making process during the formulation of the original mandate.[22] Through his efforts the major powers eventually came to agree on the somewhat ambiguous wording of ONUC's mandate. On the one hand, to secure western support for the authorisation of the operation, Hammarskjöld insisted from the outset that the sole basis for UN jurisdiction was the request by the Congolese Government for UN assistance, and not a state of hostilities between two states.[23] Hammarskjöld publicly maintained that Belgians would withdraw as soon as the UN force established law and order in their former colony. After all, Belgians had claimed that they intervened strictly because of their 'sacred duty to protect the lives and honour' of their fellow-citizens.[24] For the Soviet Union, on the other hand, the wording of the mandate alluded to the UN's enforcement role. Both the Congolese Government and the Soviet Union had consistently accused Belgium of aggressive behaviour.[25] In other words, the UN force had to do what the UN was constitutionally supposed to do against acts of aggression. Consistent with the Government's request, ONUC had to ensure, by whatever means necessary, Belgium's immediate withdrawal.

Consensual focus on external dimension: SC Resolution 145

The second SC resolution came within ten days of the first one.[26] This resolution, too, dealt with the external dimension of the crisis. The main difference with Resolution 143 was embodied in its second operative paragraph:[27]

> The Security Council,
>
> 2. *Requests* all States to refrain from any action which might tend to impede the restoration of law and order and the exercise by the Government of the Congo of its authority and also to refrain from any action which might undermine the territorial integrity and the political independence of the Republic of the Congo;

The resolution established a clear link between internal unrest in the Congo and external interference. While this conception paralleled the view reflected in SC Resolution 143, this time the identity of the perceived parties to the conflict was blurred. Belgium, as conceded in the first paragraph, was clearly a party to the crisis. A second party, undoubtedly, was the Congolese Government. Yet acknowledgment was also given to the possibility that there were more state parties to the conflict. The support extended by the surrounding French and British colonies to Katanga was not unknown. Rhodesia, for instance, consistently supplied the Province with weapons.[28] More importantly, however, the resolution reflected the mutual suspicion of the two blocs. Both the United States and the Soviet Union were fearful of each other's possible direct involvement in the Congo. In adopting the second operative paragraph, then, the superpowers had acquired the legal right to criticise each other's activities in the Congo if the need arose.

On the other hand, the paragraph for the first time referred to the 'restoration of law and order' in the Congo – a phrase which was absent in Resolution 143. From the context it is clear that these words were not intended to address the intra-state dimensions of the conflict *per se*. Instead, the Security Council was trying to establish a link between domestic problems and external interference. In other words, the problem was still perceived to be the difficulty the legitimate and supposedly cohesive Congolese Government had in maintaining domestic law and order in the presence of external interference.[29] By putting the emphasis on the Congo's territorial integrity and political independence, the paragraph unambiguously conveyed the UN's primary normative objective, namely protection of the Congo's (external) sovereignty. From the perspective of the Second and Third Worlds, the key question was that of independence. The only relevant 'enemies' of territorial integrity were foreign powers with (neo)colonial ambitions.

SC Resolution 145 remained the only resolution on the Congo crisis that was unanimously adopted, without abstentions. It embodied the uneasy collective view of the Security Council on the matter, which emerged as a compromise between radically antagonistic positions. As we shall see below, the more the internal aspect of the crisis came to the fore, the more disagreements emerged between members of the Security Council as to how the resolutions should be interpreted and what the UN's objectives and authority should be.

Although consensual, the Security Council's emphasis on the external dimension of the crisis emanated from two different positions. For the Soviet bloc and some Third World countries, the resolution could not have any other emphasis, because the whole crisis was the result of colonial ambitions. From the western viewpoint, on the other hand, the UN's responsibilities did not extend to intra-state aspects of the crisis. Neither the Congo's original request nor the Security Council's response entailed any UN commitment to deal with the domestic problems of the Congo. Furthermore, the principle of non-intervention hindered such commitment.[30]

The direct Belgian intervention largely came to an end by early September 1960.[31] However, the problem of unwanted foreign presence and activities did not evaporate. In conjunction with secessionist attempts, the issue of mercenaries continued to occupy the UN's agenda. Despite the official Belgian withdrawal, many Belgian military personnel remained in Katanga, transforming themselves into mercenaries in charge of the Katangese *gendarmerie*,[32] thereby making it very difficult for the UN to establish a formal link between Belgian intervention and the Katanga question.[33]

Where 'external' meets 'internal': attempts at secession

Katanga's proclamation of independence predates the authorisation of ONUC. Similarly, Kasai's intention to become independent was made known during the first parliamentary discussions.[34] However, these secessionist movements did not enter ONUC's agenda until mid-August 1960. Tshombé declared that Katanga would resist by every means ONUC's entry into the province. Meanwhile, South Kasai proclaimed its own secession in August under Albert Kalonji's leadership.[35]

Embarking on a diplomacy of persuasion in Katanga, Hammarskjöld arrived in Léopoldville, and sent his Special Representative, Ralph Bunche (a US citizen), to Elisabethville to make arrangements for ONUC's entry into the province. His argument was that ONUC personnel were under the sole command and control of the UN.[36] ONUC was not permitted to intervene in the internal affairs of the country where they were deployed, and hence could not prejudice Katanga's position *vis-à-vis* Léopoldville. Moreover, UN peacekeepers were not entitled to use force except in self-defence. Yet ONUC's mandate applied to the whole of the Congo, including Katanga. If, despite his assurances, ONUC were denied entry, he would call an immediate Security Council meeting. Tshombé refused and Hammarskjöld duly called a meeting.[37] At about the same time, on 6 August, Lumumba's written complaint to the Security Council, and Ghana's and Guinea's criticisms of the

UN, led the Soviet Union to demand the removal of all Belgians from the Congo 'by recourse to whatever method of action' was necessary.[38] The UN was now explicitly called upon to use force against Belgian troops.

Gradual recognition of the internal dimension: SC Resolution 146

The ensuing debate led to the adoption of SC Resolution 146 on 9 August 1960, by 9 votes to 0, with France and Italy abstaining. Before SC Resolution 146, the Katanga case had not been specifically addressed by the Security Council. The emphasis of the Security Council on the external dimension of the conflict now began to shift. In line with previous resolutions, the Security Council stuck to the view that complete Belgian withdrawal from the Congo and the establishment of an effective government were both necessary. In other words, the Security Council in its collective capacity remained committed to its previous position which had emphasised the territorial integrity and political independence of the Congo.[39]

SC Resolution 146 reaffirmed that ONUC would 'not be a party to or in any way intervene in or be used to influence the outcome of any internal conflict, constitutional or otherwise'.[40] This was a re-statement of the Charter principle of non-intervention embodied in Article 2.7. Here we find not only an expression of Hammarskjöld's doctrine of impartiality/neutrality, but also the first indicator that internal unrest in the Congo was entering the UN's formal agenda. The Resolution embodied mainly Hammarskjöld's views, which for the time being suited the West's interests. The UN's impartiality *vis-à-vis* internal parties meant in concrete terms that ONUC would not disregard the views of Katanga and Kasai. This provision was especially welcome to Britain, which had cast an affirmative vote for the resolution. In other words, the UN's impartiality *vis-à-vis* the immediate parties to the conflict signified its neutrality *vis-à-vis* the North–South and the East–West conflicts. There were strong structural constraints on the normative basis of UN action.

Up until that point, the Security Council had defined its own role purely in relation to a perceived inter-state conflict. In one sense, nevertheless, the Security Council's overall attitude was quite revolutionary, since the conflict in question had emerged out of the process of decolonisation. While considerable political and normative differences separated individual members' positions, the net effect was that the Security Council, in its collective capacity, had endeavoured to create a sovereign state out of a former colony, at least on paper and in principle. Third World opposition to colonialism was so strong that it impacted on the UN's normative attitude at least as much as the East–West conflict did.

By the time discussions got under way, Belgium had already agreed not to resist ONUC's entry into Katanga, albeit reluctantly and under considerable pressure.[41] It was Tshombé and his team who were determined not to cooperate. Yet Hammarskjöld was steadfastly refusing to use force to enter Katanga. A Soviet proposal that the Secretary-General be ordered to take all necessary means of enforcement to expel the Belgians[42] was opposed by Hammarskjöld, and did not find support among western members. The continuing emphasis on the external dimension of the crisis, that is, Belgian withdrawal, no doubt accounts, at least in part, for the Soviet Union's eventual decision to vote in favour of a Ceylon–Tunisia draft. Italy and France abstained on the grounds that Belgian withdrawal was not a necessary concomitant of the UN's law and order role.[43] The French delegate had explicitly pronounced his Government's position when in the course of discussion he posed the question: 'Which of our governments would have acted differently if it had been placed in the same position [with Belgians]?'[44]

The adoption of Resolution 146 proved a turning point for the UN's Congo operation. It was interpreted in two radically different ways. To Lumumba, who welcomed the resolution, it meant that the UN together with the Central Government would end Katanga's secession. The Soviet Union, consistent with its longstanding attitude, interpreted the resolution as direct UN support for the cause of the Central Government, and voted in favour. At this stage, Soviet insistence on the need for the UN to support the 'Central Government' not only *accorded with* the letter of SC resolutions, but it also *strengthened* the slowly emerging normative view (supported by an increasing number of Third World states, and opposed mainly by the former colonial powers) that the UN should be at the service of the Central Government to protect the Congo's sovereignty against external intervention. After Mobutu's *coup d'état*, when the Central Government was no longer in Lumumba's hands (see below), this normative preference would begin to work against the Soviet bloc which would then shift its position to supporting the 'legitimate' Congolese Government.[45]

In Hammarskjöld's view, on the other hand, ONUC had to avoid collaboration with any party so far as an intra-state conflict was concerned, hence the need to adhere to the strict principle of non-intervention. ONUC had entered the Congo at the request and in support of the Central Government against an unwanted foreign presence, but not against any internal 'threats'. On 12 August 1960, Hammarskjöld drew Lumumba's attention to previous crises where elements of an external nature had combined with elements of an internal nature.[46] Part of his Interpretation of Paragraph 4 is worth quoting at length:

> The United Nations is directly concerned with the attitude taken by the provincial government of Katanga to the extent that it may be based on the presence of Belgian troops ... [Resolution 146], which reaffirmed the principle of non-

intervention, put the main emphasis on the withdrawal of Belgian troops. Therefore ... if the Belgian troops were withdrawn ... the question between the provincial government and the central government would be one in which the United Nations would in no sense be a party and on which it could in no sense exert an influence. It might be held that the United Nations is duty bound to uphold the Fundamental Law[47] as the legal constitution and, therefore, should assist the central government in exercising its power in Katanga. However, the United Nations has to observe that, *de facto*, the provincial government is in active opposition – once a Belgian assurance of non-intervention and withdrawal has been given – using only its own military means in order to achieve political aims.[48]

The Secretary-General considered each of the internal parties as equally legitimate. All along his efforts had been directed at cutting off the close links between external third parties on the one hand and internal parties on the other. That the UN should maintain general law and order in the Congo meant in Hammarskjöld's view the elimination of foreign intervention. Beyond that, however, the UN had no right to engage in direct support either of the Central Government or of the opposition. Expressed more concretely, the UN could not be expected to transport, protect, aid or in any way favour any of the parties to the conflict.

Hammarskjöld envisaged a role for the UN focusing solely on the international dimension of peace and security. While he was aware of the continuing domestic upheaval in the Congo, at the normative level he was convinced that the internal dimensions of the conflict should be handled quite separately from its international dimensions. At the analytical level he assumed that such a distinction was possible. Although he consistently tried to hold to this interpretation all through the crisis, his position stood in contrast not only to the Soviet view, but also to the rhetoric of the first two SC resolutions analysed above. As we have seen, Resolution 143 in particular implied that Security Council action was based entirely on the consent of the Central Government. Indeed, one of Lumumba's criticisms of Hammarskjöld would be that the Secretary-General had ignored the original mandate given to ONUC 'to provide the Government with such military assistance as may be necessary'.[49]

The Secretary-General's attitude led to harsh criticisms from the Soviet bloc which insisted that the secession attempts were not even remotely 'internal' in substance, from which it followed that Hammarskjöld's policy of impartiality or non-intervention were merely serving colonial interests.[50] In mid-August the Soviet Union started to provide arms to the Central Government. Some of its supporters (e.g. Ghana) warned that they would take independent action, unless the UN faithfully carried out its mandate, which they interpreted as ensuring the political independence and territorial integrity of the Congo, by whatever means necessary. In an unambiguous case of aggression, which was clearly within the purview of the UN Charter, the UN had only one course of action open to it – to impose international peace and security. To insist that ONUC should remain neutral and not intervene, the Soviet view implied, was tantamount to insisting that the UN permit violation of the Congo's sovereignty. In other words, the UN would need to abandon the norms of impartiality/neutrality and non-intervention for the sake of protecting the Congo's sovereignty which was ONUC's foremost normative objective.[51]

Towards UN intervention in 'domestic' affairs

In the wake of mounting criticism, the Secretary-General called a Security Council meeting on 21 August, which made it clear that the socialist bloc now directly opposed Hammarskjöld's policy of non-intervention. The Polish representative stated that everyone agreed that the organisation should not interfere in disputes between the Congolese Government and provincial authorities, *if* these disputes were indeed internal in character. Since in Katanga complete authority rested with the Belgians, he held, the UN should apply the doctrine of *restitutio in integrum*, and restore the conditions before the illegal Belgian actions took place,[52] that is the Congo's unity. During this meeting, the Secretary-General made known his intention to appoint an 'Advisory Committee' consisting of the troop contributing countries.

Upon the adoption of SC Resolution 146, Hammarskjöld was finally able to enter Katanga to negotiate ONUC's entry into the province. Lumumba was not pleased with Hammarskjöld's approach, for he had chosen to ignore the wishes of the Central Government, and preferred to deal directly with Tshombé.[53] The Secretary-General had also refused to take along any Government troops or officials during his visit to Katanga. The Government was now planning to end both secession attempts by force – a decision which added to the tension between ONUC and the Government.[54] Although ONUC did not have a specific mandate to maintain 'internal' law and order, it was thwarting the Government's decision to exercise its 'sovereign right' to maintain its territorial integrity by coercive measures. Before long, Congolese National Army (ANC) troops entered South Kasai. Many civilians, mostly Baluba, were killed.

The 'Constitutional Crisis'

By early September, a serious conflict had emerged between the President and the Prime Minister, the immediate reason for which was Lumumba's bloody operation in South Kasai. On 5 September, President Kasavubu dismissed

Prime Minister Lumumba and replaced him with Joseph Ileo.[55] This led to a chaotic situation where even the legality, let alone the legitimacy, of the new government was in question. This so-called 'Constitutional Crisis' would in subsequent months become a significant component of the Congo crisis.

On 6 September, with a view to maintaining law and order, ONUC took a number of emergency measures, including the closing of the Léopoldville airport and radio station.[56] This action deprived Lumumba, whose charisma had appeal in all parts of the Congo, of the means to explain the situation and seek active support for his cause.[57] On the military side, the measures also prevented Lumumba from using his aeroplanes in his campaign against Katanga. Thus, ONUC's action was considered by the Soviet bloc as an anti-Lumumba effort. Although with the easing of tension the measures were lifted the following week, ONUC had now in effect actively 'intervened' in the domestic affairs of the Congo.

By September 1960, Hammarskjöld's policy of non-intervention was working completely against ONUC. On one side, Lumumba and the Soviet Union were accusing Hammarskjöld of complete partiality. On the other side, Kasavubu was accusing the UN of still dealing with Lumumba's illegal authority. For its part, the United States was intent on conferring total legitimacy on Kasavubu. The Congo's internal politics was increasingly incorporated into the Cold War, with Lumumba representing the aspirations of the Soviet bloc and Kasavubu those of the West.[58]

On 14 September, Joseph Mobutu led a *coup d'état*.[59] He neutralised Kasavubu and Lumumba, dismissed Ileo's government, and declared that the country would be run by a *Collège des Universitaires*.[60] Taking this opportunity to get rid of Lumumba, Kasavubu cooperated with the new regime, and converted the College into a 'Council of Commissioners' – a move welcomed by the West since Lumumba was thereby removed from office. Under the Mobutu-Kasavubu arrangement, the Soviet and Czech missions in Léopoldville were closed, and Soviet technicians in Stanleyville were asked to leave. The Cold War had now fully penetrated the intra-state conflict in the Congo.

On 14–17 September 1960, the Security Council held an urgent meeting to discuss the situation. A Ceylon–Tunisia draft,[61] which reflected the Secretary-General's recommendations, was vetoed by the Soviet Union. Eventually, despite Soviet accusations of illegal action, a US draft resolution,[62] calling an emergency special session of the General Assembly, was adopted. The Soviet Union and Poland voted against the resolution. France abstained.

The emergency special session followed immediately. On 20 September, GA Resolution 1474, sponsored by 17 Afro-Asian states,[63] was finally adopted by 70 votes to 0 with 11 abstentions including the Soviet Union and France. It contained several provisions embodied in the Ceylon–Tunisia draft recently vetoed by the Soviet Union in the Security Council. This resolution was perhaps the first concrete sign that the hitherto adopted normative rhetoric was beginning to work against the political preferences of the Soviet bloc:

> The General Assembly,
>
> 2. *Requests* the Secretary-General to continue to take vigorous action in accordance with the terms of the aforesaid resolutions and to assist the Central Government of the Congo in the restoration and maintenance of law and order throughout the territory of the Republic of the Congo and to safeguard its unity, territorial integrity, and political independence in the interests of international peace and security; [64]

As we have already seen, from the outset of the UN mission, the Soviet Union consistently argued that ONUC would have to be at the service of the Central Government. Now that the Central Government was taken over by a 'hostile' regime as a result of an internal power struggle, the Soviet bloc would adopt a new line of normative argument by putting the emphasis on the 'legitimate' Congolese government. By increasingly encouraging UN action *against* the Central Government, the Soviet Union would then help to shape an 'interventionist' UN attitude. This new approach would find its expression in SC Resolution 161, which, as we shall see below, would not even once refer to the 'Central Government', and which would task ONUC with prevention of civil war in the Congo.

GA Resolution 1474 not only requested the Secretary-General to continue to take 'vigorous' action, it also called upon member states to refrain from giving direct or indirect military assistance to the parties except at the UN's request.[65] Furthermore, it called for the establishment of a body to assist the Congolese factions specifically in the settlement of their 'internal' conflict.[66] The resolution in its entirety assigned exclusive authority to the UN for handling the crisis. Again, Third World voices were crucial in the re-definition of the UN's role.

The creation of the so-called Conciliation Commission is important in two respects. First, it highlights the belief of the UN membership that the internal and external aspects of the ongoing crisis were distinct from each other. Secondly, it confirms that the majority of members eventually prescribed a role for the UN beyond protection of 'external' sovereignty. This point has serious implications for the principle of non-intervention. In relation to this latter point, the Soviet Union had argued in the General Assembly that the Congolese might interpret the proposed line of action as interference in their internal affairs.[67] Similarly, France had objected strongly to the UN addressing the internal problems of the Congo.[68] Nevertheless, a great many Third World countries, several of them non-aligned, were now willing to tolerate a minimum level of UN intervention in the Congo's 'internal' affairs for the sake of maintaining 'international' peace and security in the face of the rapidly escalating bipolar rivalry.

Three days after the special emergency session, the General Assembly convened for its regular annual session, with the participation of 32 heads of state or government.[69] The Credentials Committee had to decide who would represent the Congo. Guinea's proposal that the seat be occupied by the representatives of the Lumumba Government was endorsed by seven other Afro-Asian countries with contingents in ONUC,[70] and supported by the Soviet Union. Argentina, reflecting the western view on the issue, opposed seating Lumumba's representatives. In the end, the General Assembly ruled in favour of Kasavubu's representatives,[71] a result which favoured the Anglo-American position. In effect, the Mobutu regime had been legitimated by the UN. An important minority, including the troop-contributing African countries and the Asian neutralists, remained opposed to this decision. A number of countries, which had a special interest in UN peacekeeping, were unconvinced and abstained.[72]

In his speech of 23 September, Khrushchev attacked the 'imperialist' powers, which had 'been doing their dirty work in the Congo through the Secretary-General of the United Nations and his staff'.[73] He targeted not only the person of Hammarskjöld but also the office of the Secretary-General, and proposed an alternative executive body consisting of one representative each from three groups of countries: western, socialist and neutralist. The harsh Soviet attack on the office of the Secretary-General did not find any supporters, as would become apparent during subsequent deliberations in February 1961.

By November 1960, ONUC had become a military target for some factions.[74] Towards the end of the month, an incident took place which added to the controversy about the UN presence: Lumumba and two other senior politicians were detained while under ONUC protection.[75] Shortly after Lumumba's arrest, his intellectual heir, Antoine Gizenga,[76] proclaimed the reestablishment of the 'legal government of the Republic of the Congo' in a new capital, Stanleyville.[77]

Transition in authority

During the Security Council meeting of 7–14 December 1960, the Soviet Union and the Afro-Asian group demanded direct UN action to release Lumumba and to disarm Mobutu's ANC. The Soviet bloc and several non-aligned members were calling for UN action against the Central Government – a measure opposed by Hammarskjöld on the grounds that such use of force would constitute an internal intervention unauthorised by existing UN resolutions. Unless the Security Council expressly invoked Chapter VII for enforcement purposes, he argued, the safeguards against intervention in

Article 2.7 could not be suspended.[78] A draft resolution sponsored by Argentina, Britain, Italy, and the United States, which merely emphasised the rights of arrested persons, was vetoed by the Soviet Union, while a Polish draft, which would have requested the Secretary-General to undertake the necessary measures to obtain Lumumba's immediate release, was rejected by 6 to 3, with 2 abstentions.

During the General Assembly meeting two days later, two principal views emerged as to how the UN should now proceed. On one side was the Anglo-American draft requesting the Secretary-General to assist President Kasavubu in establishing favourable conditions for the Parliament to function. This draft also expressed the hope that the roundtable conference being called by Kasavubu and the pending visit to the Congo by the UN Conciliation Commission would help to resolve internal conflicts by peaceful means.[79] The language of this draft, which conferred legitimacy on the military regime backed by Kasavubu, was consistent with the US position which gave pride of place to the principle of non-intervention:

> As for the status of Mr. Lumumba in the political system of the Republic of the Congo ... [i]t is a problem of internal Congolese jurisdiction and not one for the Security Council or the General Assembly to judge; it is not for the Security Council or the General Assembly to choose between sides in an internal conflict and interfere in the internal affairs of a sovereign Member State.[80]

On the other side, an eight-member[81] draft resolution urged the immediate release of all political prisoners; the immediate convening of Parliament; and measures to prevent 'armed units from interfering in the political life of the Congo'. This draft, which in essence questioned the whole legitimacy of the Kasavubu–Mobutu regime, called on the UN to take the initiative in restoring the rightful government of the Congo. The Congolese people had given clear support to Lumumba, and the military regime, installed by imperialist powers, could not be recognised as legitimate. Neither resolution was adopted.[82] No consensus emerged as to what exactly the UN should do in response to the crisis. There was, nevertheless, growing pressure against the position taken by the West.

Interestingly, Kasavubu, who was supported by the United States, was also calling for more active UN intervention, though for a completely different reason. Following Lumumba's arrest and rumours that he had been tortured and killed, Stanleyville had substantially transformed its campaign into a military one. Kasavubu threatened that if the UN did not stop these attacks, he would seek outside assistance.[83] He had already made an attempt to take over the Kitona base from ONUC. Rajeshwar Dayal, Bunche's Indian successor, however, with the Katanga precedent in mind, replied that ONUC could not intervene in a dispute between a central and a provincial government.[84]

On 3–7 January 1961, six Third World countries, contributing troops to ONUC, attended a conference at the level of heads of state in Casablanca.[85] They adopted a declaration, which demanded that Mobutu's soldiers be disarmed, Lumumba and his friends be freed, the Parliament be re-convened, all Belgian military and paramilitary personnel be removed, and all airports and other establishments be returned to the 'legitimate' government of the Congo. These countries further reaffirmed their intention to withdraw from ONUC, should the UN not respond to their demands. The UN was now explicitly invited to play a defining role in the 'domestic' affairs of a member state, since it was called upon to convene a dysfunctional parliament and to re-install a 'legitimate' government.

Security Council paves the way: SC Resolution 161
Upon the announcement of Lumumba's killing, the Security Council held a meeting on 15–21 February, which resulted in SC Resolution 161 of 21 February 1961. Drafted by Ceylon, Liberia and the UAR, the Resolution was adopted by 9 votes to 0, with the Soviet Union and France abstaining.[86] The resolution was radically different from the previous resolutions in two important respects. First, it put the main emphasis on the internal dimension of the crisis. Secondly, the resolution outlined how the UN had to respond to the latest developments in the theatre of conflict, whereas the choice of operational targets had in previous resolutions been left largely to the Secretary-General. The reason for this shift was not only the dissatisfaction of some member states with the Secretary-General, but also Hammarskjöld's belief that specific endorsement by the Security Council of prescribed methods of action, involving especially the use of force, would eliminate attacks on his interpretation of ONUC's mandate.[87]

At the beginning of the session Hammarskjöld gave his reply to the Soviet Union, which had held him personally responsible for Lumumba's death, demanded his dismissal from the post of the Secretary-General, and called for an end to ONUC within one month.[88] This time Hammarskjöld, referring to Khrushchev's 'troika' proposal, accused the Soviet Union of trying to change the structure of the UN to increase its own influence. He vigorously defended his interpretation of ONUC's mandate, arguing that he came under attack because the UN had not *exceeded* its mandate. He insisted that the UN 'had neither the power nor the right' to liberate Lumumba from captivity. 'I say the UN,' he continued, 'because to my knowledge not even this Council or the General Assembly would have such a right, much less did it exist for the UN representatives in the Congo.'

Soviet criticisms of Hammarskjöld were not widely shared by other actors. India, for instance, rejected the Soviet invitation to support its position on the Congo, declaring instead its confidence in the Congo operation and in the

Secretary-General. In March, India would contribute a brigade to ONUC.[89] This support was important in that it came from a respected member of the Afro-Asian group and a leading non-aligned country, which had not been at all uncritical of the UN's Congo policy.[90]

Notwithstanding his defence, Hammarskjöld was aware that expectations of ONUC had changed since the outset of the operation. In response to growing Soviet and Third World demands, he proposed a more assertive line of action for ONUC: Lumumba's death should be investigated; civilians should be protected regardless of their background;[91] all means short of force should be used to stop clashes, including the establishment of neutral zones and cease-fire agreements; the ANC should be withdrawn from politics; the Belgian political as well as military elements should be removed from the Congo. The Secretary-General went on to propose that the Parliament be reconvened, capital movements be controlled, and means of transportation be inspected to prevent supply of arms. Hammarskjöld, acting through his representatives, had previously opposed the disarming of the ANC on the grounds that this required the Government's consent. He had, in other words, appealed to a stricter interpretation of 'sovereign rights'. As events unfolded, his concern over the maintenance of peace and security would take precedence over strict respect for sovereignty.

Hammarskjöld's recommendations, taken together with the decision to create a Conciliation Commission, point to a crucial notion, which would assume increasing importance for the UN's peacekeeping agenda, namely national (re)conciliation. During the Congo episode, the UN gradually began to define its role as a comprehensive conciliator. A growing number of states endorsed, implicitly or explicitly, an unprecedented role for the UN, that is, creating, within a 'sovereign' state, the conditions for a relatively coherent and harmonious society. This idea would be explored, systematised, and applied with greater sophistication in the 1990s peacekeeping missions, not least those in Angola and Cambodia.

Another idea that would be more systematically examined in the 1990s was temporary UN administration in war-torn societies. Pakistan, for instance, recommended to the Security Council during the February discussions that the UN administer the Congo as a trust territory until such time as 'the Congolese people may be enabled to achieve their own political settlement'. Similarly, an independent, non-official American study found that the UN was now dealing with a problem which in the past had been solved by a trusteeship arrangement or some other form of external administration.[92] But given the opposition to colonialism and the strong Third World insistence on 'independence', Congolese leaders and the majority of the UN membership did not embrace the idea.

By Resolution 161, the Security Council for the first time expressed concern over 'the danger of a widespread civil war and bloodshed in the Congo'. Part A of the resolution authorised ONUC to take 'all appropriate measures to prevent occurrence of civil war in the Congo'. The Security Council, no longer able to ignore the internal tensions in the Congo, made prevention of civil war the main mandate for ONUC. The whole preamble and the first operative paragraph of Part A were devoted to the issue of civil war.[93]

Resolution 161 defined the following functions for ONUC: arrangements for a cease-fire; halting of all military operations; prevention of clashes (these three functions were prescribed by the Security Council in relation to the possibility of a widespread civil war, and were complemented by the authorisation of 'use of force, if necessary, in the last resort'); evacuation of all non-UN foreign personnel from the country; immediate and impartial investigation of Lumumba's killing; punishment of Lumumba's murderers;[94] protective measures to enable the reconvening of the Congolese Parliament; and arrangements to ensure that Congolese armed units and personnel were reorganised and brought under control.[95]

In contrast to the previous resolutions, Resolution 161 referred only to 'the Congo' instead of 'the Government' or 'the Republic' of the Congo. The whole of Part B of the Resolution highlighted 'the imperative necessity of the restoration of the parliamentary institutions in the Congo'. The purpose was to bring the parties, which were in a formal sense equally respected, to the negotiation table. However, neither Kasavubu nor Gizenga was pleased with the new role and methods that the Security Council had prescribed for ONUC, which had significantly departed from the original mandate.

With the authorisation of the use of force, the Security Council's adherence to the norm of non-use of force was now open to question. A shift had occurred from Hammarskjöld's notion of peacekeeping towards that of peace enforcement, as originally demanded by the Soviet Union. Resolution 161, like the previous resolutions, was not adopted under Articles 41 or 42.[96] Despite fears that international peace and security would be endangered by a civil war in the Congo, the situation was not formally perceived to be sufficiently threatening to warrant an active enforcement mandate. Nevertheless, with the authorisation of the use of force for purposes other than self-defence, the Security Council's response had turned ONUC into a 'Chapter six and three-quarters' operation, giving it greater authority than originally envisaged.

It is worth noting that Resolution 161 could have been vetoed by Britain, had Hammarskjöld not reassured the Security Council that the new authority did not extend to any objective other than the prevention of civil war. The resolution could not be used, in his opinion, to impose any political solution on the parties. It did not even give ONUC the right to search incoming trains or planes for mercenaries or weapons.[97]

General Assembly endorses

Changes to ONUC's normative basis were driven not only by the Security Council, but also by the General Assembly. On 21 March 1961, the Conciliation Commission[98] published its report and recommended the following:[99] redrafting of the 'incomplete and ill-adapted' *Loi fondamentale* 'especially in the direction of greater decentralisation'; reconvening of the Parliament under UN protection; reorganisation of the ANC in isolation from politics; and convening of a summit meeting of African leaders. The Commission further expressed its opinion that only a federal form of government could preserve the national unity and integrity of the Congo.

The Commission's recommendations all related to the domestic affairs of the host country, and suggested that the envisaged role for the UN in the Congo clearly went beyond promotion of 'external' sovereignty. Slowly, an anomalous normative position, indeed a normative dilemma, was emerging, which would not fully crystallise until the 1990s: the UN was now expected to promote 'internal' sovereignty (i.e. create an effectively functioning government that enjoyed a reasonable degree of legitimacy) by casting aside respect for 'external' sovereignty (i.e. by violating the principle that it could not tell a government what to do in its domestic affairs).

Despite heavy criticism by Kasavubu on the one hand and Tshombé on the other,[100] the General Assembly adopted on 15 April 1961 three resolutions which gave clear support to SC Resolution 161. The first explicitly stated that the central factor in the grave situation in the Congo was the continued presence of foreign military personnel, political advisors and mercenaries.[101] The second provided for 'national reconciliation and a return to constitutionality',[102] acknowledging the illegality and unconstitutionality of the Kasavubu–Mobutu–Ileo regime.[103] The third appointed the members of the commission of investigation into Lumumba's killing set up by the Security Council.[104] These resolutions reflected largely the concerns of the Casablanca group about developments in the Congo. The General Assembly's formulation was more in line with the overall Soviet view than the western view in that issue was taken with the UN policy of 'non-intervention'. Moreover, the notion that the UN had a role to play in the process of 'national (re)conciliation' became firmly established. The tendency in the General Assembly was towards a more assertive UN role in the Congo. However, the resolutions were not adopted by wide margins, with a significant level of opposition registered for each of the three resolutions, as indicated by the large number of negative votes and abstentions.

ONUC did not implement the February resolution until September 1961. In late March, when the Katangese *gendarmerie* occupied the positions of the Nigerian contingent, ONUC did little beyond reiterating that it was entitled to oppose and resist such a move.[105] Between April and August, UN representatives in Katanga repeatedly tried, without success, to convince the provincial authorities that the February resolution would be implemented. It was only after the establishment of the Adoula Government that ONUC would eventually resort to force.[106] Despite the push by the Casablanca powers, one reason for ONUC's hesitation to resort to coercion was the concerns of another group of African states led by Cameroon, Liberia, Nigeria and Togo, which held a meeting in Monrovia on 8–12 May 1961. The 'Monrovia group' would soon include 22 African countries. These states were more moderate in their approach towards the Congo. In general, their insistence on pan-Africanism was not as 'enthusiastic' as that of the Casablanca group.[107]

On 22 July 1961, the Congolese Parliament reconvened. Most members of parliament were brought to Léopoldville under ONUC's protection. On 2 August, a Government of National Unity was constituted by Cyrille Adoula at Kasavubu's request. The Constitutional Crisis, at least on paper, had come to an end. On 7 August, Gizenga himself recognised the Adoula Government as the sole legal government of the Republic and was simultaneously appointed deputy prime minister.[108] In mid-September, ONUC proceeded to round up the mercenaries for deportation.[109] The unexpected resistance turned the operation into a military action. The optimistic atmosphere rapidly changed as hostilities against UN personnel increased.[110] On 17 September 1961, Hammarskjöld died in a plane crash on his way to meet Tshombé.[111]

SC Resolution 169: forceful protection of sovereignty
Escalation of violence led to another Security Council meeting. Ceylon, Liberia and the UAR submitted a draft resolution,[112] which included the following operative paragraphs:

> The Security Council,
> 2. Further deprecates the armed action against United Nations forces and personnel in the pursuit of such activities; ...
> 11. Requests all Member States to refrain from any action which may directly or indirectly impede the policies and purposes of the United Nations in the Congo and is contrary to its decisions and the general purposes of the Charter.

The United States proposed the following amendments to the above paragraphs:[113]

> The Security Council,
> 2. Further deprecates all armed action against United Nations forces and personnel and against the Government of the Republic of the Congo; ...
> 11. Requests the Secretary-General to assist the Government of the Republic of the Congo to re-organize and retain Congolese armed units and personnel to assist the Government to develop its armed forces for the tasks which confront it.

Both amendments attempted to establish a closer relationship between the Central Government and the UN, and their wording was in conformity with the previous SC Resolutions. These amendments were vetoed by the Soviet Union which was no longer willing to encourage active UN support for the new Central Government. Nonetheless, the ninth operative paragraph, building on the precedent set by SC Resolution 145, would make it clear that the Security Council was determined to assist the Central Government to maintain law and order and national integrity.

On 24 November 1961, after ten days of intense discussions, the original three-power draft was adopted as SC Resolution 169 by 9 votes to 0, with Britain and France abstaining. ONUC's mandate changed once again. The primary task was not to put an end to external interference or prevent civil war. Instead, it was to suppress secessionist activities, especially those in Katanga.[114] By this resolution, the Security Council '*completely rejected* the claim that Katanga was a sovereign independent nation'.[115] The first operative paragraph deprecated 'the secessionist activities illegally carried out by the provincial administration of Katanga'. The eighth operative paragraph declared that 'all secessionist activities against the Republic of the Congo were contrary to the *Loi fondamentale* and Security Council decisions' and specifically demanded 'that such activities which were taking place in Katanga should cease forthwith'.

Like the previous resolutions, SC Resolution 169 intended to restore 'law and order' in the Congo, and to remove any impediments to the Government's exercise of its authority. While the overall wording of the earlier resolutions was retained, much had changed in terms of the underlying perceptions. The Katanga question was now considered an 'internal' question, as reflected in the formulations of Resolution 169. Whereas Resolution 146 had called upon 'the Government of Belgium to withdraw immediately its troops from the Province of Katanga',[116] Resolution 169 referred to 'secessionist activities and armed action being carried on by the Provincial Administration of Katanga with the aid of external resources and foreign mercenaries'.[117] The perceived parties to the problem had changed. Now Katanga rather than Belgium was seen as the relevant party to the dispute. More to the point, while the UN had carefully avoided 'intervention' in matters between the central and provincial governments at the initial stages of the mission, it was now expected to intervene.

In Resolution 169, the requirement of consent was reserved for the Central Government. As a result of the lengthy discussions over the space of one and a half years, protection of the Congo's sovereignty, by which was meant ensuring its territorial integrity and unity, eventually emerged as ONUC's dominant normative objective alongside maintenance of international peace and security. The Security Council did pronounce its verdict as to what should be the political solution: Katanga simply had to continue to be part of the Republic of the Congo.

With Resolution 169, the Security Council further authorised ONUC to 'take vigorous action, including the use of requisite measure of force, if necessary, for the immediate apprehension' of all non-UN foreign personnel. The United States demanded that ONUC be given the authority to render useless hostile war machines such as aircraft, and to prevent their use against ONUC or civilians. The United States also wanted the UN to mediate in the internal political conflict, thus making it possible for other secessionist challenges to be taken into account. Unable to resist the ever-growing Second and Third World pressure to suppress Katanga's secession attempt, the United States tried to make the most of the anti-secessionist sentiment and drew attention to the 'secessionist' Stanleyville movement led by pro-Soviet Gizenga. By November 1961, both the Soviet Union and the United States were supporting moves to end the secession problem.[118]

Following the termination of ONUC, the US Assistant Secretary of State for African Affairs identified six key factors underlying US opposition to an independent Katanga.[119] First, under Belgian rule, Katanga had always been an integral part of the Congo – a judgement clearly accepted by the Brussels Round Table Conference of 1960. Second, secession would disrupt the Congo's economic fabric and destroy its potential for economic viability. Third, though Tshombé was anti-communist, there were other moderate Congolese leaders of the same quality. Fourth, if Katanga were allowed to secede, other regions might follow it, resulting in a chaotic situation which would invite communist penetration. Fifth, if the problem of Katangan secession were solved, it would strengthen Léopoldville's capacity to cope with communist Gizenga. And sixth, to enhance America's stature in the eyes of the emerging nations, Washington had to oppose Tshombé's attempted secession which most Afro-Asians believed to be a product of western neo-colonialism.

The last three factors offer perhaps a more plausible explanation for the US attitude towards Katanga, which shifted from 'toleration' to 'opposition'. The first three were present all along. As the crisis unfolded, potential ramifications of Katanga's secession became clearer. Furthermore, the sensitivity of the newly born states to the issue of sovereignty, with particular emphasis on territorial integrity and political independence, became ever more visible as indicated in General Assembly discussions. As a consequence, the United States re-evaluated its position and adopted an anti-Katanga policy at the expense of its allies Belgium, Britain and France.

Britain continued to oppose ONUC's involvement in internal political problems on the grounds that such a 'military solution' would create a 'very dangerous precedent' for any state seeking to suppress a dissident faction.[120] A month later, the British Foreign Secretary would argue that the UN might 'sow the seeds of its own destruction' if it neglected its primary duty, that is maintenance of peace and security, and turned instead to 'the acceleration of independence and the eradication of colonialism, which is a subsidiary issue'.[121] Britain abstained from the Resolution. France abstained on similar grounds: '. . . no doubt that the use of force could bring nothing but results contrary to that which is sought by the Council'.[122]

The authority assigned to ONUC did not change after the adoption of SC Resolution 169. In December 1961 fighting broke out between ONUC personnel and Katangan forces. ONUC's success led to the signing of the Kitona Declaration, which was the first concrete step towards ending Katanga's secession. In August 1962, U Thant, Hammarskjöld's successor, proposed a 'Plan of National Reconciliation' which took the idea of a Conciliation Commission one step further. In this plan he set out the details of a possible arrangement between the Central Government and the Provincial Government, designed to resolve the secession problem once and for all.[123]

In September 1962, U Thant finally ensured the acceptance of the plan by both Adoula and Tshombé. On 11 December, Katanga having demonstrated its unwillingness to implement his plan, U Thant requested member states to impose economic sanctions on the Province, in particular by stopping its export of copper and cobalt. On 28 December another round of clashes took place between ONUC and Katanga.[124] Following ONUC's military success, Katangan authorities sent a message to U Thant, agreeing to end the secession.[125] On 17 January 1963, Tshombé signed a document and undertook to facilitate the peaceful entry of ONUC into Kolwezi. The secession of Katanga had formally ended. At Adoula's request, a small UN force of about 3,000 men remained in the Congo through the first half of 1964. On 30 June 1964, ONUC withdrew completely.

Concluding observations

The Congo crisis and the UN's response to it developed in the geopolitical context of the North–South and East–West conflicts. Two competing normative attitudes, reflecting two different sets of interests, defined the UN's objectives and authority. While the (neo)colonial powers strongly favoured the newly born 'peacekeeping' doctrine, the socialist bloc pressed for what might be loosely referred to as collective security action against 'external' threats to the Congo's sovereignty. The socialist position revolved around two distinct but closely related political goals: gaining support among newly independent Third World countries which opposed colonialism, and weakening the western foothold in Africa.

The United States, under pressure from the anti-colonialist and non-aligned South, played a key role in bridging these diverse interests and normative preferences. The US political attitude underwent significant change in the course of the mission, and heavily impacted on the emergence of 'dominant' normative views at critical moments of the crisis, particularly with respect to ONUC's authority in the handling of the conflict. At first, the United States favoured the Hammarskjöld formula, in line with (neo)colonial interests. However, as time passed, it redefined its priorities in the face of the mounting threat of unilateral Soviet intervention in the Congo and growing dissatisfaction among non-aligned states in general, and Afro-Arab states in particular. It now applied more and more pressure on its (neo)colonial allies and on the UN with a view to 'appeasing' the Soviet bloc and the Third World. As a consequence, ONUC's authority expanded and Katanga's attempt at secession was eventually defeated. The one constant in an otherwise fluctuating US position was the determination not to let the Soviet Union score a victory in the global contest for power and influence.

ONUC's authority was redefined in all its four dimensions. The requirement of consent by *all* parties was eventually abandoned. The UN was called upon to pass judgement on the rights and wrongs of the conflict, set aside strict adherence to neutrality, declare the secessionist attempts illegitimate, and eventually have these decisions implemented by ONUC. Force was used to suppress Katanga's secession: that is, for purposes other than self-defence. The increase in the UN's authority was also evident in the expansion of its functions. When, after Lumumba's death, 'civil war' became a critical issue, the UN developed a step-by-step plan for 'national conciliation'. Hammarskjöld's Afro-Asian Conciliation Commission, which was endorsed by the General Assembly, and U Thant's Plan of National Reconciliation were important milestones in the embryonic development of the UN's national (re)conciliation agenda, which we shall have occasion to revisit in the context of the Angola and Cambodia case studies. Both Secretaries-General, their non-intervention rhetoric notwithstanding, contributed to the UN's increasing authority *vis-à-vis* the Congo. Perhaps more importantly, ever deeper UN involvement in the Congo's internal affairs was encouraged both by the Security Council and the General Assembly in their collective capacity.

The change in authority, however, did not entail a change in objectives. Maintenance of *international* peace and security was the main preoccupation of the international community throughout the ONUC episode – even when ONUC was required to maintain domestic law and order. While international actors remained largely silent on human rights during the Congo operation, the principle of state sovereignty, perceived in its 'external' dimension and with the emphasis very much on territorial integrity and political independence, informed international normative expectations of the UN. Yet the manifestations of this concern were strikingly diverse.

So far as the colonial powers were concerned, the main import of the sovereignty principle was that the UN had no right to address the Congo's internal affairs, including the problem of secession. For the socialist bloc and a large group of non-aligned states, on the other hand, the UN was required to 'intervene' (that is, both to deploy forces and to address the so-called domestic issues) precisely because protection of state sovereignty was one of the UN's main responsibilities. The United States, in an effort to accommodate these conflicting positions, did not itself adopt a clear stance on these questions, preferring to advance its interests by adapting to the changing international environment, in which anti-colonialist and anti-secessionist sentiment in the Third World now exerted a substantial influence.

In normative terms, the 'resolution' that emerged in the context of the Congo operation was more a spontaneous synthesis than a lasting resolution or reconciliation. The positions adopted by virtually all relevant actors pointed to contradictory interests and value preferences. What they were arguing for, normatively speaking, was not clear. In some cases ambiguity and contradiction described the twists and turns of policy on the part of individual actors. More fundamentally, however, these tensions had a structural underpinning. They were all shaped in close interaction with each other. Taken in isolation they lost their meaning. Taken together, on the other hand, they suggested that the double peaks of the East–West and North–South conflicts had given rise to a particularly tense international environment, in which any resolution of competing norms and interests would be at best partial and provisional.

NOTES

1 Derived from the initials of its full name in French: *Organisation des Nations Unies au Congo*.

2 E. W. Lefever, *Uncertain Mandate: Politics of the U.N. Congo Operation* (Baltimore, MD: The Johns Hopkins Press, 1967), p. 3.

3 The estimated population of the Congo in 1960 was 15,310,000: see United Nations, *World Population Prospects 1990* (New York: UN Population Studies No. 120, 1991), p. 602. The ratio of ONUC's strength to the local population was 13/10,000.

4 Exact figures cited in United Nations, *The Blue Helmets: A Review of United Nations Peace-keeping*, 2nd edn (New York: UNDPI, 1990), p. 435.

5 King Léopold II colonised the Congo in competition with other colonialist powers, in particular Britain. Eventually Léopold's ownership of the Congo was endorsed in the Berlin Conference of 1885.

6 Katanga was rich in copper and cobalt, and had been the principal supplier during World War II of uranium for the US atomic bomb programme. Kasai, on the other hand, produced 80 per cent of the world's industrial diamonds. By 1960, the former province was generating 80 per cent of the Congo's export revenues and half of its total income.

7 Union Minière and its partners dominated practically every aspect of administration in Katanga and its vicinity. Forminière, a subsidiary of Union Minière, was in control of substantial mines near Bakwanga in South Kasai: see J. K. Gordon, *The United Nations in the Congo: A Quest for Peace* (New York: Carnegie Endowment for International

Peace, 1962), p. 52. For a survey of US and British business interests in the Congo in general, and in Katanga in particular, see D. N. Gibbs, *The Political Economy of Third World Intervention: Mines, Money, and U.S. Policy in the Congo Crisis* (Chicago, IL: The University of Chicago Press, 1991).

8 In January 1959, a major riot broke out in Léopoldville (Léopoldville was the name of both the Congolese capital, that is, today's Kinshasa, and the western province in which the capital was located).

9 In March 1960, an 'Executive College' of six Congolese political leaders was formed to serve as a transitional regime and to draft a constitution. This provisional government was led by Belgian Governor-General Henry Conelis: see Kanza, *Conflict in the Congo*, p. 177.

10 The Congolese MPs came from 24 different parties. The strongest party won 41 seats, whereas none of the others could go beyond 15. The 22 ministers of the emerging Congolese Government represented 12 different parties: see S. R. Weissman, *American Foreign Policy in the Congo 1960–1964* (Ithaca: Cornell University Press, 1974), p. 19; and C. Young, *Politics in the Congo: Decolonization and Independence* (Princeton, NJ: Princeton University Press, 1965), p. 302.

11 Kasavubu was the leader of Alliance des Bakongo (ABAKO), the political organisation of the Bakongo peoples. Established in 1950 (i.e. the oldest political organisation represented in the Parliament), ABAKO was particularly powerful in the western Province of Léopoldville: see Young, *Politics in the Congo*, p. 304; Gibbs, *The Political Economy of Third World Intervention*, p. 74.

12 Lumumba, the leader of Mouvement National Congolais (MNC), was of Mutetela ethnic origin. He was certainly a nationalist and allegedly a communist, and aroused considerable antipathy in the West. Established in October 1958, his party quickly ensured significant popular support. Gaining 41 seats in the parliament, MNC appeared as the most successful party in the elections. The stronghold of the party was Stanleyville: see, in general, Gibbs, *The Political Economy of Third World Intervention*; and Weissman, *American Foreign Policy*, p. 18.

13 Moise Tshombé was the leader of the Confederation des Associations Tribales du Katanga (CONAKAT). Established in October 1958, CONAKAT was the voice of the Lunda and Bayeke peoples in Katanga. Yet it was dominated by the white community, by Union Minière: see Young, *Politics in the Congo*, p. 304; Gibbs, *The Political Economy of Third World Intervention*, p. 85.

14 SC Resolution 143 of 14 July 1960 was adopted by 8 votes to 0, with three abstentions. The United States and the Soviet Union were the only two permanent members of the Security Council to vote in favour. The next day the first party of the UN Force (90 Tunisian officers and soldiers) landed at Léopoldville, followed by the remainder in the next few days. ONUC was initially welcomed by the local population as saviours from the Belgians: see L. P. Bloomfield, 'Political control of international forces in dealing with problems of local instability', in A. J. Waskow (ed.), *Quis Custodiet? Controlling The Police in a Disarmed World* (Washington, DC: Peace Research Institute, 1963), p. E-4.

15 The two telegrams by Kasavubu and Lumumba on 12 and 13 July 1960 (reproduced in S/4382 of 13 July 1960), which initiated the resolution process in the Security Council, clearly underlined that their demand was related to the Belgian 'aggression', and not to the restoration of the internal situation in the Congo. Prior to these official requests, several oral requests had been directed by individual Congolese leaders to the UN as well as to major powers.

16 Weissman, *American Foreign Policy*, p. 62.

17 The Republic of the Congo had been recommended for UN membership by an SC resolution on 7 July 1960 as a country made up of 6 provinces, one of which was Katanga: see Gordon, *The United Nations in the Congo*, p. 19. Formally, the Congo became a UN member on 20 September 1960, that is, more than two months *after* the adoption of SC Resolution 143.

18 See G. Abi-Saab, *The United Nations Operation in the Congo 1960–1964* (Oxford: Oxford University Press, 1978).

19 Weissman, *American Foreign Policy*, p. 63.

20 L. B. Ekpebu, *Zaire and The African Revolution* (Ibadan, Nigeria: Ibadan University Press, 1989), p. 55.

21 The first sought to 'condemn the armed aggression by Belgium'. The second required 'immediate' Belgian withdrawal. And the third demanded that all UN troops be supplied by African members: Ekpebu, *Zaire and The African Revolution*, p. 131.

22 I. J. Rikhye, 'Hammarskjöld and peacekeeping', in R. S. Jordan (ed.), *Dag Hammarskjöld Revisited: The UN Secretary-General as a Force in World Politics* (Durham, NC: Carolina Academic Press, 1983), p. 95.

23 T. M. Franck and J. Carey, 'Working paper: the role of the United Nations in the Congo – a retrospective perspective', in L. Tondel Jr. (ed.), *The Legal Aspects of the United Nations Action in the Congo* (New York: Oceana Publications, 1963), p. 16.

24 S/PV.873 of 13/14 July 1960.

25 The Soviet affirmative vote to ONUC's authorisation – despite the mandate's failure to refer explicitly to what the Soviet Union perceived to be aggression – reflected an understanding which did not clearly distinguish between 'peacekeeping' and 'peace enforcement'.

26 SC Resolution 145 dated 22 July 1960.

27 The essence of Resolution 143 was encapsulated in the first operative paragraph of Resolution 145, which repeated the previous call upon Belgium for withdrawal of their troops and authorised the Secretary-General to take all necessary action to this effect. The fourth operative paragraph was addressed to the specialised agencies of the wider UN system, which were hereby invited to render to the Secretary-General such assistance as he might require.

28 Sir Roy Welensky, Prime Minister of Rhodesia, reportedly told a British journalist just before independence that 'a vast and rich part of the Belgian Congo that will become independent on July 1 could throw off its old ties and join the Federation': see Gordon, *The United Nations in the Congo*, p. 34. Welensky remained a strong supporter of Katanga. When the British attitude changed in response to American pressure in the later stages of ONUC, Britain would expend enormous effort to change Welensky's mind: see A. James, *Britain and the Congo Crisis, 1960–63* (Houndmills: Macmillan, 1996), pp. 138, 142.

29 The fifth preambular paragraph reflected this conception of law and order, and maintained 'that the complete restoration of law and order in the Republic of the Congo would effectively contribute to the maintenance of international peace and security'.

30 Throughout the crisis Britain would strongly advocate the idea that 'the UN force should keep itself detached from the internal politics of the Congo'; see James, *Britain and the Congo Crisis*, p. 78.

31 In August, Belgian troops withdrew from the Congo with the exception of their two military bases in Kitona and Kamina.

32 The total estimated strengths of Katanga's *gendarmerie* and the Government's ANC (Armee Nationale Congolaise; formerly known as the Force Publique during the

colonial administration) were 18,026 and 24,300 respectively: see T. S. Soo, *The Malayan Special Force in the Heart of Africa* (Malaysia: Palanduk Publications, 1989), Appendices I and II.

33 From one perspective, the mercenary problem was simply the continuation of the Belgian intervention. Indeed, there were clear links between the two problems. From another perspective, however, the mercenary problem added a different logic to the development of the crisis. First, the mercenaries in Katanga came not only from Belgium, but also from countries as diverse as South Africa and Poland (see, for instance, Ekpebu, *Zaire and The African Revolution*, p. 110). Secondly, not all Belgian mercenaries were ex-officers of the Belgian army. There were also a significant number of volunteers. Although the UN did manage to deal effectively with the problem of direct Belgian intervention, the mercenary problem continued up until the end of ONUC, and even beyond.

34 See, Kanza, *Conflict in the Congo*, pp. 100–1.

35 The so-called 'Mining State' or 'Diamond State' covered approximately one-third of the Kasai Province. Although Kasai's attempt resembled the Katanga secession in that it involved vested foreign economic interests, the Kasai case had more significant tribal roots. Kalonji's Baluba movement was a reaction to the continued Lulua actions against the Baluba in Kasai.

36 For the detailed exchanges between Hammarskjöld, Tshombé, Bunche and Belgian authorities, see S/4417 of 6 August 1960.

37 Gordon, *The United Nations in the Congo*, p. 38.

38 Gordon, *The United Nations in the Congo*, p. 32.

39 The wording of the preambular paragraphs in particular reveals that the diagnosis of the previous two resolutions was essentially retained. SC Resolution 146 identified the problem as the continuing Belgian presence in one part of the Congo. The issue at stake was still considered to be external interference rather than internal unrest. This conclusion is corroborated by the second and third operative paragraphs. Accordingly, the Belgian intervention in the Congo was now confined to Katanga which was a province of the unitary Republic of the Congo.

40 Operative para. 4.

41 Gordon, *The United Nations in the Congo*, p. 39.

42 See S/PV 885 of 8 August 1960, pp. 58–60.

43 Franck and Carey, 'Working paper', p. 19.

44 Lefever, *Uncertain Mandate*, p. 114.

45 See, for instance, the Soviet statement in S/PV.920 of 13 December 1960, p. 11.

46 He was mainly referring to the Lebanon crisis of 1958: see S/4417/Add.6 of 6 August 1960, para. 2.

47 The Congolese constitution (*Loi fondamentale*).

48 S/4417/Add.6 of 6 August 1960, para. 6.

49 See Gordon, *The United Nations in the Congo*, p. 45.

50 The Soviet Bloc and African nationalist states grew increasingly sceptical of Hammarskjöld's 'impartiality'. First Bunche and then Hammarskjöld himself had entered Katanga by permission of Katangan authorities. Hammarskjöld even found himself in a position where he had to listen to the Katangese 'national anthem'. Impartiality had gone too far; it was now working to the detriment of the Congo's sovereignty.

51 Hammarskjöld would argue the exact opposite in his *Introduction to the Sixteenth Annual Report* of 17 August 1961: 'It is a thankless and easily misunderstood role for the Organization to remain neutral in relation to a situation of domestic conflict and to

provide active assistance only by protecting the rights and possibilities of the people to find their own way, but it remains the only manner in which the Organization can serve its proclaimed purpose of furthering the full independence of the people in the true and unqualified sense of the word': GAOR, 16th Session, Supl No.1A (A/4800/Add.1).

52 See C. Hoskyns, *The Congo Since Independence: January 1960–December 1961* (London: Oxford University Press, 1965), pp. 176–7.

53 M. G. Kalb, *The Congo Cables: The Cold War in Africa – From Eisenhower to Kennedy* (New York: Macmillan, 1982), p. 48.

54 Congolese soldiers began to harass UN personnel: see, for instance, Kalb, *The Congo Cables*, pp. 52–3. By the end of the month, the reform programme for the ANC, which had been initiated at Lumumba's request, would be interrupted: see Gordon, *The United Nations in the Congo*, pp. 49–50.

55 Rikhye, *The Theory and Practice of Peacekeeping*, p. 83.

56 These measures were taken on the initiative of the acting Special Representative, Andrew Cordier, another US citizen. For an analysis of Cordier's role in the crisis, see C. J. L. Collins, 'The Cold War comes to Africa: Cordier and the 1960 Congo crisis', *Journal of International Affairs*, 47:1 (Summer 1993), 243–69.

57 Kasavubu had no such need anyway. Even if he had, the facilities in the neighbouring French Congo would be made available to him: see, for instance, James, *Britain and the Congo Crisis*, pp. 70–1.

58 Franck and Carey, 'Working paper', p. 22.

59 After the Congo Crisis, on 23 November 1965, Mobutu would conduct a second *coup* and become the dictator of 'Zaire'.

60 The *Collège* was to be drawn from the university students and graduates, whose number was extremely small.

61 S/4523 of 16 September 1960.

62 S/4526 of 17 September 1960.

63 Ceylon, Ethiopia, Ghana, Guinea, Indonesia, Iraq, Jordan, Lebanon, Liberia, Libya, Morocco, Nepal, Saudi Arabia, Sudan, Tunisia, the UAR, and Yemen.

64 Operative para. 2.

65 Operative para. 6.

66 Operative para. 3.

67 Gordon, *The United Nations in the Congo*, p. 61.

68 Lefever, *Uncertain Mandate*, p. 116.

69 These included Castro, Eisenhower, Khrushchev, Macmillan, Nasser, Nehru, Nkrumah, Sukarno, Tito and Touré.

70 Ceylon, Ghana, India, Indonesia, Mali, Morocco, and the UAR.

71 On 20 November 1960 by 53 votes to 24, with 19 states abstaining.

72 For example, Canada and Sweden.

73 GAOR, 15th Session, 869th Plenary Meeting.

74 On 8 November, for instance, a patrol of Irish peacekeepers was ambushed in northern Katanga and eight of them died.

75 On 3 December the detainees were transferred to Elisabethville: Gordon, *The United Nations in the Congo*, p. 86.

76 Gizenga, one of the leaders of the Parti Solidaire Africain (PSA), was an influential figure in the Congolese politics and Lumumba's Deputy Prime Minister.

77 Gordon, *The United Nations in the Congo*, p. 92.

78 Franck and Carey, 'Working paper', p. 26.

79 Ekpebu, *Zaire and The African Revolution*, p. 132, nn. 26–7.

80 US statement quoted and criticised by the Indian representative before the Security Council; see S/PV.917 of 10 December 1960, p. 92.

81 Ceylon, Ghana, India, Indonesia, Iraq, Morocco, the UAR and Yugoslavia.

82 The former was rejected by 42 votes to 28, with 27 abstentions; the latter by 43 to 22, with 32 abstentions.

83 In the 1990s a similar attitude would be exhibited by dos Santos in Angola and by Sihanouk in Cambodia, both of whom would be recognised by the UN as legitimate office-holders and both of whom would be denied enforcement support against their rivals, but would be given coercive support in the form of sanctions.

84 Gordon, *The United Nations in the Congo*, p. 94.

85 Algeria, Ghana, Guinea, Mali, Morocco and the UAR. Representatives of Ceylon and Libya also participated.

86 On 12 January 1961, upon allegations that the Belgian authorities in Ruanda–Urundi were actively supporting Kasavubu, the Security Council had met at the Soviet request. However, the Ceylon–Liberia–UAR draft introduced at that meeting had not been adopted although no one actually voted against it (4 votes in favour to 7 abstentions).

87 Hoskyns mentions that as early as the end of October 1960, ONUC was (*de facto*) authorised to use force if attempts were being made: (a) to force it to withdraw from a position already held; (b) to disarm UN troops; (c) to prevent from carrying out their orders; (d) to violate UN installations or to arrest/abduct UN personnel: see Hoskyns, *The Congo Since Independence*, pp. 294–5.

88 The Soviet draft resolution of 14 February (S/4706) was rejected with 8 votes against and 2 abstentions. Not even Poland gave its support to the Soviet Union which cast the only affirmative vote.

89 E. W. Lefever, *Crisis in the Congo: A United Nations Force in Action* (Washington, DC: The Brookings Institution, 1965), p. 57.

90 On 12 December 1960, for instance, Nehru had demanded Lumumba's release, accused Belgians of neoimperialism, and charged the UN with being too passive: see Lefever, *Crisis in the Congo*, pp. 61–2.

91 The UN had already protected – outside of its specific mandate – a large number of civilians who sought refuge with ONUC during the August 1960 massacres.

92 Lefever, *Crisis in the Congo*, pp. 68–9.

93 The previous concern over the presence of external interference was reflected only in the second operative paragraph, which urged that measures be taken for the removal of all non-UN foreign personnel from the territory of the Congo.

94 SC Resolution 161A: operative paras 1, 2, 3.

95 SC Resolution 161B: operative paras 1, 2.

96 This interpretation, which argues that the original resolution must have been authorised under Article 40 and not Article 41 or 42, is advanced by Hoskyns, *The Congo Since Independence*, pp. 120–1.

97 Lefever, *Crisis in the Congo*, p. 55.

98 The Commission consisted of 12 uncommitted Afro-Asian members. Its president was Jaja Wachuku of Nigeria.

99 Franck and Carey, 'Working paper', p. 29.

100 In March 1961, the Tananarive Conference was convened at Tshombé's initiative. It envisaged a confederated form of government, which was rejected by Léopoldville. In response, Kasavubu organised the Coquilhatville Conference in April–May 1961, and called for the establishment of a federal system, which was strongly opposed by Tshombé.

101 GA Resolution 1599, sponsored by 21 Third World governments (Burma, Cambodia, Ceylon, Ethiopia, Federation of Malaya, Ghana, Guinea, India, Indonesia, Iraq, Liberia, Libya, Mali, Morocco, Nepal, Saudi Arabia, Sudan, Togo, the UAR, Yemen and Yugoslavia) was adopted by 61 votes to 5, with 33 abstentions. The Soviet Union voted in favour, Belgium cast a negative vote, and Britain, France, the United States and the Congo abstained.

102 GA Resolution 1600, sponsored by 16 governments (Burma, Central African Republic, Chad, Ethiopia, Federation of Malaya, Iran, Japan, Libya, Nigeria, Pakistan, Senegal, Somalia, Sudan, Tunisia, Turkey, Upper Volta), was adopted by 60 votes to 16, with 23 abstentions. Britain and the United States voted in favour, the Soviet bloc voted against, and Belgium, France, and the Congo abstained.

103 Ekpebu, *Zaire and The African Revolution*, p. 100.

104 GA Resolution 1601, sponsored by Ceylon, Ghana, India and Morocco, was adopted by 45 votes to 3, with 49 abstentions. The Congo voted against, while Belgium and the Permanent Five abstained.

105 Hoskyns, *The Congo Since Independence*, pp. 391–2.

106 Bloomfield argues that, despite all the propaganda to the contrary, this clash occurred only after the severest provocation, and that the UN had no tanks or bombs during the fighting: see Bloomfield, 'Political control of international forces', pp. E-50–1.

107 See Emeka Anyaoku (Commonwealth Secretary-General), *Keynote Address* at the Conference on African Diplomacy in the 21st Century (London, 24 March 1999), available online at www.thecommonwealth.org/htm/info/info/speeches/1999/993-1.htm (3 May 2001).

108 This settlement would not last long.

109 This controversial operation (codenamed *Morthor*) was initiated by Conor Cruise O'Brien, the Irish diplomat who was at the time the UN representative in Elisabethville.

110 On 11 November 1961, in a particularly brutal incident (reminiscent of Somalia in the 1990s) thirteen Italian aircrew members were killed in Kindu: see Soo, *The Malayan Special Force*, pp. 55–9.

111 For the recent findings of South Africa's Truth and Reconciliation Commission about whether Hammarskjöld fell victim to a western plot, see 'Letters Say Hammarskjöld Death Western Plot', *Reuters* (19 August 1998) and 'UN Assassination Plot Denied', *BBC* (19 August 1998).

112 S/4985/Rev.1. of 20 November 1961.

113 S/4989 of 20 November 1961.

114 By that time, Gizenga too became a 'secessionist' in the eyes of Léopoldville authorities.

115 Preambular para. 4: emphasis original.

116 Operative para. 2.

117 Preambular para. 5.

118 See Lefever, *Crisis in the Congo*, p. 99.

119 G. M. Williams cited in Lefever, *Uncertain Mandate*, p. 82.

120 Lefever, *Crisis in the Congo*, pp. 92–3.

121 Lefever, *Crisis in the Congo*, p. 99.

122 Franck and Carey, 'Working paper', p. 38.

123 See SCOR, 17th year, Supl. for July, August and September 1962, S/5053/Add.11, para. 91.

124 The ONUC operation was codenamed *Grandslam*.

125 The message was sent through the Belgian Government channels on 14 January 1963.

6

The UN in the Cyprus conflict: UNFICYP

T HE CYPRUS CONFLICT, too, emerged out of a colonial context. In Cyprus, some 6,500 peacekeepers were deployed at a time when, as a result of the Congo experience, several international actors were sceptical of UN peacekeeping.[1] As of 2002, the Cyprus mission was still continuing. However, its nature had changed considerably since the Turkish intervention in 1974. This chapter focuses on the early years of the operation, when the intra-state dimension of the conflict was arguably more visible. Until the status quo of 1974, the UN Peacekeeping Force in Cyprus (UNFICYP) exhibited more than 'inter-positionary' peacekeeping, which indicates that it had the potential to assume multiple functions and expanded authority, making it a highly instructive case for this study.

As with the Congo, the Cyprus conflict was diagnosed differently by different actors. This chapter will first look at these diverging diagnoses, and then proceed to an examination of how they impacted on the normative synthesis underpinning UNFICYP's operations. Our focus will be on the ambiguous nature of UNFICYP's mandate which arose out of the tensions between the different interests at stake and the normative preferences that accompanied them. The chapter will conclude by examining the implications of this ambiguity for the ensuing normative synthesis.

Historical background

Cyprus, the home of a Hellenic civilisation, became part of the Ottoman Empire in 1571. The island came under British rule in 1878. During the decolonisation decade, the trilateral Zurich and London Agreements of February 1959 between Britain, Greece and Turkey created the independent 'Republic of Cyprus' in 1960. The 1960 constitution provided for strict power-sharing between the Greek and Turkish Cypriot communities. The latter, constituting roughly one-fifth of the total population, was granted veto powers over all major legislation, and entitled to a share in governmental, administrative and military services. Archbishop Makarios was elected President by the Greek Cypriots. Dr. Küçük was elected Vice President by the Turkish Cypriots.

In November 1963, Makarios introduced a thirteen-point proposal to amend the constitution in a way that would ensure decision-making by the Greek Cypriot majority, which was rejected by the Turkish community. Inter-communal violence soon erupted,[2] and the Turkish Cypriot ministers and other officials eventually withdrew from the government. As Clerides, a Greek Cypriot leader, put it in his memoirs:

> Just as the Greek Cypriot preoccupation was that Cyprus should be a Greek Cypriot state, with a protected Turkish Cypriot minority, the Turkish Cypriot preoccupation was to defeat any such effort and to maintain the partnership concept, which in their opinion the Zurich Agreement created between the two communities. The conflict, therefore, was a conflict of principle and for that principle both sides were prepared . . . to fight, rather than compromise.[3]

While Greek nationalists called for union with Greece (*enosis*),[4] Turkish nationalists devoted their efforts to the idea of permanent partition of the island (*taksim*).[5] Perhaps the root cause of the conflict was that neither community would agree to be Cypriot and nothing else.[6] British and UN sponsored mediation efforts failed to restore order. In March 1964 the Security Council would authorise a peacekeeping operation (UNFICYP) on the island.

Prelude to active UN involvement

The internal strife in Cyprus was first brought to the notice of the Security Council on 26 December 1963 in a letter from the Government of Cyprus, which listed perceived acts and threats against the territorial integrity and sovereignty of Cyprus, and requested the UN to protect the country from unilateral military intervention.[7] The Cyprus Government, which was by then exclusively in the hands of Greek Cypriots,[8] declared that it feared a Turkish invasion.

As a result of intensive British diplomacy, on 2 January 1964 Cyprus accepted a proposal by the British, Greek and Turkish governments to take part in a conference in London concerning the future of the island. Britain informed the Secretary-General that the governments of Britain, Greece, Turkey and Cyprus wanted him to appoint a UN observer in Cyprus.[9] Nevertheless Britain and the United States repeatedly produced plans which largely excluded the UN but included NATO.

Opposition to the NATO option

Following the deadlock in London, two Anglo-American proposals for NATO peacekeeping in Cyprus were refused by Makarios:

> The position of Archbishop Makarios could be summed up as follows: the principle that an international force should be created and stationed in Cyprus was accepted; such a force, whose composition might be agreed upon in advance, should be under the Security Council; Greek and Turkish units should not participate in the force; and in its terms of reference should include the protection of the territorial integrity of the Republic of Cyprus and assistance in restoring normal conditions.[10]

According to the substantially revised second plan, the proposed peacekeeping force would not be composed exclusively of NATO troops; UN approval would be sought; Britain would send regular reports to the UN Secretary-General; and the Cyprus Government would be kept informed of developments.[11] However, Makarios made it clear that he would not consent to an international force unless it were placed under the effective authority of the Security Council. Britain and the United States reportedly exerted enormous pressure on the Cypriot Government, even to the point of threatening to obstruct Makarios' efforts at the UN, if he chose to reject the idea of NATO peacekeeping.[12]

Cypriot scepticism of the desirability of a NATO action was understandable, given that Cyprus was a newly decolonised and non-aligned country. However, other considerations had in all probability also motivated Makarios' rejection of the idea of NATO peacekeeping.[13] In the first place, he felt that in the event of a NATO operation NATO interests would take priority over Greek Cypriot interests. A NATO-based solution would tend to favour Turkish Cypriots as he believed had been the case with the Zurich and London agreements.[14] Among other things, he also wanted to 'escape from the straitjacket of new negotiations with the three guarantor powers alone', make the UN directly 'responsible for' the solution of the Cyprus problem, and isolate the Turks who had fewer friends in the UN than in NATO.[15] Furthermore, the decolonisation sentiment prevailing in the UN might even give Makarios the opportunity to have the London and Zurich agreements (both created under *de facto* NATO auspices) nullified.

Makarios' position found support especially from the socialist bloc, but also from the non-aligned countries. Soviet policy over Cyprus had been based on two interlinked objectives: to prevent incorporation of the island into NATO, and ensure the abolition of the so-called British sovereign bases in Cyprus.[16] The Soviet Union saw the prospect of UN peacekeeping as offering the pretext for intruding into an intra-NATO dispute in the eastern Mediterranean. In an all-NATO affair the Soviet Union would have little or no say, whereas a UN mission would mean active Security Council involvement, hence an active role for the Soviet Union. Secondly, the situation would give the Russians ammunition to criticise the 'imperialist' tendency of NATO powers. In the Soviet view, the whole crisis typified an imperialist manipulation. First and foremost was Britain's role as the former colonial power which did not want to lose its colonial privileges. In this assessment, Britain was the most important factor contributing to the conflict. The disputed Cyprus Constitution, the argument ran, was specifically designed and imposed by Britain for the express purpose of maintaining its hegemony over the island.[17] For its part Turkey was seen as harbouring hostile intentions in relation to Cyprus' territorial integrity.

Though de Gaulle's France was at the time more favourably disposed towards the UN than towards NATO, following the fallout of the Congo operation it was less than enthusiastic about the creation of a new UN peacekeeping mission. For France, no external involvement was desirable in Cyprus, whether it be by regional state parties to the conflict (Greece and Turkey), the world powers (especially Britain), NATO, or the UN. Such an attitude would, of course, sooner or later result in *enosis*. France was indeed on record as favouring *enosis* as a solution to the Cyprus problem.[18] If, however, some sort of international involvement was absolutely necessary – and this seemed to be the case – France's preference was to counterbalance Anglo-American influence over any likely outcome. Given its veto power at the Security Council, the UN option was preferable to the NATO option.[19]

The Anglo-American position

The United States was mainly concerned to keep and resolve the Cyprus crisis within NATO boundaries.[20] Greece and Turkey, the guarantor powers of the 1959 agreements, were both within the NATO family, and escalation of the crisis might even cause a war between two neighbours and geostrategic allies. US handling of the situation had to be based on a delicate balance between the Greek and Turkish points of view.[21] In the presence of an ever stronger non-aligned 'bloc', whose anti-colonial and anti-western orientation was encouraged and provoked by the Soviet Union, the Greek Cypriot case found considerable support among the UN membership. The United States had to be particularly careful not to offend the Turkish side publicly.[22]

A second American consideration was the necessity to counter the Soviet rhetoric of 'NATO aggression'. As the leader of NATO, the United States could not permit Turkey or Britain to be labelled aggressors. NATO's prestige was at stake. Yet another reason for the slight American tendency to support Turkey's viewpoint was Greece's peculiar position. Greece had strong cultural and historical links with Russia, not least in terms of their common Orthodox heritage. In addition, both countries had for centuries considered the Ottoman Empire as their common enemy. Moreover, notwithstanding its NATO membership, Greece was home to an influential socialist movement – the American backed Greek junta of 1967 had not yet been installed in Athens.[23]

Britain was opposed to a UN force, because it might diminish Britain's influence in Cyprus. British Defence Minister Thorneycroft had stated in the House of Commons that Cyprus remained the principal base for the British striking airforce, which supported CENTO, and for some substantive units of Britain's worldwide network of military communications.[24] The strategic importance of the island was unquestionable.[25] Thanks to its continuing military presence on the island, Britain hurriedly operationalised its own independent 'peacekeeping' operation, which lasted from 21 December 1963 to 27 March 1964.

The British Government brought the situation before the Security Council only when its own troops were no longer able to control the escalating crisis, and when the Greek Cypriot side firmly rejected alternative courses of action.[26] Britain had not been keen to see a UN peacekeeping operation in the Congo either. In the face of rapid decolonisation, the British tried to maximise their political dominance in what they perceived to be their sphere of influence. With the situation deteriorating, the British delegation finally requested an early meeting of the Security Council. The same day the Cyprus Government asked the Security Council to proceed with the examination of its complaint. These two requests together would form the agenda for the subsequent discussions of the Cyprus question at the Council.[27]

The attempts to resolve the crisis under NATO auspices having failed, the West was left with no choice but to bring the issue to the UN. However, since much was at stake, neither Britain nor the United States could risk leaving the matter entirely in the hands of the General Assembly, where the majority of states were suspicious of possible western neocolonialist intentions. The General Assembly was therefore virtually sidestepped quite early in the process, all the more easily as it was not in session at the time. The General Assembly's formal contribution to the orientation of UNFICYP remained limited.

Resolving two divergent diagnoses

Two completely different versions of the history of the dispute were presented by the two communities before the Security Council. Largely in response to efforts of the non-permanent members, the Council would choose in its resolutions to ignore the substance of the matter, that is, the root causes of the conflict. The emphasis was instead put on avoidance of renewed violence.[28] The discussion of UN intervention in Cyprus revolved around concerns over peace, security and sovereignty. The overwhelming majority of the statements made in the Security Council (as well as the General Assembly) focused on the unity, territorial integrity and political independence of Cyprus. Could UN involvement be directed towards attainment of any other normative objectives? The consensual answer seemed to be in the negative.

For the Soviet bloc, the issue at stake was protection of the territorial integrity and sovereignty of the new Republic of Cyprus against external aggression. While Turkey's claims that it had the right to intervene unilaterally on behalf of the Turkish Cypriot community was identified as the immediate source of the threat, wider NATO interests were considered the actual source of the aggression:

> The dispatch of foreign troops to Cyprus has pursued and continues to pursue but one purpose: the actual occupation by the military forces of NATO of the Republic of Cyprus ... The Security Council must ensure the maintenance of peace in Cyprus and in the eastern part of the Mediterranean region. But it is not possible to ensure peace in Cyprus without ending the interference from outside.[29]

In keeping with this view, the Soviet bloc, which insisted on the inter-state dimensions of the conflict, held that the main protagonists were the Governments of Cyprus, Turkey and Britain:

> What other interested party in Cyprus, apart from the Government of Cyprus itself, can there be? There is one lawful government in Cyprus, and its representatives are recognized ... as the only lawful representatives of the Republic of Cyprus ... Denktas' ... claim to represent some sort of interested party in Cyprus was clearly an unsuccessful attempt, and one that was not likely to succeed.[30]

The Turkish Cypriots, according to this view, were nothing but a pawn of NATO's imperialist policies. The sovereignty of the Cypriot state rested with the constitutional Cypriot Government,[31] against whose wishes no UN action could be taken. Since the Soviet bloc defined the Cypriot conflict in terms of 'aggression', it maintained that the Security Council, given the provisions of Chapter VII, had the authority to tell who in the dispute was in the right and who was in the wrong. The UN presence on the island was intended to protect the Cypriot Government, the party alleged to be in the 'right', against the external Turco-British threat.

For the United States, on the other hand, the UN was confronted with a primarily intra-state conflict. The task was to restore domestic law and order by putting an end to the inter-communal strife:

> No one is threatening to take the territory of Cyprus, no one is threatening its independence – Turkey or Greece or anyone else ... I repeat that the urgent business before the Council and the responsibility of the Government of Cyprus is to restore communal peace and order and to stop the bloodshed. The sooner that we in the Security Council turn our attention to this, the better it will be for all.[32]

The western camp was also more inclined to consider the Turkish Cypriots as a legitimate party to the conflict. Although the Turkish Cypriot community was not explicitly endorsed by the Security Council as a 'party' to the conflict, its representative was granted the opportunity to make a statement before the Council. The difficulty arose from the fact that the Turkish side did not enjoy the legal status of a government. The British representative, nevertheless, took the following position:

> The discussion now before us, which arises out of the serious deterioration of relations between the two communities in the Republic of Cyprus, will be materially assisted by hearing a statement from the representative of the Turkish community.[33]

While several representatives would implicitly admit in their speeches that the Turkish Cypriot side was a *de facto* party to the conflict, and should be recognised as such, there was no specific attempt on the part of the Security Council to identify in any formal sense the parties to the conflict. This would in due course create significant complications for UNFICYP. The agreement, for example, between the UN and the Turkish Government for the re-commencement of the rotation of the Turkish contingent and the parallel removal of roadblocks on the Kyrenia road would provoke great anger amongst the Turkish Cypriots. Regardless of the position taken by the Turkish Government, the Turkish Cypriot leadership held they had not been duly consulted about the agreement. And the road remained blocked.[34]

The overarching concern common to both the socialist and western camps was that, should the Cyprus conflict escalate, peace and stability in the entire eastern Mediterranean would be endangered. In other words, maintenance of international peace and security appeared as the chief concern. However, the situation was so complex that it was simply impossible to determine whether the root causes of the conflict were intra-state or inter-state. As events unfolded, the non-permanent members of the Security Council became convinced that there was little to be gained from trying to establish a causal relationship between the external and internal aspects of the conflict. Instead, the complexity of the situation should be duly acknowledged, and its potential danger for regional stability immediately addressed.

For the non-aligned countries, the most important aspect of the crisis was not the complex interplay between the external and internal dimensions of the conflict, but its implications for the non-aligned cause in the Cold War environment. The representative of Morocco would put the idea in a nutshell: 'From Lattaquie to Tangier, as non-aligned nations, we are deeply attached to the desire that our part of the world should be less and less exposed to the dangers of the cold war'.[35] The critical issue in this regard was state sovereignty, because the will of the newly independent states to choose their own political regime was best captured by this principle. The concept of sovereignty, it was believed, had to include the freedom of a country 'to be the only propounder of its Constitution and to put within that Constitution that which best reflects the rights and guarantees of all communities and citizens'.[36] Non-alignment was a legitimate choice for a country, and the only way to secure that choice was to avoid foreign interference.

Peace and security coupled with sovereignty

These different views manifested themselves in a common rhetoric, in which several countries, with the exception of the Soviet bloc, preferred to characterise the UN's normative objective as the 'restoration of peace' within Cyprus rather than maintenance of *international* peace and security. This rhetorical preference resulted mainly from the enormous difficulty in distinguishing between the inter-state and intra-state dimensions of the conflict. Largely as a result of Soviet persistence, however, successive Security Council resolutions would keep their focus on international peace and security.[37] And given the actors' overarching preoccupation with regional stability, it would be fair to argue that maintenance of *international* peace and security was indeed the consensual objective prescribed for the UN.

Another characteristic of the UN's response to the Cyprus conflict was the dominance of the sovereignty discourse. Especially in the early stages of Security Council deliberations, all members, regardless of their political stance on the issue, repeatedly referred to such principles as sovereignty, territorial integrity, political independence and non-intervention. There was hardly any reference to human rights, and virtually none to socio-economic development.

The primacy of sovereignty was especially evident in the statements of the socialist bloc representatives:

> Our understanding follows from the fundamental principles of the Charter. We are convinced that the Security Council, proceeding from these principles, must deal with the solution of the question before us unequivocally from the point of view of safeguarding the security, independence, sovereignty and territorial integrity of Cyprus . . . All other interests must be subjected to this primary objective.[38]

The socialist camp, consistent with its attitude during the Suez and Congo crises, insisted that the UN had to respect and reinforce the sovereignty of Cyprus as embodied in its constitutional government. With frequent references to the colonialist past of some prominent members of the western bloc, the Soviet Union and its allies used every opportunity to cite the 'imperialist' attitude of the NATO allies as the main threat to other states' sovereignty, and hence to international peace and security.

The principle of human rights was subordinated to sovereignty during the early Security Council deliberations. As the Bolivian representative put it, the Cypriot Government had 'reiterated the unlimited recognition of human rights and the guarantee of individual freedom to all citizens of Cyprus', but 'the importance of this question ha[d] not been debated in the Council'.[39] Although there was some mention of 'minority rights' in the search for a resolution to the conflict,[40] systematic emphasis on the importance and promotion of human rights was lacking.[41] It was not until the news had arrived of several Greeks being deported from Turkey in retaliation for Greek Cypriot ill-treatment of Turkish Cypriots, that the members of the Council began to make specific reference to the necessity of protecting human rights. What is striking is that the scale of the refugee problem on the island was actually comparable to several post-Cold War cases: an estimated 20–25 per cent of the Turkish Cypriot population had become internally displaced or refugee in the course of just a few months.[42]

Even after human rights had entered the discussion, the actors' insistence on the primacy of sovereignty and related principles remained intact. Any reference to human rights was almost always complemented by a more prominent reference to state sovereignty and territorial integrity. This attitude found its parallel in relevant UN resolutions as well. Perhaps the most vivid example was GA Resolution 2077 (XX) of 18 December 1965. In its fifth preambular paragraph, the resolution underlined the importance of the full application of human rights to all citizens of Cyprus, irrespective of race or religion. In the first two operative paragraphs, however, it immediately proceeded to stress the 'sovereignty, unity, independence and territorial integrity of the Republic of Cyprus' and 'the fact that ... Cyprus ... should enjoy full sovereignty and complete independence without any foreign intervention or interference'.[43] Equally important, the role prescribed for UNFICYP did not encompass human rights or humanitarian aid. The efforts of the UN mission, including both UNFICYP and mediators, were directed towards attainment of 'peace and security', but these concepts were not explicitly linked to the promotion of human rights. Nor is there much evidence to suggest that there was any implicit linkage.

It is also worth noting here that the actors did not necessarily perceive a tension between state sovereignty and human rights. In the words of the Bolivian representative, while the concepts of independence and sovereignty could not be altered and had to prevail over other norms, the Charter also imposed certain obligations on its members, such as respect for human rights. 'In one word,' he asserted, 'the Charter has all the principles and the elements required whereby Cyprus can develop as an independent State and achieve political integration of its inhabitants.'[44] In the context of the Cyprus conflict, international actors did not regard as problematic the reconciliation of these seemingly 'incompatible' principles; they did not entertain any tension arising between the requirements of state sovereignty and those of human rights.[45]

Breaking the non-intervention barrier

Non-intervention was a particularly sensitive issue. The socialist bloc maintained that the essential element, discernible in all decisions of the Security Council on Cyprus, was the confirmation of the principle of non-intervention in the internal affairs of Cyprus and respect for its sovereignty.[46] Indeed, the potential dangers associated with external interference in Cypriot affairs were a widely shared concern. The Soviet Union and its allies, who were the most outspoken exponents of this view, maintained that no one should be allowed to intervene in the domestic affairs of the new Republic, whether it be a state, a bloc, or, for that matter, the United Nations itself:

> Only the people of Cyprus have the right to decide upon their domestic affairs . . . The Soviet Union in principle is negatively disposed toward the dispatch to Cyprus of any foreign military forces including United Nations forces . . . In order to meet the wishes of the Government of Cyprus, the Soviet delegation is prepared not to hamper the adoption of this draft resolution.[47]

The Soviet Union implied that it actually considered even the initial deployment of UN forces as 'intervention' in Cyprus' domestic affairs. This view indicated a normative dilemma inherent in the Soviet position, in that the UN was expected both to protect the sovereignty of Cyprus against external 'aggression' and not to deploy its forces. Given the request by the Cyprus Government, however, the Soviet Union would eventually tolerate the authorisation of UNFICYP.

The view that the UN should take extreme care in holding on to the principle of non-intervention was shared by France, whose perspective nevertheless differed somewhat from that of the Soviet bloc. Because of its bitter experience in the face of accelerating decolonisation, France was reluctant to support intervention by multilateral organisations. In the end, France would support the authorisation of UNFICYP, but not without reiterating its normative commitment to the principle of non-intervention:

> Having regard to the unanimous agreement of the parties concerned on this point, France has not opposed the suggestion despite its reservations concerning the principle of intervention by the United Nations in a military form, particularly if this were to lead to operations involving the use of force.[48]

Not long before, during the Suez crisis, UN intervention had proved detrimental to vital French interests in the canal zone. In the Congo, too, the French saw how Belgium's colonial interests had been endangered by an operation shaped primarily by American and Soviet influences. Non-intervention, therefore, was considered a necessary requirement for the protection of French interests.

Soviet and French reservations on UN intervention notwithstanding, several actors did envisage from the outset an active role for the UN in the rapidly-escalating intra-state conflict in Cyprus. These actors did not invoke the principle of non-intervention in the context of Cyprus. Nor did they link UN intervention to the potential international ramifications of the dispute. In other words, they did not necessarily or consistently advocate that the UN, and the Security Council in particular, confine its overall mandate to the maintenance of *international* peace and security which, as we have pointed out, was the main preoccupation of the western and socialist blocs. The likelihood of the conflict spreading to the international sphere or threatening regional stability was not seen as a precondition for active UN involvement in the conflict. Given the circumstances, the Security Council was simply obliged to act. The statement by the Norwegian representative strikingly illustrates the point:

> My Government is deeply concerned over the developments in the area. I would like to say ... what my Government means by "in the area". We mean the situation in the territory of the Republic of Cyprus itself. The Norwegian people and Government do not believe in violence and bloodshed as a means of solving problems within a state;[49]

The Soviet and French insistence on non-intervention was eventually side-stepped thanks in part to the proactive stance taken by those countries which were not in the same camp as the United States and Britain but which were nevertheless in agreement with the Anglo-American policy of introducing the UN into the conflict. No doubt one important element of their support for UNFICYP's establishment was the increasing willingness of the internal parties to see a UN force on the island.

The Turkish side had from the outset demanded an intervention to deal with the 'internal' conflict in Cyprus.[50] The Greek request, in contrast, had been directed towards the removal of a perceived 'external' threat. As time went on, however, the Greek emphasis shifted slightly towards a preference for a stabilising UN force on Cypriot territory.[51] The growing willingness of the Greek Cypriot Government to involve the UN in the maintenance of internal law and order was no doubt an important factor in the support given by Third World members to the authorisation of UNFICYP. While extremely sensitive to the issue of sovereignty, as symbolised by the government, the Third World members of the Security Council were not necessarily insistent on the maintenance of *international* peace and security.[52]

An ambiguous mandate acceptable to all concerned

The Security Council's authorisation of UNFICYP came on 4 March 1964 with the adoption of Resolution 186:[53]

> The Security Council,
> 5. *Recommends* that the function of the Force should be in the interest of preserving international peace and security, to use its best efforts to prevent a recurrence of fighting and, as necessary, to contribute to the maintenance and restoration of law and order and a return to normal conditions;

The mission had an ambiguous mandate. In the first place, it was not clear how the force would prevent the recurrence of fighting. Secondly, it was not clearly spelt out what 'law and order' and 'normal conditions' referred to. For the Cyprus Government, this meant disarming the so-called Turkish 'rebels'. For the Turkish Cypriots, it meant a return to the order envisaged by the original Cyprus constitution. The Security Council did not provide clarity on these points.

The different expectations of the Greek Cypriots and Turkish Cypriots were reminiscent of the Congo Conflict where Lumumba had assumed that ONUC came to the Congo to enforce his government's authority over all parts of the newly independent state. In Cyprus, Makarios held the same belief with reference to what he portrayed as the Turkish Cypriots' 'secessionist' activities. In the Congo, the Katanga authorities (and after the outbreak of the civil war, the Lumumbist Stanleyville forces) thought that ONUC's duty would be impartial maintenance of law and order without prejudice to their political claims. Similarly, in the Cyprus episode Turkish Cypriots held that UNFICYP should not try to superimpose a political solution on them. The Turkish side's main expectation of the UN was physical protection and prevention of hostilities.

In addition to UNFICYP, SC Resolution 186 authorised a UN Mediator who would 'use his best endeavours ... for the purpose of promoting a peaceful solution and an agreed settlement of the problem confronting Cyprus ... having in mind the well-being of the people of Cyprus as a whole and the preservation of international peace and security'.[54] The Mediator was to report periodically to the Secretary-General. He would be the political wing of the UN mission in Cyprus. In this authorisation the overarching concern for *international* peace was explicitly spelt out.

UNFICYP's authorisation resulted from intense discussions. Although the Soviet Union and France preferred a UN force to other alternatives, they were not particularly keen to finance another large-scale and long-term UN force, especially if the objectives of the force were not totally acceptable to them. Their adherence to the principle of non-intervention partly resulted from this consideration. Given the strong British concerns over Cyprus and the

American interest in keeping NATO affairs out of the UN's sphere, neither the Soviet Union nor France could realistically hope to define the objectives of the proposed UN peacekeeping as they saw fit. Moreover, the parties to the conflict had different expectations of a UN mission.

In these circumstances, UNFICYP's terms of reference were defined rather vaguely. In the words of its sponsors,[55] the resolution was 'the result of lengthy negotiations, much give-and-take and compromise'.[56] While it failed to give entire satisfaction to any party, it was not totally unacceptable to them. The subsequent resolutions would share the same fate. At a later stage, one of the sponsors of a subsequent draft resolution would complain that the text they had prepared was so vague as to give the impression that what they were trying to do was to elude or evade debate. Yet this was the only way of achieving agreement and maintaining the mission.[57] Apart from the vagueness of the mandate, two factors helped overcome the veto threat: unlike the controversial Congo mission, UNFICYP was authorised only for a limited period (three months),[58] and on the principle that its costs would be met by voluntary contributions.

On 16 January 1964, U Thant appointed Lt-Gen. Gyani of India as his representative in Cyprus. With the adoption of Resolution 186, Gyani became UNFICYP commander. He would be replaced by his countryman Gen. Thimayya on 27 June 1964. In addition to the appointment of Sakari Tuomioja of Finland as UN Mediator, the Secretary-General also sent his successive 'personal representatives' to Cyprus.[59] In September 1964, the appointment of Galo Plaza (the then personal representative) as the new UN Mediator would give way to a practical merger between the two posts in the form of the Secretary-General's Special Representative.

Authority: expansion within severe constraints

From the outset, the functions of the UN mission were defined in terms of short-term and long-term tasks. The former belonged with UNFICYP, while the latter was considered more the responsibility of the Mediator. In any case, the scope of the operational tasks was pretty narrow. UN peacekeeping was expected to address the immediate peace and security problems, that is, prevention of active fighting. The Mediator, on the other hand, was tasked with the preparation of a negotiating environment conducive to a permanent resolution of the conflict.

Since UNFICYP's formal mandate was not adequately clear, the Secretary-General felt it necessary to translate that mandate into a clearer set of guidelines and objectives. First, he issued a significant *aide-mémoire* to the governments concerned.[60] This document laid down, above all, guiding principles as to the command structure of the operation and principles of self-defence. Three weeks later, the Secretary-General would elaborate on the functions of UNFICYP.[61] The *aide-mémoire* authoritatively stated that UNFICYP should avoid any action designed to influence the political situation in Cyprus, but contribute to a restoration of order, and create an improved climate in which political solutions might be sought.[62] In other words, UNFICYP would be a typical limited-scope security mission. It was the Mediator's job to address the political aspects of the situation. In accordance with SC Resolution 186, the *aide-mémoire* restated that the activities of UNFICYP and of the Mediator were 'separate and distinct undertakings' and should be kept so.[63]

Although the tasks of the force and the Mediator were distinguished by the Secretariat and by several actors, the close and necessary relationship between the two was not overlooked. Norway would argue that:

> the immediate and urgent aim must be to prevent the situation in Cyprus from deteriorating and to restore peaceful conditions in the island ... The long-range aspect of the problem, however, must be to create conditions in Cyprus which will remove the distrust, the fear and the lack of confidence now prevailing between the parties, and we believe that the peace force would have very important effect in that regard also. It is with this in view that a proposal has been made for the appointment of an impartial mediator.[64]

There were signs that UN peacekeeping was expected to contribute to a long-term coexistence of the parties by performing wider functions reminiscent of peacebuilding. The Secretary-General did indicate that the two components of the UN's peace mission were not quite separable. If the Force was able to ensure order, this would help the Mediator. If the Mediator made progress, this would facilitate UNFICYP's mandate. The initial distinction between Force and Mediator reflected also the membership's reaction to the Congo experience, where ONUC had become increasingly entangled in the internal military–political struggle. In Cyprus, it was believed, thanks to the careful separation of functions, political problems would be settled by the conflicting parties themselves with the assistance of UN mediation efforts. The effects of the principle of non-intervention were clearly visible here. Solution of domestic problems was the business of the internal parties.

The post of Special Representative was created to relieve the Force Commander of the burden of non-military and political negotiation. It became increasingly apparent that UNFICYP could perform its duties only in direct interaction with synchronised political efforts. Both the Force Commander and the Special Representative would be appointed by the Secretary-General, and the latter would be the chief of the mission. The 1990s would see a systematic application of this method. The two broad functions of peacekeeping and peacemaking would be frequently integrated through Special

Representatives of the Secretary-General. Furthermore, peacekeeping missions would include a number of political and civilian affairs officers.

The UN Force in Cyprus generally relied on negotiation skills rather than the use or show of force in performing the tasks entrusted to it. In July 1966, in the village of Mora, the commander of the Finnish contingent, Col. Koskenpalo, would ease the escalating tension by shuttle diplomacy rather than deployment of his contingent. At about the same time, another crisis would be prevented in Melousha through similar efforts. While the commander of the Swedish contingent negotiated with the Greek Cypriot guards in the field, UNFICYP's Chief of Staff, Brig. Harbottle, would conduct negotiations with Greek Cypriots at a higher level.[65] The main implication of such lengthy negotiations between UNFICYP and the internal parties was that, although UNFICYP approached the matters on hand from a technical perspective, both Cypriot communities were wary of the political ramifications of such negotiations.

Formally, UNFICYP had neither a civilian mandate nor an administrative capacity (as would be the case with UNTAC in Cambodia).[66] Despite the lack of a formal civilian mandate and the absence of formal multifunctional duties, UNFICYP was operationalised by the Secretary-General in a more extensive manner than was originally intended. The Secretary-General's refinement of UNFICYP's vague mandate produced a large number of non-military tasks for the Force.[67] Stegenga distinguishes between UNFICYP's pacification and normalisation functions.[68] Whereas the former included mainly military objectives, the latter roughly corresponded to the Force's non-military tasks, such as ensuring freedom of movement throughout the island; eliminating economic restrictions against the Turkish Cypriots; preventing the 'separate' economic development of the two communities; administering the public services; reopening schools and industries; finding land records; getting the judicial system to function normally; facilitating agricultural activities; opening up local and export markets; and supporting human rights.[69]

Soon after deployment, the situation on the ground dictated that UNFICYP perform a great many functions beyond its limited mandate. Faced with a rapidly-evolving situation, the Secretary-General and his experts in theatre also felt that the Security Council should provide a clearer definition for UNFICYP's functions.[70] The Secretary-General appealed to the Security Council with a request to expand UNFICYP's mandate beyond persuasion and military assistance. If law and order were to be maintained, he argued, the UN personnel should enjoy a greater degree of freedom of action, including complete freedom of movement all over the island, the right to dismantle fortified positions, and the authority to create neutral zones.[71] The proposed expansion of the UN's authority in the peacekeeping theatre attracted strong opposition from the Soviet bloc:

We categorically oppose any expansion of the mandate of the United Nations forces in Cyprus in comparison with the way in which that mandate is set forth in the resolution of 4 March. It is quite obvious to us that this would indubitably lead to interference in the internal affairs of the Republic of Cyprus.[72]

In the Soviet view, the UN presence in Cyprus was intended merely to strengthen the competence of the Greek Cypriot Government to maintain law and order. The Soviet Union had made sure that SC Resolution 186 contained a provision to the effect that responsibility for the maintenance and restoration of law and order belonged to no one but the Cyprus Government.[73] Were UNFICYP to be assigned additional functions, including governmental duties, it might begin to challenge the authority of the Cypriot Government.[74]

From the outset of the mission, 'return to normal conditions' proved a particularly problematic operational objective. Preservation of the status quo could hardly be considered a return to normal conditions. On the whole, the UN tried to avoid a political interpretation of this phrase and concentrated instead on day-to-day economic and social problems. The Secretariat seemed to interpret UNFICYP's mandate beyond military duties. In the view of Osorio-Tafall, the Secretary-General's Special Representative, the return to normal conditions should enable the two communities 'to resume their normal relations and make it possible for all Cypriots of both communities to go about their normal daily occupations anywhere in the island in greater freedom and unimpaired security'.[75] For U Thant, too, this phrase referred to a normalisation of civilian life.[76]

More was expected from the normalisation of civilian life than the mere absence of immediate violence. Although that much was clear, the parties entertained quite different notions as to the meaning and content of normalisation. The Turkish interpretation foresaw a return to the situation that had existed before the fighting began in December 1963 and a restoration of the original 1960 Constitution. It was the proposed changes to that Constitution that gave rise to the conflict in the first place. For the Greek side, normalisation meant, first and foremost, the removal of *de facto* Turkish enclaves, and preferably a radical reorganisation of the constitutional system of the Republic.

The vague wording of the mandate did leave the door open to a wider interpretation – especially the provisions for normalisation and order. The situation on the ground more or less dictated that, if peace were to be achieved, the UN would have to deal with more than just territorial integrity. One example where UNFICYP performed non-military duties involved the work of economic officers attached to UNFICYP contingents. The task of these officers was to find ways in which Turkish-owned factories in the Greek sector and Greek-owned factories in Turkish towns would be free to operate. UNFICYP also helped with Greek–Turkish joint projects for soil conservation and water development. The mission was concerned, at least in an embryonic sense, with establishing the socio-economic preconditions of peace and security.[77]

UNFICYP, to a certain degree, assumed two functions which have traditionally belonged to governments: physical protection of individuals and provision of services.[78] The mission affected Cyprus' economy as well. In these circumstances it was unrealistic to expect UNFICYP not to intervene in the domestic affairs of the host state. To be more precise, it was not realistic to exclude the possibility that some parties to the conflict and some UN members would consider UN efforts as intervention in Cyprus' internal affairs. As one analyst puts it, 'any agency that provides police protection and welfare to a dislocated society cannot remain neutral politically'.[79] In the 1990s, however, the objection to this notion of non-intervention would diminish. The inclusion of numerous tasks within the job description of UN peacekeepers, although not always appreciated by the conflicting parties, would become less and less objectionable for the UN membership.

A very early warning as to the limitations of UN authority (as exercised by the Security Council) *vis-à-vis* intra-state conflicts came from non-permanent members of the Council:

> There is no merit in the Council discussing whether these treaties and the Constitution that was adopted were good or bad. It is the view of my Government that it is not for the Security Council to pronounce upon the Constitution of a Member State, nor to pass judgment on a set of treaties which were negotiated as an integral part of the whole process of granting independence to that State.[80]

Lengthy debates about the domestic arrangements and the constitutional order in Cyprus were considered neither useful nor appropriate. It was not the business of the Security Council to pronounce what was 'good' or 'bad' for the internal functioning of a member state. Typically, the creation and nature of a country's constitution were considered integral to its domestic affairs.[81]

The British attitude, however, was more 'interventionist' in that it pointed to certain expectations as to proper governmental conduct. Britain held – though without questioning the legal standing of the Greek-held Government – that the Government in Cyprus, like any other government, was under an obligation to maintain security within its territory and to observe the Constitution under which it was created and which authorised its representatives to speak on behalf of the Republic.[82]

The Secretary-General's *aide-mémoire* had moved towards asserting the UN's normative authority. Having maintained that UNFICYP should 'undertake no functions which are not consistent with the definition of the function of the Force ...', paragraph 9 dealt with the question as to *who* would judge whether proposed actions were consistent with the mandate or not: 'Any doubt about a proposed action of the Force being consistent with the definition of the function set forth in the resolution must be submitted to the Secretary-General for decision'. Despite the scepticism of some influential members, among them the Soviet Union and France, the Secretariat was asserting the UN's referee role embodied in the person of the Secretary-General.[83] It was obvious from the beginning that the Greek and Turkish interpretations of UNFICYP's mandate differed substantially, and that the two sides had different expectations of the mission. The Secretary-General was of the view that the UN, in his person, should have the final say over the course of action to be taken. Not every decision could be left to the parties' consent.

Paragraph 13 underlined the clear distinction to be drawn between the troops of the British contingent in UNFICYP and the other British military personnel in Cyprus. The Secretariat was thereby trying to dissociate UNFICYP from one of the international parties to the conflict, which also happened to be a permanent member of the Security Council. Taken together with paragraphs 4–7, on the other hand, paragraph 13 gave the clear message that the British contingent in the Force would be under the exclusive command and control of the Secretary-General through the intermediary of the Force Commander. The Secretary-General went even further in his *aide-mémoire*, expressing the desire to see both Greek and Turkish troops stationed in Cyprus brought under overall UNFICYP command, even though, as he clearly admitted, the UN had no specific mandate to require this.[84]

UNFICYP was quite hesitant to use or threaten force in the performance of its functions. In November 1967, during the notorious Kophinou incident, the Force chose not to intervene in the fighting in the face of a determined and large-scale Greek Cypriot offensive. The guidelines for self-defence and for the use of armed force, which were outlined in the *aide-mémoire*,[85] were more detailed than those in the Congo operation. The key provisions were that the use of armed force was permissible only in self-defence, and that the principle of minimum force should be applied. As a general rule, UNFICYP was allowed to use force only when all peaceful means of persuasion had failed.[86] The Force was prohibited to take any action which was 'likely to bring [it] into direct conflict with either community in Cyprus'. However, it was authorised to use force 'where specific arrangements accepted by both communities [had] been, or in the opinion of the commander on the spot [were] about to be, violated, thus risking a recurrence of fighting or endangering law and order'.[87] Examples in which troops might be authorised to use force included 'attempts by force to prevent [UNFICYP personnel] from carrying out their responsibilities as ordered by their commanders'.[88]

The guidelines, as expressed in paragraphs 17 and 18, had created a vast space in which the issue of the use of force could be entertained. In a sense, rather than actually specifying the conditions for the use of force, these guidelines had established the justification of any line of action, and added to the UN's authority in Cyprus. If UNFICYP intended to take enforcement action against either party, for instance, these two provisions might provide an excellent umbrella, though, as demonstrated in the case of Kophinou, it would not be realistic to anticipate coercive UN action, given the likely international repercussions.

In a subsequent report, U Thant provided further specifications for the use of force,[89] in particular the specification that UNFICYP was 'reasonably entitled to remove positions and fortified installations where these endanger the peace . . .'. It was not, however, altogether clear whether the peace in question would have to be *international* to warrant UN action. He also added that UNFICYP could demand 'that the opposing armed forces be separated to reasonable distances in order to create buffer zones . . .'.[90] Though these clarifications were more explicit than the ones before, the ambiguity surrounding the principle of non-use of force persisted. In any given situation, UNFICYP might or might not choose to use force, and both choices would be equally and perfectly justifiable within the available guidelines.

Concluding observations

The UN's involvement in the Cyprus conflict reflected a dominant preoccupation with the maintenance of regional stability, and in that sense *international* peace and security. A second principle that featured prominently, as in the Congo case, was state sovereignty, expressed almost exclusively in its external dimension. Here again a striking silence surrounded the issue of human rights, which was only sporadically addressed – usually in terms of 'minority' rights.

Considerable tension emerged between two opposing views as to the nature of the conflict and the approach to be adopted by the UN. As with the conflict in the Congo, this tension was best symbolised by the Anglo-Soviet disagreement. Britain again strongly favoured the Hammarskjöldian 'peacekeeping' formula, insisting on strict adherence to the principle of impartiality/neutrality. The Soviet Union, in line with the attitude it took during the ONUC episode, initially emphasised the prevention of 'external' threats to Cyprus' sovereignty, portraying the Turkish Cypriot claims as 'secessionism' fuelled by colonial/imperial ambitions. The socialist bloc, whose position was again directed towards securing the support of the non-aligned world, endorsed the Hammarskjöldian formula only after the Greek Cypriot Government had extended its consent to UN peacekeeping. One factor behind the eventual Soviet toleration was, no doubt, the fact that the Cyprus conflict was taking place practically within the US sphere of influence rather than in a relatively 'neutral' zone, with Greece and Turkey directly involved.

The US role was again crucial in synthesising diverse normative prefer-ences. Washington carefully supported the British and Turkish positions, moderated the Greek attitude, and counterbalanced Soviet pressure. The ambivalent voices from the South also contributed to the reconciliation of conflicting interests and normative prescriptions. In the ensuing normative synthesis, consent emerged as the critical factor. Value was attached both to the *de jure* consent extended by the Government and the *de facto* consent extended by other parties to the conflict. For UNFICYP to materialise the polit-ically indispensable element was certainly Greek Cypriot consent. Yet what was crucial to the *normative* synthesis was the consent given by both the Turkish Cypriot community and Turkey. Given the Anglo-Soviet disagree-ment and the Third World's ambivalent position, this ensuing normative 'synthesis' may not have emerged, had either party to the conflict adopted a negative attitude, as was the case in the Congo. The normative preferences expressed by international actors were all along premised upon this dual consent.

At the local/regional level the Greek and Turkish sides as well as Greece and Turkey, and at the geopolitical level the western and socialist blocs had different expectations of UNFICYP. The mission was authorised and opera-tionalised in a way that was acceptable to the Greeks and Turks on the one hand, and to Britain and the Soviet Union on the other. Predictably, UNFICYP's mandate was surrounded by ambiguities – what might be called 'resolution by ambiguity'. The authority assigned to the UN was necessarily constrained, because the interests that were temporarily reconciled through the introduction of a UN presence on the island were diametrically opposed to each other, and a stronger multilateral intervention would have been deemed by all parties concerned, including the superpowers, to be prejudicial to their interests.

The vague wording of the formal mandate, with its ambiguous references to 'normalisation' and 'law and order', made it possible for UNFICYP to adapt to the changing conditions in the peacekeeping theatre. The UN's role in 'governance' remained, however, negligible throughout. A more flexible and slightly expanded implementation of the mandate was tolerated and even encouraged, but only so long as the *de facto* consent of the parties continued. In general, the UN's authority in Cyprus was defined within the parameters of the Hammarskjöldian formula. UNFICYP was expected to use force only in self-defence, and most importantly, to remain 'neutral'. Taken at face value, neutrality simply meant not favouring one intra-state party at the expense of the other. At a deeper level, it meant refraining from taking sides in the context of either regional (Greece vs. Turkey) or global (United States vs. Soviet Union) conflict.

The Cyprus mission demonstrated a sharp contrast with the Congo, and was for this period more the 'rule' than the 'exception'. Active UN involvement was attributable partly to the fact that Britain was desperate to maintain its foothold in Cyprus, and partly to the special ties that Greek and Turkish Cypriots had with Greece and Turkey respectively, both of which, it should be stressed, were part of the US alliance system. Having experienced the tensions and contradictions associated with the Congo episode, the international community, and especially the key actors, were wary of involving the UN in the active 'settlement' of the conflict. The emerging normative synthesis reflected minimalist prescriptions for the UN, in which consent and neutrality emerged as the key factors.

NOTES

1 The estimated population of Cyprus in 1965 was 582,000: see United Nations, *World Population Prospects 1990*, p. 368. The ratio of UNFICYP's strength to the local population was 110/10,000.

2 On 21 December 1963, Greek Cypriots, acting in accordance with a 'top secret' plan, attacked the Turkish Cypriots. The Akritas Plan was first published in the Greek Cypriot newspaper *Patris* on 21 April 1966 'with the professed intention of exposing the mishandling of the Greek Cypriot cause by Archbishop Makarios': see Z. M. Necatigil, *Our Republic in Perspective* (Nicosia: Tezel, 1985), p. 4. For full text of the Akritas Plan, see A/33/115-S/12722 of 30 May 1978.

3 G. Clerides, *Cyprus: My Deposition*, vol. 3 (Nicosia: Alithia, 1990), p. 105.

4 All Greek Cypriot newspapers on 28 October 1964 covered Makarios' statement: 'Greece has come to Cyprus, and Cyprus is Greece. I firmly believe that the Pan-Hellenic struggle for the union of Cyprus with motherland Greece will shortly be crowned with success. This success will be the beginning of a new era of Greek grandeur and glory'. See www.turkishforum.com/cyprus/enosis_statements1.html (27 March 2001).

5 Reportedly, Dr. Küçük was of the view that the partition of the island might be the only solution to the Cyprus problem: see M. Wall, 'Agreement on Neutral Zone in Cyprus', the *Guardian* (31 December 1963).

6 This diagnosis by the Togolese delegation seems fairly accurate: see GAOR, First Committee, 1409th meeting (13 December 1965).

7 S/5488 of 26 December 1964.

8 Dr. Küçük and the three Turkish Cypriot ministers kept their titles until 1967, but were prevented from returning to their offices by the Greek Cypriot national guard: see A. C. Gazioglu and M. A. Demirer (eds), *Cyprus: The Island of Sustained Crises*, 2nd edn (Nicosia: CYREP, 1999), p. 17.

9 S/5508 of 8 January 1964.

10 The British representative outlined both proposals (dated 31 January 1963 and 12 February 1964 respectively) before the Security Council: see S/PV.1095 of 18 February 1964, pp. 22–45; quotation from pp. 32–3.

11 *Keesing's Contemporary Archives*, 14:2 (13–20 June 1964): 20117.

12 J. A. Stegenga, *The United Nations Force in Cyprus* (Ohio: Ohio State University Press, 1968), p. 179.

13 See J. S. Joseph, *Cyprus: Ethnic Conflict and International Concern* (New York: Peter Lang, 1985), pp. 202–5.

14 G. S. Kaloudis, *The Role of the U.N. in Cyprus from 1964 to 1979* (New York: Peter Lang, 1991), p. 35.

15 Stegenga, *The United Nations Force in Cyprus* pp. 57–8.

16 R. McDonald, *The Problem of Cyprus* (London: IISS, Adelphi Paper No. 234, Winter 1988/89), p. 67.

17 In this regard, the Kenyan representative at the UN saw a parallel with the original constitution of Kenya at independence, which created an artificial distinction between 'major tribes' and 'pastoral small tribes' and was allegedly designed to weaken the Central government *vis-à-vis* the semi-autonomous provinces: see GAOR, First Committee, 1409th Meeting (13 December 1965).

18 P. Windsor noted by Stegenga, *The United Nations Force in Cyprus*, pp. 46, 199.

19 The pro-Greek, anti-NATO stance of France is noted in Joseph, *Cyprus: Ethnic Conflict and International Concern*, p. 180.

20 Upon intensifying criticism, the US Secretary of State, Dean Rusk, felt it necessary to deny publicly that the United States was in fact afraid to let the Cyprus issue come before the Security Council: see *US Department of State Bulletin* (2 March 1964), pp. 332–3.

21 George Ball, the then US Under-Secretary of State, writes: 'Cyprus was a strategically important piece of real estate at issue between two NATO partners: Greece and Turkey. We needed to keep it under NATO control.' See W. G. Ball, *The Past Has Another Pattern: Memoirs* (New York: W. H. Norton, 1982), p. 342.

22 Behind the scenes, however, one of the strongest warnings to Turkey came from President Johnson in his letter to the Turkish Prime Minister (5 June 1964); for the full text and a comment, see E. Erner, *Davulun Sesi: Disislerinde 44 Yil* (Ankara: Bilgi, 1993), pp. 104–6, 256–64.

23 In November 1999 Clinton publicly expressed his regret for the US support to the Greek junta of 1967. 'When the junta took over in 1967,' Clinton said, 'the United States allowed its interests in prosecuting the Cold War to prevail over its interest, I should say its obligation, to support democracy, which was, after all, the cause for which we fought the Cold War. It is important that we acknowledge that.' See http://cjonline.com/stories/112199/new_usgreece.shtml (29 March 2001).

24 See *The Times* (London) dated 20 February 1964 cited in the Soviet statement in S/PV.1097 of 25 February 1964, pp. 97–100.

25 The island was strategically important also for the overall NATO umbrella. Reportedly, the CIA had constructed monitoring stations in Cyprus in 1949 under an agreement with Britain. Furthermore the presence of British troops on the island was expressly described as being in the interest of NATO: see McDonald, *The Problem of Cyprus*, p. 55.

26 The British Secretary of State for Commonwealth Relations and for the Colonies, Duncan Sandys, tried to justify his Government's attitude as follows: 'There seemed to us to be serious objections to the proposal that the United Nations should be asked to assume full responsibility for creating and controlling the required international force. The transfer of the argument to the Security Council would not in itself solve the difficulty in reaching agreement upon the composition and terms of reference of the force.' See UK House of Commons, Hansard Debates, Fifth Series, vol. 689, cols 840–3.

27 Both letters were dated 15 February 1964: see S/5543 and S/5545 respectively.

28 The Bolivian representative pointed out that the Security Council chose not to examine the substance of the matter, in view of the fact that new violence must be avoided at all costs: see S/PV.1139 of 20 June 1964, p. 16.

29 Soviet statement before the Security Council: see S/PV.1096 of 19 February 1964, pp. 13–15, 22.

30 Soviet statement before the Security Council: see S/PV.1099 of 28 February 1964, p. 12.
31 Czechoslovakia maintained that the constitutional Government of Cyprus was 'the sole representative of the national sovereignty': see S/PV.1139 of 20 June 1964, p. 7.
32 US statement before the Security Council: see S/PV.1096 of 19 February 1964, p. 36.
33 British statement before the Security Council: see S/PV.1098 of 27 February 1964, p. 21.
34 A. Duncan-Jones, 'The civil war in Cyprus' in E. Luard (ed.), *The International Regulation of Civil Wars* (London: Thames & Hudson, 1972), pp. 160–1.
35 See S/PV.1097 of 25 February 1964, pp. 18–20.
36 See the statement by Morocco in S/PV.1097 of 25 February 1964, pp. 13–15.
37 The exception was SC Resolution 193 of 9 August 1964, which called upon the parties to cooperate in the 'restoration of peace and security'.
38 Statement by Czechoslovakia before the Security Council: see S/PV.1097 of 25 February 1964, pp. 38–40.
39 S/PV.1139 of 20 June 1964, p. 12.
40 Ironically, the 'minority rights' discourse was in any case not acceptable from the Turkish perspective. All along the Turkish Cypriots had made it clear that they 'must not be regarded as a minority, but accepted as a separate community, on an equal footing': see A. C. Gazioglu, *Two Equal and Sovereign Peoples: A Documented Background to the Cyprus Problem and the Concept of Partnership* (Nicosia: CYREP, 1997), p. 43.
41 See also General Assembly First Committee discussions in A/C.1/1407–1414 of 11–15 December 1965.
42 See K. Kyle, *Cyprus: In Search of Peace* (London: Minority Rights Group International, 1997), p. 12; Turkish Ministry of Foreign Affairs, *Cyprus: 7 Questions and Answers* (Ankara: July 1999), p. 10.
43 The resolution was adopted by 47 to 5, with 54 abstentions. It was mainly the non-aligned countries which voted in favour. Turkey, the United states, Albania, Iran, and Pakistan voted against. The 54 abstentions included both the western and the socialist bloc, both of which were reluctant to further irritate Turkey: see J. S. Joseph, *Cyprus: Ethnic Conflict and International Politics – From Independence to the Threshold of the European Union* (Houndmills: Macmillan, 1997), p. 110.
44 S/PV.1098 of 27 February 1964, p. 97.
45 The primacy assigned to sovereignty was, nevertheless, apparent in such statements as the one made by the Ivory Coast: 'The sovereignty and territorial integrity of a Member State ... cannot be subordinated to anything whatsoever ... We should, in conformity with the Charter, reaffirm the sovereignty and territorial integrity of Cyprus as well as the need, flowing from respect for human rights, to protect and guarantee the rights of the minority.' See S/PV.1097 of 25 February 1964, pp. 52–5.
46 Soviet statement in S/PV.1153 of 17 September 1964, pp. 43–5.
47 Soviet statement before the Security Council: see S/PV.1102 of 4 March 1964, pp. 3–6.
48 French statement before the Security Council: see S/PV.1102 of 4 March 1964, p. 21.
49 While Norway made it clear that it did 'not believe in intervention from the outside in order to bring about a certain solution to tragic differences between various parts of the population of any Member state', these words were not intended to discourage UN inter-vention. Rather they underlined the normative position that no outside solution could be *imposed* on the parties: see S/PV.1103 of 13 March 1964, p. 72.
50 See the Turkish statement in S/PV.1099 of 28 February 1964, p. 72.
51 The Cyprus Government held that the UN force could enter Cyprus to help the

Government in restoring internal peace and normal internal conditions: see S/PV.1099 of 28 February 1964, p. 71.

52 The Ivory Coast held: 'The Security Council must immediately put an end to the massacres ... According to press reports, the Government of Cyprus hopes to see a United Nations force ... May we take this as an invitation to the United Nations to intervene? My Government believes so.' See S/PV.1097 of 25 February 1964, p. 51.

53 The mission's mandate would be hardly modified in the following two years; see SC Resolutions 187 of 13 March 1964; 192 of 20 June 1964; 193 of 9 August 1964; 194 of 25 September 1964; 198 of 18 December 1964; 201 of 19 March 1965; 206 of 15 June 1965; 207 of 10 August 1965; 219 of 17 December 1965.

54 Operative para. 7.

55 Bolivia, Brazil, Ivory Coast, Morocco and Norway, that is, all non-permanent members of the Security Council except for Czechoslovakia.

56 See the statement by Brazil in S/PV.1100 of 2 March 1964, pp. 4–5. In due course, this vagueness would hamper the mission's effectiveness and even constitute another source of conflict as was argued by the Ivory Coast in S/PV.1155 of 21 September 1964, p. 16.

57 This point was explicitly spelt out by Bolivia: see S/PV.1159 of 25 September 1964, pp. 12–15.

58 UNFICYP's continuation was subject to periodic Security Council approvals. This would create a significant difficulty for peacekeepers, since they did not know, until a few days before a mandate was due to expire, whether the mission would continue: see Lt. Col. Martin's remarks in Stegenga, *The United Nations Force in Cyprus*, p. 163.

59 Spinelli, Plaza and Bernardes.

60 S/5653 dated 10 April 1964.

61 S/5671 dated 29 April 1964.

62 Para. 2.

63 Para. 15.

64 S/PV.1097 of 25 February 1964, p. 26.

65 Duncan-Jones, 'The civil war in Cyprus', p. 153.

66 N. Sambanis, 'The United Nations operation in Cyprus: a new look at the peacekeeping–peacemaking relationship', *International Peacekeeping*, 6:1 (Spring 1999), 91.

67 See S/5671 dated 29 April 1964.

68 J. A. Stegenga, 'UN peace-keeping: the Cyprus venture', *Journal of Peace Research*, 8:1 (1970).

69 Kaloudis, *The Role of the U.N. in Cyprus*, pp. 59–60.

70 See the statement by Ivory Coast in S/PV.1159 of 25 September 1964, pp. 7–10.

71 See the supportive statement by Morocco in S/PV.1155 of 21 September 1964, p. 22.

72 Soviet statement before the Security Council S/PV.1153 of 17 September 1964, pp. 48–50.

73 Operative para. 2 asked 'the Government of Cyprus, which has the responsibility for the maintenance and restoration of law and order, to take all additional measures necessary to stop violence and bloodshed in Cyprus.'

74 Czechoslovakia had earlier maintained that the coexistence of the two communities was the exclusive 'responsibility of the Cypriot Government': see S/PV.1097 of 25 February 1964, pp. 41–5.

75 UN Press Release CYP/521 of 25 June 1968.

76 'A great deal remains to be done to bring about real progress towards a return to normal conditions in civilian life': see S/9233 of 3 June 1969.

77 Duncan-Jones, 'The civil war in Cyprus', p. 161.

78 Heye notes that 'an important part of the work of the military peacekeepers in UNFICYP was to negotiate the restoration of public services and ensure that they operate efficiently, and establish clinics and stock them with medical supplies'. See Heye, 'United Nations peacekeeping', p. 12.
79 Stegenga, *The United Nations Force in Cyprus*, p. 150.
80 Norwegian statement before the Security Council S/PV.1097 of 25 February 1964, p. 22.
81 In addition to Morocco's view mentioned above, see the statement by Ivory Coast in S/PV.1097 of 25 February 1964, p. 51.
82 S/PV.1098 of 27 February 1964, pp. 43–5.
83 The Soviet Union was especially critical of the extensive role the Secretary-General was given. This objection owed much to the Congo experience. Here we should recall the acrimonious Khrushchev–Hammarskjöld debates about the functioning of ONUC. As a result of the objections raised by the Soviet Union and France, paragraph 4 of SC Resolution 186, which defined the role of the Secretary-General in relation to the Cyprus mission, was subjected to a separate vote, but in the end adopted.
84 Para. 11.
85 Paras 16–19.
86 Para. 18.
87 Para. 17 (c).
88 Para. 18 (c).
89 S/5950 dated 10 September 1964.
90 Para. 215.

7

The UN in the Angola conflict: UNAVEM

THE UN'S ANGOLA MISSION underwent four phases, starting with the first UN Angola Verification Mission (UNAVEM I) in 1988, through UNAVEM II and III, and ending with the UN Observation Mission (MONUA) in 1999.[1] Angola is an illuminating case, not only because it is a point of temporal comparison with the Congo and Cyprus cases, but also because the evolution of the mission itself illustrates how an ever-expanding political space was created for the UN in relation to the conflict. In this chapter, we pay particular attention to the second phase of the operation, UNAVEM II, which marked a transition from inter-state peacekeeping to intra-state peacekeeping. During this transitional period the scope and size of UNAVEM were significantly altered – a fact which is likely to shed light on possible changes in its normative basis, especially in terms of authority.

Another interesting aspect of the UN presence in Angola is the doubt that it casts on the 'evidence' of normative shift suggested by the so-called 'humanitarian interventions'. Such UN operations as the ones in Somalia, Bosnia and Rwanda are frequently taken to imply that human rights had by the early 1990s exceeded international concerns over sovereignty. Over 300,000 people died in Angola in 1993 in the presence of UNAVEM II, thus making it the second deadliest civil war (after Rwanda) between 1992 and 1996.[2] Yet the international community did not authorise a 'humanitarian intervention'. Does that mean that the tension between the norms of state sovereignty and human rights were resolved in favour of the former? It is mainly with this question in mind that we examine the UNAVEM episode.

Historical background

Angola was colonised by Portugal in 1575. In January 1975, after two decades of struggle for decolonisation, Portugal finally initiated talks for Angola's transition to independence.[3] The talks at Alvor (Portugal) took place with the participation of three separate Angolan liberation movements: the MPLA, UNITA, and FNLA.[4] The Alvor Agreement soon fell apart, and the three groups began to fight one another, with the FNLA subsequently losing its military importance. The MPLA emerged as the strongest of the three groups, and on 11 November 1975 established the People's Republic of Angola. Soviet and Cuban support for the MPLA was countered by South African and US backing for UNITA.[5]

Although the Angola conflict developed into a proxy war for the superpowers, it did have other dimensions, not least the ethnic divide reminiscent of both the Congo and Cyprus cases. UNITA drew its support primarily from the Ovimbundu ethnic group which made up some 40 per cent of the total Angolan population,[6] while the MPLA was sometimes perceived as representing the Umbundu people which accounts for some 23 per cent of the population.[7]

The situation in Namibia played a significant role in the development of the Angolan conflict. In the 1970s, South Africa was convinced that pre-emptive attacks on the camps of the Namibian liberation movement, the South West African Peoples' Organisation (SWAPO), inside Angola would be necessary to stop these fighters from crossing into Namibia. South African attacks were only partly directed against SWAPO. They were also aimed at capturing key points in southern Angola and consolidating UNITA as a buffer. With the so-called Total National Strategy becoming official South African policy in 1979, attacks on Angola intensified.[8] By September 1980, South Africans had managed to set up UNITA headquarters in southeast Angola.

Soon after President Carter's inauguration in January 1977, the United States played an important role in constituting an informal grouping to be known as the western 'Contact Group' to deal with the complex of southern African crises.[9] Reportedly, in the next few years the US Government had an ambiguous attitude to the settlement of these conflicts. Such notable figures as Cyrus Vance and Andrew Young were of the view that South Africa had to withdraw from Namibia. Otherwise, the Cuban troops would not withdraw, and an inescapable clash between Cuban and South African troops could spill over into other parts of the region, especially Rhodesia, where the United States 'would be virtually powerless to prevent immense damage to American political, economic and strategic interests'.[10] While the Carter administration did not at any stage accept the notion that South African withdrawal from Namibia should precede Cuban withdrawal from Angola, this line of thinking played a considerable role in the search for a diplomatic solution to the problem.

A second grouping to address these conflicts, particularly in relation to Namibia, comprised several OAU states: Angola itself, Botswana, Mozambique, Tanzania and Zambia. In 1975, the OAU had delegated its authority over southern Africa to these states – a formal *ad hoc* committee of the OAU's assembly of heads of states – whose primary aim was to contain South Africa.[11] Both the Contact Group and the OAU emphasised the regional ramifications of instability in Namibia and Angola. Neither the causes nor the possible effects of such instability were considered to be primarily intra-state in nature.

Towards active UN involvement

In June–August 1977 the United States presented a settlement plan, which provided for free elections open to all Namibian political parties and the presence of a UN special representative. South Africa would begin a phased withdrawal of its troops, to be completed upon independence. The active role envisaged for the UN in settling southern African conflicts was initially spelt out in the context of the Namibian pillar of the regional problem rather than the Angolan one.

Julius Nyerere of Tanzania accepted the twin principles of elections and universal suffrage, but pointed out that the OAU's and SWAPO's main concern was that the elections should be free and fair. The answer would be to strengthen the role played by the UN which should assume legal responsibility for the territory during the transition period. UN administrative staff would need to replace the South Africans and the local authorities. According to Vance, Nyerere insisted that there should be a large UN peacekeeping force and that South Africa should be required to withdraw not part but all of its troops.[12] On the day of independence SWAPO would have to take over from the UN and not from South Africa.[13]

The OAU approach was important in two respects: first, it explicitly accepted, even demanded, that the power vacuum in the territory be filled by the UN. No other third party was considered a suitable candidate to perform this task. Secondly, it defined the problem as an 'international' conflict, and in that sense invited the UN to perform a relatively uncontroversial task, that is, to remove the threat posed to international peace and security, which resulted from an unfinished project of decolonisation. In the meantime, Waldheim sought the agreement of Angola, Zambia and Botswana for UNTAG representatives to be established in their countries in order to facilitate the implementation of the Namibia plan. Though Angola considered a UN presence on its territory to be an infringement of its sovereignty,[14] the day would come when it would consent to hosting a large UN peacekeeping mission.

In the 1980s, the Reagan administration introduced the notion of 'linkage',[15] according to which the resolution of the Angola crisis would be more explicitly linked to the resolution of the Namibia question. While the notion was not at first well received by the Security Council,[16] the United

States nevertheless persisted with its attempts to get the countries concerned to negotiate a set of agreements encompassing both Namibian independence and Cuban withdrawal from Angola. By this time, South Africa had realised that it could not win a military victory in Angola,[17] while the economically devastated Soviet Union had signalled its intention to halt the supply of arms to the MPLA.

Addressing the international dimension

US-mediated talks between Angola, Cuba and South Africa eventually led, on 22 December 1988, to the signing of two agreements.[18] In a tripartite agreement, the three countries undertook to commence implementation of SC Resolution 435.[19] In a bilateral agreement, Angola and Cuba agreed upon a timetable for the withdrawal of the 50,000 Cuban troops from Angola. The UN Secretariat, for its part, conducted consultations with delegations from Angola and Cuba, resulting in an agreement on a set of modalities which would enable UN military observers to keep a record of Cuban troop movements. At the request of both governments, SC Resolution 626 authorised the establishment of UNAVEM on 20 December 1988.[20]

The UN's peacekeeping mission in Angola started, then, in traditional fashion. Like the Congo and Cyprus situations in the 1960s, the Angolan crisis was initially addressed in terms of inter-state relations. Although the conflict had obvious global, regional and domestic dimensions, the UN's prescribed role was, at first, entirely limited to the inter-state dimension of the crisis.[21] In this sense, the influence of continuing Cold War constraints was all too visible.

UNAVEM's original mandate included verification of the redeployment and withdrawal of Cuban troops;[22] inspection and supervision of ports, airports and bases where Cuban soldiers were deployed; and conduct of *ad hoc* inspections at the request of the Security Council or the UNAVEM Chief Military Observer.[23] The mission, which comprised unarmed military observers, was not provided with 'rules of engagement' as the mandate did not envisage the use of force. To ensure liaison between the parties and the UN, a Joint Commission was established consisting of the Chief Military Observer as chairman, and two senior officers – one appointed by Angola and the other by Cuba.

In general, the provisions of the Angolan–Cuban agreement were complied with[24] and the entire process was completed one month ahead of schedule.[25] UNAVEM was based on genuine agreement between the Angolan and Cuban governments, that is, between two friendly parties and between two state parties. In Angola, at least initially, the UN did not become involved in the intra-state dimensions of the conflict. The withdrawal of the Cuban troops did not require any concession or undertaking on the side of UNITA.

Gradual transformation of the UN's role

The origins of the Angolan conflict could not be attributed solely to the foreign presence. In January 1989 President dos Santos made an offer of peace to UNITA, which led to peace negotiations in Gbadolite (Zaire), brokered by eight African countries, on 22 June 1989. However, while dos Santos and Savimbi shook hands and signed a cease-fire agreement, within one week the parties were accusing each other of violating the cease-fire. Between April 1990 and May 1991, six rounds of negotiations between the MPLA and UNITA were convened in Lisbon, in the presence of a Portuguese mediator and US and Soviet observers.

Estoril to Bicesse: no place for the UN in intra-state conflict

These initiatives did not involve active UN participation. When it came to the intra-state dimension of the conflict, international mediation efforts were conducted largely outside the confines of the UN. At this stage, the prominent role played by Portugal, the Soviet Union and the United States was perhaps a symbolic reminder of the continuing structural influence exerted upon the conflict by decolonisation and Cold War concerns. The solution to the Angola conflict would have to reflect a particular resolution of these concerns in the light of the changing power configuration in world politics.

The first concrete example of the UN's exclusion from the peace process was the Protocol of Estoril, eventually signed by the Government and UNITA on 1 May 1991. The Protocol provided for a cease-fire to be monitored by a Joint Political–Military Commission (CCPM), composed of the MPLA and UNITA as members, and of Portuguese, Russian and US representatives as observers. According to Provision II.5, which set out the composition of the CCPM, the UN would not be an essential part of the process: 'The United Nations may be represented, in the capacity of invited guest.'

On 31 May 1991 the Government and UNITA formally signed the Bicesse Peace Accords,[26] which consisted of four main documents: the Cease-fire Agreement; the Fundamental Principles; the Concepts; and the (now ratified) Protocol of Estoril.[27] The UN's functions were kept to an absolute minimum. Article 4 of the Cease-fire Agreement summarised the essence of the UN's military role: 'United Nations personnel ... will verify whether the monitoring groups are assuming their responsibilities.' The Fundamental Principles and the Concepts referred to the UN only once each. While the former practically restated that the UN 'might' be invited to participate in the meetings of CCPM,[28] Article 2 of the latter established a special link between the UN and one of the internal parties: 'The United Nations will be invited to send monitors to support the Angolan parties, at the request of the Government of Angola.'[29] The Government, recognised as such by the General Assembly, was given a privileged position, in contrast to the other provisions of the same Article, which treated both internal parties as equals: 'Overall political supervision of the cease-fire process will be the responsibility of the Angolan parties ... The Governments that are to send monitors will be chosen by the Angolan parties ...'.

Although politically both internal parties enjoyed the same status, the MPLA, by virtue of holding government, seemed to be *primus inter pares* when it came to getting the UN involved in the process legally. Here we need to recall that in practically every case of intra-state conflict, including the Congo, Cyprus and, as we shall see, Cambodia, the UN sought to deal with one 'accountable' government, which it considered the guardian of the state's sovereignty. Where government was the subject of acute contestation, including in civil war situations, the UN, as an inter-governmental organisation, much preferred to deal with a 'nominal' government until an internationally uncontested, authoritative government would emerge out of the peace process.

Bicesse to UNAVEM II: a place for the UN after all

On 17 May 1991 the Angolan Government requested UN participation in verifying the implementation of the Peace Accords. This was in effect an invitation from the host-state for the UN to become actively involved in its domestic affairs, no matter how minuscule the UN's prescribed duties would be. The Government, which once rejected an UNTAG presence in its territory on the grounds that it would violate sovereignty, came to accept the deployment of a verification mission to oversee its own domestic situation. Even though the mediators and the parties were at first not particularly keen to introduce the UN, or any other actor, into the conflict, the resolution of their differences – in interest and in viewpoint – necessitated that they make use of a suitable 'mechanism'. They also needed further legitimacy by taking into account the interests and preferences of regional powers. The UN readily suggested itself as a relatively neutral, sufficiently accountable, comprehensively multilateral and reasonably transparent option for the reconciliation of diverse positions.

On 30 May 1991, UNAVEM was given a new mandate (henceforth to be known as UNAVEM II).[30] The mandate in this second phase of the Angola mission was to verify that the joint monitoring groups, composed of Government and UNITA representatives, were carrying out their responsibilities. The joint monitoring groups were to observe the cease-fire, the troops' confinement in the assembly areas, and the disarming and demobilisation of forces.[31] The neutrality of the Angolan police was to be observed by monitoring teams similar in composition, and their work verified by UNAVEM II police observers. The role of UNAVEM II was limited to observing the monitors, and did not involve organising, regulating, or enforcing observance[32] – a role described by one observer as 'watching the watchers'.[33]

Addressing an intra-state conflict

Gradually, the UN's active involvement in the intra-state dimension of the Angolan conflict came to be considered legitimate. During UNAVEM I and II, concern over 'respect' for sovereignty of the Angolan state was paramount. If one of the reasons for the limited observation role assigned to UNAVEM II was the failure of the Bicesse Accords to include the UN more prominently in its provisions, the other reason was that the implementation as well as direct supervision of the Angolan peace process was considered a responsibility of the Angolan people.[34] In a Presidential Statement the Security Council re-emphasised that 'Angola being a sovereign and independent country, the organisation and supervision of all tasks under the Peace Accords is the responsibility of the Angolan parties themselves'.[35]

At all stages of the mission, it was beyond dispute that the Angolan situation had clear-cut internal dimensions. At the very least, as one delegate put it, UNITA was not a foreign creation; it was and would remain an Angolan creation.[36] Cuba, which was itself a state party to the southern African crises, would draw attention to two different but complementary dimensions of the situation in Angola. On the one hand, the Council was preparing to renew the mandate of UNAVEM II on the basis of the Secretary-General's report, which was primarily concerned with the internal aspects of the situation. On the other hand, the Council was meeting in response to President dos Santos' request that the issue of foreign interference in Angola's internal affairs be taken up.[37] Having thus acknowledged the interplay between the internal and external issues, Cuba did not object to the UN's involvement in the conflict's intra-state dimensions. Neither did any other participant in Security Council deliberations.[38]

Premature multi-functionalism

On 6 February 1992, the Secretary-General appointed Margaret Anstee as his Special Representative to coordinate UN activities in connection with the Peace Accords. Given the scarce resources at her disposal,[39] Margaret Anstee would compare her position with flying 'a 747 with only the fuel for a DC 3'.[40] The appointment of a Special Representative was perhaps the UN's first acknowledgment that dealing with this intra-state conflict would require substantial coordination, involving several issue areas in which the mission would have to be active. UNAVEM II's experience on the ground confirmed this, and the mission increasingly tended to go beyond mere observation of observers.

The major problems during the attempted implementation of the peace plan were in fact of a non-military nature for both sides. Transport to remote assembly areas had proved a significant problem. Shortage of food and medicines in the assembly areas, and poor accommodation were among other reasons cited by several soldiers who revolted and ran back to their homes, depleting the number of troops in the assembly camps.[41] Military personnel, who were often accompanied by their families, continually delayed mass mobilisation, citing among other reasons lack of civilian clothing.[42] UNAVEM officials and teams found that they had to play a role beyond their observation mandate: in order to play a part in the maintenance of peace and security they found it necessary to address several non-military, indeed civilian, tasks. They often took the initiative, arranged countings, organised meetings, or mediated over disputes. UNAVEM was also instrumental in getting the UN and other organisations to assist in supplying food to the assembly areas.[43]

Although UNAVEM II was not given the necessary authority and resources to conduct extensive field operations, none of the UN's competent organs, including the Security Council and the Secretariat, raised any objections to the relatively flexible interpretation by their field officers of UNAVEM II's mandate. Indeed, a Presidential Statement on behalf of the Security Council urged 'Member States as well as United Nations agencies to display flexibility and pragmatism' in the performance of the required tasks in the field.[44]

On 24 March 1992, at the request of the Government, the Security Council expanded UNAVEM II's mandate to include observation of the elections,[45] without, however, making the necessary resources available. In keeping with its new mandate UNAVEM II was enlarged to include an Electoral Division. Here again the role of the UN was to observe and verify the elections, not to organise them (as would be the case in Cambodia). The expanded mission's tasks included verifying the impartiality of the electoral authorities; ensuring freedom of organisation, movement, assembly, and expression for political parties; and monitoring fair access by all political parties to State radio and television. In addition, electoral observers would monitor all activities related to the registration process, the organisation of the polls, the actual polling and the counting of the ballot.[46] Although only in a monitoring capacity, the UN's Angola mission nevertheless involved promotion of political rights and civil liberties.

In a Presidential Statement the Council called on all parties 'to work closely with the Special Representative and all UN specialised agencies engaged in the electoral process to ensure that voter registration is conducted in accordance with established procedures and completed in a timely manner'.[47] The additional electoral role allocated to UNAVEM II was generally supported.[48] UNAVEM II officials played a role beyond their 'verification/

monitoring' mandate in relation to their electoral mandate, too. They gave active assistance to the electoral process. Although their pragmatic attitude in the peacekeeping theatre was not specifically endorsed by the Security Council, it would enjoy considerable support from the UN membership, and attract favourable comments: 'The functions being discharged by UNAVEM II at the present time, although they do differ from those in its original mandate, are a vital factor in the peacemaking process.'[49] The electoral process was supported by technical assistance provided by UNDP experts and consultants. Elections were held on 29–30 September 1992, with 18 parties running for office, and 12 parties securing representation in the Parliament. Though UNITA had gained 70 seats, making it the largest opposition party,[50] it did not accept the results and returned to its military campaign against the MPLA government. The Bicesse process had failed.

Increasing emphasis on human rights and humanitarianism
In late April 1993, a UN Humanitarian Assistance Coordination Unit (UCAH) was set up in Luanda to serve as the coordinating body for all humanitarian operations. It was to support the efforts of the operational UN agencies, while mobilising increased participation by other organisations. Some 50 UN agencies and NGOs conducted humanitarian operations in Angola. To cite a few examples, Médecins Sans Frontières ran a hospital in Cuito, Halo Trust engaged in de-mining, Swedrelief built bridges, and Save the Children was commissioned work by the World Food Program (WFP).[51] The WFP's operation in Angola was reportedly its most complex operation and largest airlift to date.[52] The organisation delivered food and other aid all over the country, flying across combat zones.

The arguments for more active humanitarian assistance and for a strengthened and expanded peacekeeping presence indicate that UNAVEM II's involvement in Angola was intended to go beyond mere observation, and beyond the performance of traditional military tasks. In 1993, the Portuguese delegate explicitly acknowledged the widening of the UN's peacekeeping agenda: 'We believe that the role of the United Nations is and will continue to be crucial not only in the search for peace but also in bringing emergency humanitarian assistance to all Angolans.'[53]

While UNAVEM II's mandate recognised that the verification of democratically-held elections was the ultimate requirement for instituting peace in Angola, it did not include supervision of human rights.[54] The mission's human rights activities remained limited and indirect, as exemplified by its support for a one-week human rights seminar held by the Swedish Raoul Wallenberg Institute. UNAVEM II's police contingent, tasked with monitoring the organisation, operation and neutrality of the new Angolan police force, was not equipped to perform this duty.[55] Margaret Anstee would express regret that UNAVEM II did not have an effective human rights monitoring component.[56]

Britain and the United States seemed wary of UNAVEM's involvement in humanitarian and human rights issues. When UNAVEM II came physically under attack, the British held that the emphasis would have to be on the diplomatic role of the Special Representative rather than on UNAVEM II's earlier functions, which it proved incapable of fulfilling.[57] Although Britain admitted that the deterioration of the human rights situation was regrettable, it did not favour an explicit link between the UN presence in the field and the 'indiscriminate killing of civilians', which 'simply [had] to stop'.[58] The US position was even more revealing. Madeleine Albright stated that the strength (and, by implication, the scope of functions) of UNAVEM II should not be increased until conditions were established that would make the exercise of its mandate feasible.[59] In other words, for the UN to be active in such fields as humanitarian assistance, a reliable cease-fire would first need to be achieved. Here, of course, the effects of the Somalia syndrome were all too visible.[60] In effect, the Anglo-American view was a restatement of a familiar normative position: *first* peace and security, *then* human rights and humanitarianism.

Notwithstanding UNAVEM II's inadequacies in mandate and resources, and the Anglo-American hesitation, there was growing normative encouragement for the UN mission to get more actively involved in humanitarian and human rights issues. The Spanish delegate's response to a report by the Secretary-General was typical in its emphasis on the importance of improving humanitarian and human rights conditions in Angola:

> My delegation wishes to express its support for the emergency plan drawn up by the United Nations Humanitarian Assistance Coordination Unit in Luanda ... I must express my country's grave concern about the Secretary-General's references in his report to: 'massive human rights violations and other atrocities committed against unarmed civilians in the course of events'.[61]

Yet it was generally the Third World countries that established a clear and insistent link between UNAVEM and provision of humanitarian and human rights assistance. The overall support given by smaller and middle powers to the enlargement and expansion of UNAVEM II highlighted the importance they gave to the UN's performance of multiple tasks, especially humanitarian assistance.[62]

Perhaps the sharp contrast with the US view was best expressed by the Namibian delegation which argued:

> To link the extension of the mandate and enlargement of UNAVEM II to the restoration of the cease-fire is a question of the chicken and egg, and in the process, more and more Angolans will be caught in a vicious circle. Therefore, Namibia calls for a sizeable and effective United Nations presence in Angola ...[63]

Implicit in this line of thinking was the inseparability of the UN's two crucial normative objectives, that is, maintenance of peace and security and promotion of human rights and humanitarian goals. Since there was no prospect of achieving one without the other in Angola, the UN would need to pursue both objectives simultaneously. Interestingly, human rights and humanitarianism, which had been given the status of a main international concern during the mid-1970s by the persistent efforts of western (in particular US) governments, were by now adopted by a wide range of Third World countries, and imposed structural constraints on the Anglo-American position which became increasingly difficult to maintain.

Creating space for judgement
During Security Council discussions, several actors suggested that the UN's intervention in Angola was subject to both parties' consent.[64] Others, however, implied that the parties' continuous consent might not be a prerequisite for the mission's viability or legitimacy. Zimbabwe advanced the argument that an increased UN presence in Angola should pursue its peacekeeping role until the objective, that is, the full implementation of the Bicesse Accords, was achieved.[65] In Angola, the UN was eventually entrusted with the task of overseeing an intra-state peace agreement, regardless of how exactly that agreement came into being. That the UN did not participate in the formation of the Accords was of no consequence. Once the UN was assigned a role in settling the conflict, it should go all the way until 'peace' was achieved. By implication, peace within the boundaries of a state was considered the UN's legitimate business. This attitude, as we shall see, would be even more systematically applied in the case of Cambodia.

A significant tendency among the UN membership during the UNAVEM II episode was the perceived need to confer on the UN a referee role through its mission in the field. As a consequence, the UN's search for peace and security was now thought to depend, at least in part, on judgements as to the 'rights' and 'wrongs' of a particular conflict. Impartiality could not be taken to mean neutrality. The UN, and its extension on the ground UNAVEM, should be impartial in its evaluation of the situation, but it should not hesitate, when required, to pronounce a verdict. The Hammarskjöldian interpretation of the principle of impartiality/neutrality, as exemplified in the Congo, had been effectively abandoned.[66] In the absence of the Cold War and colonial rivalries, the structural need to observe strict neutrality had evaporated.

After the elections especially, the unanimously expressed normative position of the UN was to draw a line between the 'right' party and the 'wrong' one. The Government of Angola was now considered the only legitimate authority in Angola, holding office after a 'free and fair election' endorsed by the UN.[67] The more UNITA insisted on non-compliance with the results, the more UN members called for coercion against what they now considered the 'spoiler' party.[68] Such diverse countries as Brazil, Hungary, Portugal, Russia and Zimbabwe were all calling for some form of enforcement against the party in the wrong.[69] The United States, hitherto the most important supporter of UNITA, though at first unwilling to resort to sanctions, could no longer ignore the emerging normative consensus that the UN had the responsibility to pronounce on the rights and wrongs of a particular conflict.[70] Eventually the United States would support the decision to impose sanctions against UNITA.

Unlike UNAVEM I, UNAVEM II is generally considered a failure. UNAVEM II's limited mandate did not match the operational objectives of the UN's involvement. In the first place, the UN was not allowed to play an active role in the negotiation process that led to the Accords. According to Margaret Anstee, 'the UN had only a very peripheral role in these negotiations so that at the end it was faced with a *fait accompli*'.[71] In addition, the Bicesse Accords envisaged no formal role for the UN in the actual settlement of the Angolan crisis. The peace process was made entirely dependent on the adversaries, not unlike the Cyprus case or the early stages of the Congo case, where international actors were cautious about possible UN violations of sovereign rights. The UN was expected to be an impartial observer, a distant third party.

UNAVEM II marked, however, a significant transition from UNAVEM I to UNAVEM III. These latter operations were in stark contrast to each other. UNAVEM I was a small-scale observer operation, a classical exercise in inter-state peacekeeping, a relatively straightforward undertaking with limited functions. UNAVEM III, which we shall briefly discuss below, was a relatively large-scale operation with an intra-state mandate and multiple functions.

The Lusaka process: transformation completed

Following the breakdown of October 1992, Margaret Anstee succeeded in arranging two rounds of talks between the two sides: in Addis Ababa and in Abidjan. In Anstee's own assessment, their ultimate failure was due to the UN's reluctance at that stage to underwrite the large international presence demanded by UNITA.[72] In her view, the fundamental reason was that although the countries most closely concerned with Angola genuinely sought peace, they wanted a 'quick fix' – particularly the two superpowers whose strategic priorities had changed.[73] A third round of negotiations took place at the initiative of Anstee's successor, Alioune Blondin Beye, in Lusaka in October 1993 – one year after the resumption of fighting, and one month after the Security Council had imposed sanctions against UNITA.[74]

Towards greater authority

In Lusaka, in contrast to Bicesse, the UN maintained a central role through Beye's chairmanship. The UN authority was asserted by the threat of further sanctions against UNITA in order to bring it to the negotiating table. Conceptually, the UN's role was now expanded so as to incorporate an active element of coercion. The observation operation, UNAVEM II, was functionally 'associated' with a particular form of enforcement – sanctions – against one of the parties.

Under pressure Savimbi agreed that the basis of the negotiation would be acceptance by UNITA of the validity of the 1991 accords and of the 1992 elections. However, as the talks shifted from short-term military to longer-term political arrangements, both sides tried to gain the upper hand on the battlefield to pave the way for an advantageous final settlement. By the end of September 1994, the Security Council would declare any further obstruction or procrastination as 'unacceptable'.[75] With additional pressure exerted on UNITA by the Observer States, and despite continued fighting, the Lusaka Protocol was eventually signed on 20 November 1994, and a cease-fire declared. The Protocol acknowledged the continuing legitimacy of the Bicesse Accords and of the 1992 electoral process,[76] and addressed key military and political questions, as detailed in its 10 thematic annexes.[77] In contrast to the Bicesse Accords, it embodied a reasonably detailed notion of national reconciliation as set out in Annex 6 with its 5 general and 18 specific principles, and 11 modalities.

Annex 8 of the Protocol, unlike the 1991 agreement, carefully laid out the precise role of the UN in the implementation process. The stark contrast with the Bicesse Accords was observable from the very beginning:

> The Government and UNITA invite the United Nations to perform, in addition to its missions of good offices and mediation, the tasks defined in the present mandate with a view to the full implementation of the Acordos de Paz para Angola (Bicesse) and the Lusaka Protocol. The Observers of the peace process (the United States of America, Portugal and the Russian Federation) give their full support to this invitation.[78]

At first, the Observer States had been reluctant to continue negotiations through UN channels.[79] However, the strong regional pressure paved the way for more direct UN involvement. As the representative of Zimbabwe put it, the Africans were 'concerned that the involvement of many negotiators [might] actually retard progress'. They therefore urged 'that discussions continue to take place under the auspices only of the United Nations and the OAU'.[80] In contrast to the Bicesse Accords, which were orchestrated by Angola's former colonial rulers and Cold War interventionists, that is the three Observer States, the Lusaka negotiations resulted from the efforts of Africans to solve an

African crisis.[81] Once the internal dimensions of the crisis came to the fore-front, the proposed alternatives to UN mediation were no longer the Observer States, whose influence on the intra-state parties was increasingly open to question, but such African personalities as Miguel Trovoada, President of Sao Tome-Principe.[82] Trovoada, however, made it known that he had no intention of replacing the United Nations as peace mediator in Angola, and that Sao Tome-Principe was completely at its disposal for whatever the UN would ask it to do.[83]

The persistent efforts of regional actors aside, the two internal adversaries became increasingly amenable to active UN involvement in their country – partly in order to buy time (in the case of UNITA) and legitimacy (in the case of the MPLA). Although the UN had imposed sanctions on UNITA and was largely perceived as a hostile force by this party, a stronger UN presence in Angola would stabilise the military confrontation in the short term, and enable UNITA to re-organise itself in its strongholds.[84] An election under UN auspices, on the other hand, would give the MPLA a much higher degree of legitimacy on the international stage, which it could then use to exert pressure on its rival. After all, for years the MPLA (in ways reminiscent of the Phnom Penh Government in Cambodia, about which more later) had been in control of the administrative apparatus which it hoped it could mobilise to win elections. Furthermore, UN sanctions and monitoring mechanisms might do precisely what the MPLA itself could not do, that is, restrict UNITA's activities. Thus it was that the UN was brought into the equation at a particular moment when the short-term interests of the internal parties overlapped with the superpowers' willingness to end a protracted 'proxy war' and with the mounting concern of African states over the regional ramifications of the conflict. The UN, it seemed, was the only strategically-placed actor which could simultaneously reconcile internal, regional, and global interests.

The UN, in the person of Blondin Beye (an African himself), was to chair the paramount institution in the implementation process: the Luanda-based Joint Commission made up of Government and UNITA nominees and Observer States' representatives.[85] The UN's role was set out under four headings. The 'military issues' constituted the most detailed set of tasks assigned to the UN mission, and included 34 articles. The UN was to be directly responsible for 'overall supervision, control and verification of the cease-fire', in contrast to the vaguely defined monitoring role assigned to it in 1991. In addition, it was to have responsibility for the quartering and demobilisation of UNITA forces and reception of surrendered weapons.

The other three functions were as yet less typical for a peacekeeping operation. They related to issues which would normally be considered as falling within the domestic jurisdiction of states. Verification and monitoring of various 'police activities' constituted the second set of tasks assigned to

UNAVEM. The UN's role in 'national reconciliation activities' involved certification that the requisite conditions for the normalisation of state administration had been fulfilled. The UN mission was charged with one other major function: to verify and monitor the successful 'completion of the electoral process'.

Although politically both the MPLA and UNITA had agreed to create a wider space for UN involvement in Angola, military hardliners on both sides were unenthusiastic about the agreement. Particularly on the Government side, military advances in 1993–94 had created an expectation of ultimate victory against UNITA. On the other side, a number of UNITA generals saw the agreement as the beginning of the end for the movement. The UN's next step in Angola was decided in this uncertain climate.

Extension and expansion: consensual support for UNAVEM III

Before, during and immediately after the Lusaka negotiations, there was a powerful temptation on the part of the UN membership to extend and expand the UN presence in Angola. Several countries were convinced that the necessary re-deployment of UNAVEM II under deteriorating conditions on the ground should not be interpreted as a lessening of the UN commitment to Angola.[86] The UN presence should continue. The African countries in particular held the view that the UN's withdrawal from Angola was simply inconceivable. The overall African stance was well expressed by Namibia:

> The issue at hand is ... not just the numbers themselves but a visible and effective United Nations presence ... Just two days ago, the Secretary-General of the Organization of African Unity ... appealed to the international community to give full support to the United Nations peacekeeping operations in Angola, and he further added that this was the time to strengthen the United Nations presence instead of withdrawing or reducing it, if Angola is to be prevented from sliding into a state of anarchy similar to that in Somalia.[87]

Indeed, African states called for a stronger and more comprehensive UN presence.[88] In essence, the African position found considerable support from such extra-regional powers as Brazil,[89] Hungary,[90] and perhaps more importantly, the European Union (Community).[91] Eventually the Observer States, too, gave their support to the extension and expansion of the UN's Angola mission,[92] though US support was cautious in that the envisaged operation, no matter how much expanded, should not involve active enforcement on the ground. Referring to what would become SC Resolution 804, the US representative commented that while the United Nations was about to assume more authority and flexibility to fulfil its responsibilities, the Secretary-General, UNAVEM II and concerned nations could not 'impose peace where the will for peace does not exist'.[93] The United States was not against UN coercion; it would support sanctions against one of the parties. What it opposed was coercion in the form of military enforcement.

With the deteriorating situation in the theatre of conflict, UNAVEM III was eventually authorised by SC Resolution 976 of 8 February 1995. African efforts, again crucial in the expansion of the UN's role in Angola, enjoyed the support of several middle powers. Apart from the group of African countries who had requested that they be given the opportunity to participate in Security Council deliberations leading up to the adoption of SC Resolution 976,[94] a number of sympathetic extra-regional governments were also involved in discussions.[95] These countries pressed for an expanded UNAVEM role.[96] Speaking on behalf of the OAU Council of Ministers, Malawi called for 'urgent and appropriate measures' to be taken by the UN, and urged the Security Council to facilitate the speedy establishment and deployment of an enlarged UN mission.[97]

UNAVEM III was given a far more comprehensive mandate than UNAVEM II. In line with the Secretary-General's recommendations, UNAVEM III involved five main components: military, political, civilian police, humanitarian and electoral.[98] Perhaps as important as these five main components envisaged in the Secretary-General's report was the creation of a human rights component, directly attached to the Office of the Special Representative with various posts throughout the country. The activities of these components would be coordinated and integrated under the authority of the Special Representative. The UN's political and peacemaking activities would be performed by the Special Representative who was also in charge of a military presence. In other words, a clearer operational linkage was established in this third phase between the military and non-military functions of the UN peacekeeping mission.

The importance of such tasks as humanitarian relief and mine-clearing was expressed in numerous speeches at the Security Council. Despite the considerable expansion of its scope, however, the UN mission was still expected to perform primarily traditional military tasks, which were considered the most important step towards a political process of 'national reconciliation'.[99] A fundamental flaw in the implementation of the Bicesse Accords lay in the failure to keep military disengagement and demobilisation tied to the advance of the electoral programme. As a consequence, in October 1992 UNITA was still militarily capable of returning to war following the elections. In UNAVEM III, the inter-linkage was, conceptually, more effectively maintained. The primary target of the political process, backed by the performance of military duties, was the formation of a coalition government designed to enhance national reconciliation.

In this third phase, the mission's mandate became more comprehensive and enjoyed consensual support. Britain, which had been sceptical of UNAVEM's assumption of multiple functions, now welcomed the Secretary-General's proposal for an expansion in the human rights component of UNAVEM III. The additional human rights observers would have an important role to play in helping ensure that basic rights were respected.[100]

Paul Hare, the US special envoy on Angola and an active participant of the Lusaka Protocol, would claim that 'human rights was a subtext in the negotiations' in Lusaka, but that during implementation human rights had not been given the same priority as had been given to other pressing issues, such as monitoring of the cease-fire. He strongly advocated the balancing of human rights initiatives against other measures to prevent large-scale violence. Holding the two sides to human rights standards would have jeopardised delicate negotiations.[101] Nonetheless, the anticipated difficulties in implementation did not prevent normative insistence on the observance of human rights, as evidenced by the inclusion of several human rights provisions in the formal agreements and operational arrangements.

Arguably, an important reason why insistence on human rights could not be dropped easily at critical moments of the Angolan negotiations was precisely the support that Washington had extended to pro-UNITA civil society campaigns throughout the 1970s and 1980s. While providing active help for UNITA's cause against the Angolan Government in the broader context of the Cold War, such organisations as the American Security Council (ASC), the Heritage Foundation, the World Anti-Communist League and the International Society for Human Rights had frequently invoked the human rights discourse.[102] They had steadily contributed, in other words, to the evolving ideational attributes of the international community. The changing political conjuncture in Angola in the 1990s was not in itself sufficient to resist the ever-stronger ideational attributes of the new era, which had been in the making for the past decades.

With hindsight, it is arguable that UNAVEM III was perhaps an even bigger failure than its predecessor, since several of its duties were not fulfilled. However, our focus here is not so much with success or failure but with the normative approach underlying the mission. In the case of UNAVEM III that approach drew on a broad-based consensus, promoted largely by the regional African states which, in the wake of a hegemonic human rights discourse, frequently appeared before the Security Council and contributed to its deliberations. Moreover, on this occasion the UN's authority in the settlement of a predominantly internal conflict was carefully based on a peace agreement signed by both intra-state parties as well as the Observer States. In the process, a special position was accorded to the UN, from which it could render judgements as to the rights and wrongs of the conflict.

With UNAVEM III, the UN got involved more clearly in the planned resolution of the Angolan civil war. An expanded UN role *vis-à-vis* an intra-state conflict was endorsed by the UN membership. To perform its primary duty, that is, maintenance of international peace and security, the UN began to penetrate several state functions, although not to the same extent as in Cambodia. The UN formally assumed multiple duties which would be backed by a substantial pacific military component in the field and supplementary sanctions. In June 1997, the mission entered its last phase, MONUA,[103] and its mandate expired in February 1999.

Concluding observations

Although there is little evidence of a strong international will to ensure observance of human rights in Angola, the normative emphasis put on human rights and humanitarianism was now much more visible and clearly defined than before. This is not to say that the maintenance of *international* peace and security, understood primarily as regional stability, did not persist as the international community's chief preoccupation.

Initially, the principle of non-intervention, understood as the primary manifestation of the principle of state sovereignty, had a marked impact on the UN's role in Angola. The intra-state parties were not keen to invite UN intervention – an attitude reinforced by the unwillingness of the Observer States to involve the UN. However, the mood would gradually change for two discernible and interconnected reasons. To begin with, a settlement of the Angola conflict, long considered a major contributing factor to regional instability, became a high priority of regional states. A settlement entirely dependent on the initiative of Observer States was unlikely to take sufficiently into account, let alone reconcile, the interests and viewpoints of all relevant regional actors. Secondly, the actual on-the-ground arrangements for conflict settlement needed to reconcile simultaneously the interests of local, regional and global actors. The UN readily suggested itself as the most appropriate candidate, because it combined a number of characteristics: it had global membership, hence the capacity to accommodate the viewpoints of regional and global powers; it had a political mandate; it was able to draw on the expertise of specialised programs and agencies; and it had active field experience.

Once the UN was brought into the equation, the principle of state sovereignty gradually acquired yet a different complexion. On the one hand, the parties reduced their insistence on UN non-intervention, and on the other, the internal dimension of sovereignty gained normative priority. A second parallel trend soon emerged, namely the increasing incorporation of human rights and humanitarianism into UNAVEM's normative basis. Promotion of sovereignty in its internal dimension neatly dovetailed with the promotion of human rights. In other words, the tension between two crucial norms, state sovereignty and human rights, was attenuated by stressing the internal dimension of the sovereignty principle. The UN was expected to promote the creation of a political entity (stable government) which would enjoy an acceptable level of internal and external legitimacy within a defined territory. Such legitimacy would presumably depend, at least in part, on the observance of human rights.

As events unfolded, it became clear that settlement of the conflict in a way that would suit the interests of local, regional and global actors required closer and expanded UN involvement, which meant not only greater authority for the UN in all its four aspects, but also greater insistence on ensuring 'govern-ability', as evidenced in part by the emphasis on 'national reconciliation' efforts. Aside from the expanding scope of peacekeeping functions, both in terms of depth and breadth, the increasingly generalised expectation was that the UN would no longer require the consent of all parties, that it would pronounce judgement against the party 'in the wrong', and enforce that judgement.

Interestingly, at this 'unipolar' moment, it was not the United States or its allies – as might have been expected – which drove the continuous redefinition of UNAVEM's normative basis. Without US support, no doubt, the Angola mission would not have survived. However, this support was generated through the persistent efforts of regional states and sympathetic middle powers, not to mention the indirect influence of a wide range of civil society organisations. The eventual US endorsement of sanctions against UNITA was a manifestation of this dynamic. Perhaps its most significant feature is that a coalition of actors had effectively resisted the Anglo-American preoccupation with 'peace' at the expense of 'human rights', at least at the normative level. In other words, the ideational dimension of the prevailing western hegemony imposed considerable constraints even upon the most powerful states in the system, and managed to modify their normative stance in this particular case.

NOTES

1 The estimated population of Angola in 1990 was 10,020,000: see United Nations, *World Population Prospects 1990*, p. 308. The ratio of UNAVEM III's largest authorised strength to the local population was 8/10,000.
2 See Stedman, *International Actors and Internal Conflicts*, p. 18.
3 The Angolan guerilla war for independence continued from the early 1960s until the mid-1970s. The close relationship between the liberation movements in colonial Angola and Namibia, and the corresponding close collaboration between their respective colonial powers – Portugal and South Africa – is well documented in the literature: see R. Dreyer, *Namibia and Southern Africa: Regional Dynamics of Decolonization, 1945–90* (London: Kegan Paul International, 1994), especially chs 2–3.
4 Movimento Popular de Libertaçao de Angola (established in 1956, led by Agostinho

Neto), Uniao Nacional para a Independencia Total de Angola (established in 1966, led by Jonas Savimbi), and Frente Nacional de Libertaçao de Angola (established in 1962, led by Holden Roberto) respectively.

5 As late as 1990, the official US position was phrased in the following terms: 'The US will continue to support UNITA until national reconciliation, leading to free and fair elections, is achieved. The United States looks forward to normal relations with a freely elected government in Angola. Until then, we will not recognize or establish diplomatic relations with any Angolan government.' See 'Sub-Saharan Africa and US policy', *US Department of State Dispatch*, 1:6 (8 October 1990), 171.

6 See L. Macphisa, 'UN, US biased in Angola conflict – Terra Viva', *Inter Press Service* (6 December 1999), available online at www.woza.co.za/forum2/dec99/angola6.htm (9 May 2001).

7 Furthermore, while the MPLA and UNITA were the most important internal components of the Angolan conflict, there were several other Angolan groups which pursued their own military campaigns. In the oil-rich Cabinda province alone, there were at least seven factions which fought for Cabinda's 'independence': see UNHCR, *Background Paper on Refugees and Asylum Seekers from Angola* (Geneva, October 1994), 3.3. and 3.4.

8 See Dreyer, *Namibia and Southern Africa*, p. 143.

9 This group comprised the United States, Britain, and France as well as two of the elected members of the Security Council at the time, Canada and West Germany.

10 C. R. Vance, *Hard Choices: Critical Years in America's Foreign Policy* (New York: Simon & Schuster, 1983), p. 274.

11 Although for different reasons, these five countries did support the efforts of the Contact Group; see Dreyer, *Namibia and Southern Africa*, pp. 119–22.

12 Vance, *Hard Choices*, p. 274.

13 Under OAU pressure, SWAPO accepted the principle of western mediation. In late March 1978, the Contact Group came up with its *Proposal for a Settlement of the Namibian Situation*, which would constitute the main body of SC Resolution 435 dated 29 September 1978. Eventually, both South Africa and SWAPO would accept the plan.

14 *Guardian* (14 August 1979) cited in Dreyer, *Namibia and Southern Africa*, p. 135.

15 See Dreyer, *Namibia and Southern Africa*, pp. 5, 145–66.

16 SC Resolution 566 of 19 June 1985 even rejected 'South Africa's insistence on linking the independence of Namibia to irrelevant and extraneous issues as compatible with resolution 435 (1978)'.

17 This not only prompted a rethinking of South African military strategy, but also gave rise to new diplomatic efforts to end the conflict: see www.hrw.org/reports/1999/angola/Angl998-03.htm#P439_33860 (24 May 2000).

18 For an 'official' chronology of US involvement in Angola, see N. D. Howland, 'The United States and Angola, 1974–88: a chronology', *US Department of State Bulletin* 89:2143 (February 1989), 16–24.

19 Though the UN's Namibia mission (UNTAG) had its roots in SC Resolution 435, it could not materialise until after the Cold War.

20 This would be followed by UNTAG's authorisation in Namibia.

21 This view was very much at the heart of the British position, which initially stressed the principle of non-intervention: 'We would welcome any move to establish internal peace which had the support of both sides, but it is not for us to prescribe how elections should be conducted in another sovereign state … The internal political situation in Angola is not the subject of discussion at the United Nations.' See the Government

response to an inquiry in UK House of Commons, Hansard Debates, 13 March 1989, col. 25.

22 This was set out in detail in an appendix to the bilateral agreement.

23 UNAVEM became operational on 3 January 1989.

24 The withdrawal was suspended only once, on 24 January–25 February 1990, following two attacks by UNITA against Cuban personnel during which 10 Cuban soldiers were killed.

25 It has been noted that 'as a first generation peacekeeping mission UNAVEM I was tremendously effective. It had the basic conditions outlined by Boutros Boutros-Ghali for a successful mission: a clear and practicable mandate; the cooperation of the parties; the continuing support of the Security Council, and a willingness of the Member States to contribute.' See P. Adrian, *Peacemaking and Peacekeeping in Angola 1988–1994* (Geneva: Institute Universitaire des Hautes Etudes Internationales, 1994), p. 5.

26 These accords are frequently referred to in their Portuguese original: *Acordos de Paz para Angola*. In addition to the cease-fire, the Bicesse Accords provided for: the banning of external military assistance to the MPLA and UNITA; the confinement of all troops from both sides in assembly areas; the restoration of government administration in rebel controlled areas; the release of POWs and political prisoners; the formation of new unified 50,000 armed forces (*Forças Armadas Angolanas* – FAA); the disarming and demobilisation of surplus troops; the neutrality of the police force; and the holding of free and fair multi-party elections in September–November 1992. In accordance with the peace accords the following three main commissions were established beside the CCPM: a Joint Verification and Monitoring Mission (CMVF); a Joint Commission on the Formation of the Angolan Armed Forces (CCFA); and a Political Commission. In addition, several working groups were set up to deal with demobilisation, de-mining, police, humanitarian aid and other matters.

27 The full titles, respectively, are: the Cease-fire Agreement; the Fundamental Principles for the Establishment of Peace in Angola; the Concepts for Resolving the Issues Still Pending between the Government of the People's Republic of Angola and UNITA; and the Protocol of Estoril.

28 Article 2 in the document's Annex.

29 Article 4.

30 SC Resolution 696. Algeria, Argentina, Brazil, Canada, Congo, Czechoslovakia, Egypt, Guinea-Bissau, Hungary, India, Ireland, Jordan, Malaysia, Morocco, Netherlands, New Zealand, Nigeria, Norway, Senegal, Singapore, Spain, Sweden, Yugoslavia and Zimbabwe contributed to UNAVEM II: see 'UNAVEM II created to verify peaceful transition', *UN Chronicle*, 28:3 (September 1991), 28.

31 The process of demobilisation consisted of 4 components: assembly of troops; disarmament; demobilisation of troops not joining the FAA; and the formation of the FAA. None of these tasks would be properly accomplished. And the failure to demobilise the MPLA and UNITA forces before the elections would facilitate the return to civil war. UNAVEM II, with its inadequate mandate and resources, was unable to prevent the situation from deteriorating.

32 UNAVEM II's initial strength was 350 unarmed military observers and 89 police observers provided by 24 countries. Military observers were deployed around the country at 46 assembly points as well as such critical points as ports, airports and border posts. Police observers were also deployed in all 18 provinces. The country was divided into 6 regions; the regional headquarters were located in Luanda, Huambo, Suarimo, Luena, Lubango and Mavinga with the main UNAVEM II Headquarters in Luanda.

33 Adrian, *Peacemaking and Peacekeeping in Angola*, p. 5.

34 S/24145 of 24 June 1992.

35 S/PV.3092 of 7 July 1992, p. 3.

36 See Zaire's speech in S/PV.3168 of 29 January 1993, p. 117.

37 S/PV.3168 of 29 January 1993, p. 81.

38 Cape Verde, for instance, highlighted the importance of the UN assisting the establishment of a multiparty democracy in Angola; see S/PV.3062 of 24 March 1992, p. 7.

39 'In January 1993 the annual cost of UNAVEM II was roughly estimated to be US$39 million. By contrast, UNTAG in Namibia (with only one-eighth of Angola's population) was provided with a wider mandate and a budget of US$430 million for a period of one year and some 7,150 officials. The UN mission in Mozambique, likewise, was allocated 7,500 UN observers': see V. Krška, 'Peacekeeping in Angola (UNAVEM I and II)', *International Peacekeeping*, 4:1 (Spring 1997), 94.

40 *Financial Times* (London), 11 May 1992. This was a play on words – a reference to SC Resolution 747 expanding the mandate: see www.hrw.org/reports/1999/angola/Angl998–10.htm#P1843_375081 (24 May 2000).

41 See Krška, 'Peacekeeping in Angola', p. 87.

42 See Krška, 'Peacekeeping in Angola', p. 87.

43 See Krška, 'Peacekeeping in Angola', p. 87.

44 S/PV.3092 of 7 July 1992, p. 6.

45 SC Resolution 747 was adopted unanimously.

46 UN Press Release SC/5387 of 24 March 1992.

47 S/PV.3092 of 7 July 1992, pp. 4–5.

48 See, for instance, the strong French support expressed in S/PV.3062 of 24 March 1992, p. 12. Though the United States welcomed this role, its rhetoric alluded to its unwillingness to see the elections as the UN's 'responsibility' that would be need to be carried out at all costs. The responsibility for elections should rest with the Angolans; see S/PV.3062 of 24 March 1992, p. 10. Belgium exhibited a similar attitude, stressing that the UN had intervened in Angola 'only at the explicit request of the parties' who committed themselves to the holding of free, fair and multiparty elections: see S/PV.3062 of 24 March 1992, p. 13.

49 See the speech by the Spanish delegate in S/PV.3168 of 29 January 1993, p. 54.

50 See Angola's speech in S/PV.3168 of 29 January 1993, p. 7.

51 See M. Sayagues, 'A little breathing space', *Africa Report*, 40:3 (May–June 1995), 14–17.

52 See *Africa Information Afrique* (Harare, 18 May 1994), available online at ftp://csf.colorado.edu/ipe/Thematic_Archive/newsletters/africa_information_afrique _net/Angola/940512.ang.The_Legacy_of_War (30 May 2000).

53 S/PV.3226 of 1 June 1993, p. 16; for Guinea-Bissau's appeal to UNHCR and NGOs, see S/PV.3168 of 29 January 1993, p. 106.

54 See Y. C. Lodico, 'A peace that fell apart: the United Nations and the war in Angola', in Durch (ed.), *UN Peacekeeping, American Politics, and the Uncivil Wars of the 1990s*, pp. 123–4.

55 Actually UNAVEM II's police themselves lacked training in human rights; Lodico, 'A peace that fell apart', p. 124.

56 Interview with Margaret Anstee (11 March 1998) cited in Human Rights Watch, *Angola Unravels: The Rise and Fall of the Lusaka Peace Process*, available online at www.hrw.org/reports/1999/angola/index.htm#TopOfPage (30 May 2000).

57 S/PV.3168 of 29 January 1993, pp. 49–50.

58 S/PV.3168 of 29 January 1993, p. 51.

59 Furthermore, Albright argued that before agreeing to additional commitments the United States also needed to have the Secretariat's clear advice on the costs involved and their duration; see S/PV.3254 of 15 July 1993, p. 114.

60 See, for instance, I. Ros-Lehtinen, 'Review of Clinton Administration's Performance in Africa' (Statement before the Subcommittee on Africa of the House Committee on International Relations; 26 September 1996).

61 S/PV.3226 of 1 June 1993, p. 31.

62 For Brazil's views see S/PV.3182 of 12 March 1993, p. 6 and S/PV.3206 of 30 April 1993, p. 3; for Cape Verde's views see S/PV.3226 of 1 June 1993, p. 23.

63 S/PV.3254 of 15 July 1993, p. 41.

64 Belgium, for instance, held the view that 'it must be clear that the United Nations is intervening in Angola only at the explicit request of the parties and in a precise context, namely, that of the "Acordos de Paz".' See S/PV.3062 of 24 March 1992, p. 13.

65 S/PV.3168 of 29 January 1993, pp. 88–90.

66 This normative change did, of course, attract some resistance or at least scepticism. See, for instance, Cuba's views in S/PV.3168 of 29 January 1993, pp. 83–4.

67 See, for instance, the views expressed by Mozambique, Namibia and Venezuela in S/PV.3254 of 15 July 1993 and S/PV.3168 of 29 January 1993.

68 Borrowed from S. J. Stedman, 'Spoiler problems in peace processes', *International Security*, 22:2 (Fall 1997).

69 For the views of these members, see S/PV.3130 of 30 October 1992, p. 9; S/PV.3182 of 12 March 1993, p. 19; S/PV.3226 of 1 June 1993, p. 16; S/PV.3182 of 12 March 1993, p. 11 and S/PV.3226 of 1 June 1993, p. 27; and S/PV.3254 of 15 July 1993, p. 21 respectively.

70 The United States was 'deeply concerned by the reports that UNITA [was] trying to extend its authority over parts of Angolan territory. If true, this would represent a major breach of the Peace Accords, which [the US] would condemn': see S/PV.3130 of 30 October 1992, p. 19.

71 M. Anstee, 'Angola: The forgotten tragedy, a test case for UN peacekeeping', *International Relations*, 11:6 (December 1993), 496. In her assessment of UNAVEM II in implementing the Bicesse process, Anstee insisted that 'the UN should never become involved in monitoring any peace accord where it has not taken part in negotiations ... it must have a say in drawing up its own role.' See M. Anstee, 'Angola: a tragedy not to be forgotten', *The World Today*, 52:7 (July 1996), 190–1.

72 Anstee, 'Angola: a tragedy not to be forgotten', 190. One reason for this caution was the apprehension that UNITA sought a large UN intervention as a means of containing FAA advances while it regrouped its own forces.

73 M. Anstee, *Orphan of the Cold War: The Inside Story of the Collapse of the Angola Peace Process, 1992–93* (London: St. Martin's Press, 1996), p. 533.

74 By SC Resolution 864 of 15 September 1993 (adopted unanimously) all states were required to refrain from the supply of arms and oil to Angola 'other than through named points of entry on a list to be supplied by the Government of Angola'.

75 SC Resolution 945 of 29 September 1994 was adopted unanimously.

76 See the Protocol's Annex 2 'Re-Affirmation of the Acceptance, by the Government and UNITA, of the Relevant Legal Instruments'.

77 The political settlement differed significantly from Bicesse's winner-take-all arrangement. It committed the parties to a 'power-sharing' arrangement through the formation of a Government of Unity and National Reconciliation (GURN). The 70 UNITA deputies elected to the legislature in the 1992 election would take their seats,

and the presidential election would be completed. UNITA would appoint four ministers and seven deputy ministers. It would hold several offices at the provincial level as well.

78 Article 3 under 'I. General Principles'.

79 The Portuguese statement at the Security Council is a case in point: 'The role of the United Nations is crucial . . . But the efforts of the United Nations must be accompanied by those countries with responsibilities in the process, namely the three observers . . . we therefore consider that their continued involvement in the process is essential.' See S/PV.3168 of 29 January 1993, p. 98.

80 See S/PV.3254 of 15 July 1993, p. 23.

81 Lodico, 'A peace that fell apart', p. 122.

82 Trovoada was considered the only African president on good terms with both Savimbi and dos Santos.

83 Mario Dujisin/AIA/IPS (Lisbon, 27 October 1993), available online at ftp://csf.colorado.edu/ipe/Thematic_Archive/newsletters/africa_information_afrique _net/Angola/931019.Ang.Arms_From_Zaire (30 May 2000).

84 See *Africa Confidential* (18 February 1994) cited in UNHCR, *Background Paper*, 2.2.

85 Article 5 under 'I. General Principles'.

86 See, for instance, the views expressed by Cape Verde in S/PV.3226 of 1 June 1993, p. 22, and by Cuba and New Zealand in S/PV.3168 of 29 January 1993, p. 82 and p. 33 respectively.

87 S/PV.3168 of 29 January 1993, pp. 77–8.

88 See the views of Djibouti, Nigeria and Zimbabwe in S/PV.3168 of 29 January 1993. For Zimbabwe, see also S/PV.3254 of 15 July 1993, p. 22.

89 S/PV.3168 of 29 January 1993, pp. 24–5 and S/PV.3226 of 1 June 1993, p. 19.

90 S/PV.3182 of 12 March 1993, p. 19.

91 See the Spanish speech in S/PV.3168 of 29 January 1993, p. 54.

92 See, for instance, the Portuguese views in S/PV.3130 of 30 October 1992, p. 6 and S/PV.3168 of 29 January 1993, p. 101.

93 S/PV.3168 of 29 January 1993, p. 47.

94 Algeria, Guinea-Bissau, Kenya, Lesotho, Malawi, Mozambique, Namibia, Senegal, South Africa, Tunisia, Tanzania, Zaire, Zambia and Zimbabwe.

95 Brazil, India, the Netherlands, Norway, Spain and Sweden.

96 See S/PV.3499 of 8 February 1995 in its entirety.

97 S/PV.3499 of 8 February 1995, p. 6.

98 In addition to the Special Representative, the mission's organisational structure included a Deputy Special Representative, a Director for Political Affairs who would head the political component, and a legal staff.

99 See, for instance, the French statement in S/PV.3628 of 6 February 1996, p. 12.

100 S/PV.3562 of 7 August 1995, p. 12.

101 Ambassador Paul Hare cited in 'Panel 2: Angola post-Cold War harvest, panel summary', *How Can Human Rights Be Better Integrated into Peace Process?: Conference Report* (Washington DC: The Fund For Peace, January 1998).

102 For a survey, see A. Conchiglia, *UNITA, Myth and Reality*, trans M. Holness (London: ECASAAMA, 1990), pp. 54–79.

103 The United Nations Observer Mission to Angola comprised 1,500 'rapid reaction troops' to assist 345 civilian police and 85 military observers.

8

The UN in the Cambodia conflict: UNTAC

A N EXAMINATION OF the UN Transitional Authority in Cambodia (UNTAC)[1] should prove especially illuminating for our study in that this mission points to the growing willingness of the international community to involve the UN in intra-state governance. It helps us, in other words, to scrutinise more closely the relationship between the changing normative basis of UN peacekeeping and the UN's evolving role in world politics.

The literature on the UN's Cambodia experience has rightly pointed to the 'comprehensive' nature of the mission. What is less well understood is the normative meaning and implications of this comprehensiveness, which is what this chapter seeks to elucidate. Here we explore the local, regional and global interests that impacted on the development of the idea of UN peace-keeping and the way these interacted, and at least temporarily synthesised to form a seemingly coherent normative framework for UN action. What is particularly revealing about this framework is not only the fact that the UN was given unprecedented authority in the process, but also the emergence of a complex blend of normative objectives which were partly reflected in the functions UNTAC was expected to perform.

Historical background

Cambodia became a French colony in 1887.[2] In 1945 Prince Sihanouk[3] proclaimed Cambodia's independence from France, but at the conclusion of World War II the Allied troops arriving in Cambodia restored French rule. Sihanouk pursued a diplomatic campaign to gain independence from France, in which he eventually succeeded. In the Geneva Conference of May–June 1954, Sihanouk's Royal Government was recognised as the sole legitimate political authority in Cambodia.

In March 1969, with the escalation of the Vietnam War, the United States started to bomb communist 'sanctuaries' in Cambodia. Within one year Lon Nol and Sirik Matak had staged a *coup d'état* which overthrew Sihanouk and instituted a pro-American republican regime to replace the monarchy. Meanwhile, the South Vietnamese Army and the Americans increased their raids into communist sanctuaries. These incursions finally gave rise to a full-scale US invasion in April 1970. In December 1970, largely because of domestic political concerns, the US Government brought the invasion to an end.[4] Soon after, a civil war broke out between Lon Nol's forces and the Khmer Rouge, which the latter eventually won in April 1975.[5]

The Khmer Rouge regime, led by Pol Pot and named Democratic Kampuchea in early 1976, pursued a determined campaign to eradicate all internal opposition to its Maoist programme in Cambodia.[6] The actual toll of the radical Khmer Rouge attempt to forcefully reconstruct Cambodia as a self-sufficient agricultural society, where there was no place for money, would be known only after the regime was overthrown. The number of deaths in excess of Cambodia's normal mortality rate for 1975–78 is estimated to be one million.[7]

While the Khmer Rouge instigated several military clashes with Thailand (an ASEAN member),[8] they practically waged war against Vietnam. Even though the deeper roots of the Khmer Rouge's hostility towards Vietnam lay in the historical animosity between the Khmer and Vietnamese,[9] the more recent political cause of the conflict was their relationship with Sihanouk. In the early 1970s, the Khmer Rouge had tried to get rid of Sihanouk in order to establish their own rule in Cambodia. At first, North Vietnam seemed a natural ally for the Khmer Rouge,[10] since both were trying to establish communist regimes in Indochina. As the Vietnam War intensified, however, North Vietnam needed Sihanouk who, after all, had previously allowed North Vietnamese forces to operate from Cambodia against the US and South Vietnamese forces. The Khmer Rouge's seizure of power coincided with the fall of the South Vietnam regime. As early as May 1975, Cambodia and Vietnam directed allegations against each other, and eventually, in December 1978, Vietnam invaded Cambodia.[11]

The invasion took place in the wider context of the intra-communist political tension between the Soviet Union and China.[12] The Khmer Rouge were an ideological and strategic ally of China before, during and after their short-lived reign. Hanoi, however, was sceptical about Mao's 'Cultural Revolutionary' policies abroad and Beijing's *rapprochement* with the United States in the early 1970s.[13] Vietnam's persecution of its ethnic Chinese minority and the territorial disputes between China and Vietnam were yet other reasons contributing to Hanoi's increasing alignment with Moscow.[14] On 29 June 1978, Vietnam joined COMECON. The Treaty of Friendship and Cooperation of 3 November 1978 marked the consolidation of the Soviet–Vietnamese alliance.[15]

A pro-Vietnamese government was installed in Phnom Penh, and the establishment of the People's Republic of Kampuchea (PRK) was officially proclaimed on 10 January 1979.[16] The West, China, and ASEAN[17] responded by isolating the Phnom Penh Government diplomatically and economically.[18] In June 1982, ASEAN's persistent efforts led to the formation in Kuala Lumpur of the Coalition Government of Democratic Kampuchea (CGDK),[19] which comprised the three most important groups opposed to the Phnom Penh regime: royalists (FUNCINPEC), non-communist republicans (KPNLF) and the Khmer Rouge (PDK). The CGDK lacked internal coherence, as the three factions were able to maintain their formal togetherness largely due to their pragmatic considerations.

A more organised resistance to Phnom Penh was encouraged by the external sponsors of the three factions which received open Thai support as well as more discreet US and Chinese support.[20] The formation of the CGDK was intended partly to prevent the UN from seating the new Phnom Penh regime at the General Assembly,[21] and partly to demonstrate unity and mobilise international support against Vietnam.[22] The occupant of the Cambodian seat, that is, the Khmer Rouge Government, was attracting increasingly severe criticism, especially from the western public, for its past 'genocidal' policies.[23] In the 1980s, the CGDK, acting as a government in exile, continued to occupy the Cambodian seat in the UN with the support of western and ASEAN governments.

Peacekeeping in Cambodia: the evolution of an idea

Although it is not easy to date the original call for active UN involvement in Cambodia, it can be stated with reasonable confidence that the UN became involved in the Cambodia conflict mainly through ASEAN's efforts. In June 1981, the International Conference on Kampuchea was convened by the General Assembly at ASEAN's initiative, and attended by 79 states. The refusal of Vietnam and the Soviet bloc to participate soon brought the Conference to a deadlock. Its only achievement was the establishment of an Ad Hoc Committee to undertake peacemaking efforts.[24] Peacekeeping was not yet on the agenda. In 1982, the Secretary-General began to advocate a change of strategy to deal with the Cambodia problem, pressing for discussions to be held in a much smaller forum than the International Conference and limited to those local, regional and global powers directly affected.[25]

Contemplating peacekeeping – mainly with Hanoi in mind

Until the late 1980s, it was Sihanouk and ASEAN who were the primary advocates of active UN involvement in Cambodia. The main emphasis in these

181

early calls for UN intervention was on Vietnamese withdrawal – an idea which found support in neither Phnom Penh nor Vietnam. As early as 1980, Sihanouk was open to international control of Cambodia.[26] He would remain one of the driving forces behind the idea of active UN involvement in Cambodia, which would in turn gain increasing ASEAN support on the international stage. In 1983 ASEAN introduced a plan, the so-called ASEAN Appeal, which specifically mentioned 'international supervision' in relation to Vietnamese troops in Cambodia. Neither Hanoi nor Phnom Penh welcomed the idea. Over the next three years ASEAN continued with its efforts to bring an end to the regional instability caused by Vietnam's moves.[27]

On 17 March 1986, in response to ASEAN calls, the CGDK offered a peace plan, which *inter alia* called for a UN observer group to supervise the withdrawal of Vietnamese troops and the ensuing cease-fire, and to monitor the conduct of free elections. Soviet moves in April 1987 to 'normalise' Sino-Soviet relations represented the first breakthrough: the main backers of the Phnom Penh Government and the CGDK would eventually come closer to the idea of settlement. The proposal to deploy an observer group would be eventually accepted by Phnom Penh's new Prime Minister, Hun Sen. The idea of UN peacekeeping in Cambodia gained strength thereafter, with the period between 1987 and 1991 witnessing a number of formal and informal meetings between Cambodian and international parties.[28]

With his coalition partners and Beijing still hesitant to engage in negotiations with Phnom Penh, Sihanouk decided to act individually to establish a dialogue. On 2 December 1987, the first meeting between Sihanouk and Hun Sen took place in Paris.[29] Sihanouk's independent initiative put pressure on his coalition partners as well as on China and ASEAN to reconsider their uncompromising stance *vis-à-vis* dialogue.[30] By January 1988, Sihanouk was insisting on the necessity of a peacekeeping force rather than a mere observer mission as envisaged by Hun Sen.[31]

Indonesia, ASEAN's designated interlocutor on Cambodia, carried the process of negotiation one step further. During the first ever face-to-face meeting of the four Cambodian factions in Jakarta on 25–28 July 1988 (the first Jakarta Informal Meeting), the Phnom Penh Government rejected the idea of international peacekeeping. So did Vietnam, which for the first time had sent a delegation to multilateral negotiations on Cambodia. Phnom Penh and Hanoi were highly sceptical of the internationalisation of attempts to settle the dispute through the UN where there seemed no prospect of support for their cause.

The idea gains credibility: neutralisation of both Hanoi and the Khmer Rouge

All along, another obstacle in the path of finding a workable peacekeeping formula was the position of the Khmer Rouge who were well aware of the fact that the support extended to them by China and ASEAN (especially Thailand)[32] owed much to these actors' strategic interests. If these interests changed, the UN (that is to say, both the General Assembly and the Security Council) might easily turn against the Khmer Rouge. Reports and evidence documenting their atrocities were already in wide circulation in UN corridors.[33] It was not until late 1988 that the Khmer Rouge gave their explicit support to Sihanouk's demand for international peacekeepers:[34] 'An international peace-keeping force would be stationed throughout Cambodia to enforce the agreement.'[35] The assurances given by China that it would protect the interests of the Khmer Rouge, and more generally its strongly stated public position on the issue played a decisive role in this change of attitude.[36]

The three CGDK partners entered the second Jakarta Informal Meeting in relative harmony. According to the new Sihanouk proposal of 30 November 1988, a substantial international peacekeeping force, capable of preventing election frauds, was necessary. The functions envisaged for the force were: first, to ensure that the Khmer Rouge would not monopolise power; secondly, to verify Vietnamese non-aggression and non-interference; and thirdly, to prevent a civil war in Cambodia. In order to accommodate Phnom Penh's and Hanoi's wishes, Sihanouk was now willing to try and 'neutralise' the Khmer Rouge, while taking care that such a strategy did not entail a return to civil war. 'Prevention of civil war' in this sense had to be part of the mandate of the proposed UN peacekeeping force. More importantly, the idea of UN peacekeeping gained credibility only after it was placed within a wider context. UN involvement was now sought not only against Vietnam but also against the Khmer Rouge.[37]

In effect, Sihanouk's new approach called for more than the UN's traditional peacekeeping role, that is, maintenance of international peace and security and prevention of foreign intervention. We have already seen that the Security Council had made 'prevention of civil war' part of the peacekeeping mandate in the Congo. The difference is that this time the demand to include this objective in the mandate came directly from one of the intra-state parties, and emerged out of a concern to accommodate the diverse interests of opposing actors. The more diverse interests and perceptions were taken into consideration, which was necessary for a peaceful settlement of the conflict, the wider became the role prescribed for the UN.

Sihanouk's attempt to work out an acceptable solution did not immediately lend itself to unanimous acceptance of a peacekeeping role for the UN. For Phnom Penh the very idea of international peacekeepers implied an infringement of Cambodia's sovereignty. The most that Phnom Penh was prepared to accept was a 600-strong mission, with its role limited to observation of the 'external' aspect of the conflict, that is, the Vietnamese withdrawal. On 5 April 1989, a joint declaration by Phnom Penh, Vietnam and Laos called for supervision by the International Control and Supervision Commission established under the 1954 Geneva Agreements.[38] The proposed supervision would be supplemented by the chairman of the Jakarta Informal Meeting and a representative of the Secretary-General. Communist Indochina did not wish to assign a greater role to the UN, where the CGDK representative was still seated in the General Assembly, and where their only supporters seemed to be members of the Soviet bloc.[39]

Following the repeated failure of reconciliation attempts, a conference was organised at the initiative of the French Government in Paris in July 1989. In addition to the four Cambodian factions, the Permanent Five, the members of ASEAN, Vietnam and Laos (the other two Indochinese states), India and Canada (both former Control Commission states), Zimbabwe (acting chair of the NAM), Australia, Japan, and the Secretary-General all participated in the First Paris Conference on Cambodia.[40] The most significant rule of the game at the Conference was set by two rivals, that is, Vietnam and China. On their insistence, the principle of unanimity was adopted when dealing with substantive issues.[41] This arrangement effectively delivered the right of veto to the China-sponsored Khmer Rouge on the one hand, and the Vietnam-sponsored Phnom Penh Government on the other. This practical necessity would have two long-term normative implications.

First, the subsequent multilateral agreements and UN decisions on Cambodia would use rhetoric that attempted to reconcile the different interests and normative preferences of all parties. In concrete terms this meant that the language adopted would highlight the importance of both the inviolability of Cambodia's sovereignty and respect for human rights. China's normative priority was clearly the former, with an emphasis on removing Vietnamese dominance in Cambodia's internal affairs. Vietnam, on the other hand, continually stressed its concern that the previous Khmer Rouge regime, which had perpetrated gross human rights abuses, should not be allowed to recapture power in Cambodia.

Secondly, the Conference would give the first signs of enhanced UN authority in dealing with the Cambodian conflict. De Cuéllar emphatically underlines in his memoirs that the UN was a full participant at the Paris Conference, even though he signed the final document only as a witness. Full participation meant that the UN delegation was given the right to speak and to vote just as the national delegations were. It also meant that the UN had the right to veto any proposals, since all decisions were to be reached by unanimity.[42] In other words, the UN was accorded the status of an autonomous actor, which could pursue its independent agenda in relation to the settlement of the conflict.

The Conference organised itself into five working groups, each concerned with a different aspect of the conflict. Perhaps the most important of these was the fourth group – the so-called 'Ad Hoc Group' which dealt with the issues of national reconciliation and an interim authority in Cambodia. It was largely because of the disagreements within this group that the Conference came to a deadlock and was eventually suspended. One observer attributed its failure to Phnom Penh's refusal to share power in the interim period which would precede the proposed elections.[43] One of the most contested issues was partial delegation of Cambodian sovereignty to a provisional polity of which the UN would be an integral part. Although the Conference failed to break the deadlock, there was general consensus at its close that some kind of International Control Mechanism should supervise the internal aspects of a future Cambodian settlement, and that, regardless of its precise mandate, the 'mechanism' should be a UN operation.[44] On 26 September 1989, Vietnam formally withdrew from Cambodia.[45]

**Lead-up to UN 'protectorate':
from the Australian Plan to the Paris Agreement**

November 1989 proved a milestone in the international handling of the Cambodia situation. First, the General Assembly adopted a resolution calling for 'the creation of an interim administering authority'.[46] Then, on 24 November 1989, a more radical settlement proposal was put forward, which proved nevertheless more acceptable from Phnom Penh's viewpoint. Gareth Evans, the Australian Foreign Minister, gave a speech to the Australian Senate where he summarised the main points of a plan to resolve the Cambodia conflict. He envisaged a role for the UN, which went far beyond mediation and supervision.[47] In effect, Evans proposed a UN trusteeship in Cambodia. His formulation was not anti-Phnom Penh in tone. Two weeks later, Hun Sen expressed his readiness to 'consider' the Evans plan.

The third of the Jakarta meetings on Cambodia, held on 26–28 February 1990, put the Australian proposal on its agenda, by which time Australia had already turned Evans' proposal into a collection of ten separate papers laying down more detailed plans.[48] The plan, which introduced the idea that the settlement of the Cambodia problem would require a comprehensive package, sought to designate a temporary form of political authority in Cambodia.[49] Chinese and US insistence on comprehensiveness was already well established.

From the outset, the Australian plan was sensitive to the issue of the UN's image. It gave the impression that the UN's authority *vis-à-vis* Cambodia would be limited. It stated clearly that no agreement on a comprehensive settlement could decide between the competing claims as to which party constituted the legitimate government of Cambodia, or determine what would be Cambodia's constitutional order and social and political system.[50]

185

Adherence to transitional arrangements would not involve any acknowledgment that the previously asserted rights of any party were either legitimate or illegitimate, accepted or rejected.[51] As a logical corollary of this, the UN could not be expected or allowed to make judgements as to which of the parties would be the legitimate office holder. The plan proposed instead the establishment of a Supreme National Council (SNC) to be formed by the four factions. All government authority would be vested in this Council. Taken at face value, then, a strict 'neutrality' was envisaged for the UN, reminiscent of the Cold War period.

A closer reading of the plan, however, revealed that the UN would be endowed with unprecedented political authority with far-reaching normative implications for governance. The SNC was expected to devolve its legislative, executive, and judicial authority to the Secretary-General, who would be authorised by the Security Council to accept and exercise that authority. The Secretary-General would be able to delegate, and resume, this authority to such officials or external agencies as he deemed appropriate.[52] This was in effect a call for the empowerment of the UN (in the person of its Secretary-General) to exercise greater authority *vis-à-vis* the Cambodian conflict. Among other things, it reflected a concern to accommodate the expectations, perceptions and interests of two key allies, Phnom Penh and Hanoi.

For years, the Phnom Penh regime had not been seated in the UN. ASEAN-sponsored General Assembly resolutions had associated the Phnom Penh regime with the Vietnamese invasion, and steadfastly refused to confer official legitimacy to it. Vietnam, on the other hand, was widely considered an aggressor. Security Council action against Hanoi and Phnom Penh had been averted only by dedicated Soviet efforts.[53] As a consequence, Hanoi and Phnom Penh, without whose cooperation there could be no peaceful resolution, considered the UN's deliberative bodies as unfriendly, if not inimical. If, however, the UN based its actions in Cambodia on the authority of the Secretary-General, and not the General Assembly, this difficulty might be surmounted.[54] By making the Secretary-General the focal point of UN involvement, Australia had effectively removed an important barrier to settlement: Hanoi's and Phnom Penh's distrust of the organisation.

The proposed direct UN involvement in the Cambodian civil administration was in practice designed to sidestep the issue of power-sharing which had impeded progress at the Paris Conference. Temporary transfer of authority to the UN would enable the interested parties not to enter dangerous territory during negotiations, that is, the issue of which faction would get what share in Cambodia's temporary governance. This was a particularly delicate question, since it was the key to 'legitimate' re-entry of the Khmer Rouge into Cambodia. It might also have implied that Phnom Penh was expected to give up its relative advantage in bargaining, namely dismantling the country's administrative structures which were largely under Phnom Penh's control.

Soon it became clear that the envisaged interim administration would in fact serve more the interests of the Phnom Penh Government than of their major rival, the Khmer Rouge. In response to mounting domestic accusations that his plan accommodated the genocidal Khmer Rouge, Evans would argue that the plan in fact sought to constrain the role of the Khmer Rouge during the transitional arrangements.[55] Accordingly, the plan envisaged that the 'existing' civil administration in Cambodia would, as part of the search for an arrangement acceptable to Phnom Penh, be permitted to continue with its day-to-day activities.[56] Despite the weakening of its position, Phnom Penh's administrative apparatus would in effect remain largely in place. Phnom Penh would in these circumstances be willing to compromise, because such an arrangement would still give it the upper hand. Its opposition to the idea of extensive UN involvement in Cambodia gradually diminished.

Despite a number of disagreements between the factions, the third Jakarta meeting did result in the signing of the first ever joint *communiqué* by the four factions. Given the sympathetic response of the Permanent Five to the Australian Plan,[57] the factions came to accept the idea of a UN presence in Cambodia for the interim period before the elections. They also agreed to the establishment of a Supreme National Council which would embody Cambodia's 'national sovereignty and unity' for the period in question. As one might expect, both points were surrounded by ambiguities. First, the UN presence would be 'at appropriate levels' – a phrase clearly open to interpretation. For his part, Hun Sen stressed the limits of Phnom Penh's latest concessions to the emerging international support for an extensive UN role in Cambodia. In his view the UN should not go beyond organising elections; it could not be allowed to 'manage, control, or govern Cambodia'. Secondly, the formula by which the SNC should be organised was not specified. Phnom Penh opposed the dismantling of the existing governmental structure as suggested by Sihanouk.[58]

Reconciling geostrategic interests: the Permanent Five as a conjunctural 'bloc'

On 15–16 January 1990, on the initiative of the United States, the deputy foreign ministers of the Permanent Five held in Paris their first meeting on Cambodia. From that moment on, the representatives of the Permanent Five gathered on a monthly basis. The discourse of the UNTAC period was largely set during these meetings which continuously referred to 'comprehensive political settlement', 'cessation of outside military assistance', 'enhanced UN role', 'effective presence', and 'neutral political environment'. A course of action began to be specified by the Permanent Five in the light of the ideas, positions and plans already in circulation, and a summary of conclusions was issued.[59]

Until their adoption of the so-called Framework Document on 28 August 1990,[60] the Permanent Five held several meetings.[61] During this negotiation process, it was China, more than any other actor, which complicated the issue for the other permanent members. China insisted, first, that the Phnom Penh Government be totally dismantled prior to UN deployment; and secondly, that the Khmer Rouge not be excluded from the process. The first point was resisted mainly by the Soviet Union, Phnom Penh's main supporter, while the second point continued to provoke opposition from the other three powers, whose publics had long associated the Khmer Rouge with genocidal practices. A political stalemate seemingly ensued. The Permanent Five meetings had not succeeded in reconciling the positions of the relevant parties.

In March 1990, in what was perhaps a landmark move, the Permanent Five issued a call to the Cambodian factions to delegate Cambodian national sovereignty to the proposed UN mission during the transitional period. The Permanent Five referred to a UN body whose system and procedures would be 'absolutely impartial'. All Cambodian participants would have the same rights, freedoms and opportunities in the election process. Once this stance was adopted, the supporters of all four factions eventually agreed to make the necessary compromises. China gradually withdrew its insistence on up-front dismantling of the Phnom Penh administrative structures;[62] the Soviet Union dropped its reference to Khmer Rouge genocide; and the three western powers simply endorsed the obvious reality: the two rival communist Cambodian factions would have a say over Cambodia's future.

The Permanent Members came to agree in principle that the UN's role in the resolution of the Cambodian problem should be substantially 'enhanced'.[63] According to their joint statement the complete withdrawal of foreign forces had to be 'verified by the UN';[64] free and fair elections had to be conducted under 'direct UN administration';[65] an 'effective' UN presence would be required during the transition period in order to assure 'internal security';[66] the scale of the UN operation should be 'consistent with the successful implementation' of a Cambodian settlement;[67] and a Special Representative should be appointed to supervise UN activities.[68] The Secretary-General would comment:

> How far would such internal involvement extend and how would it relate to the sovereignty of the Supreme National Council as described in the principles defined by the Five? ... For more than four decades, the Permanent Members had been reluctant to give the United Nations any independent authority at all. Now they seemed prepared to have it administer a whole country, a task that was, in my view, inappropriate and beyond its capacity.[69]

Reconciliation of the Permanent Five's interests in the Cambodian context had such enormous normative implications for the UN's future that the Secretary-General felt obliged to express concern over possible ramifications. The UN had never taken direct responsibility for the maintenance of law and order within a sovereign state. Neither had it been directly responsible for the conduct of elections in an independent country. These functions meant that the UN would inevitably become involved in aspects of Cambodia's domestic affairs,[70] putting into question the UN's adherence to the principle of non-intervention.

The Secretariat's concerns notwithstanding, any interim solution other than a UN administration seemed unfeasible to the Permanent Five. Any other mechanism would serve the interests of one or another permanent member. Whether the UN was actually capable of performing such extensive functions as foreshadowed by the Permanent Five remained a point of controversy. Normatively speaking, nevertheless, the UN was assigned a role that would set a precedent for years to come.

The authority prescribed for the Secretary-General in the Australian Plan was taken one step further by the Permanent Five. The Secretariat proposed that in the event of the SNC not being able to reach consensus, the Special Representative of the Secretary-General should be entitled to make a final decision, taking fully into account views expressed in the Council. This provision gave the Special Representative, and through him the Secretary-General, 'supreme power if he chose to use it'.[71] The UN's authority in relation to the Cambodian conflict was now fully endorsed by the Permanent Five. On 26 November 1990 came their 'draft comprehensive political settlement' (the Draft Agreement),[72] which was developed directly from the Framework Document.

Reconciling regional interests

As the Permanent Five engaged in extensive consultations on Cambodia, a parallel series of meetings took place between the four factions and interested states. In Tokyo, a meeting organised by Thailand and Japan to discuss Sihanouk's nine-point proposal of 9 April 1990, reduced the gap between the positions adopted by FUNCINPEC, the KPNLF and Phnom Penh.[73] To be able to exert a degree of pressure on Phnom Penh, the two coalition partners of the Khmer Rouge were now willing to act at its expense. In a sense, Sihanouk and Son Sann, acting on behalf of FUNCINPEC and the KPNLF respectively, clearly signalled at the Tokyo meeting that they valued a compromise with Phnom Penh more than their strategic alliance with the Khmer Rouge. The Tokyo meeting did not address the issue of the proposed UN role in Cambodia, but concentrated instead on the establishment of the SNC. By the end of the meeting an agreement on the composition of the Council had begun to emerge.

The factions held another meeting in Jakarta on 9–10 September 1990, and finally established the 12-member SNC,[74] even though the question of the Council's presidency remained a bone of serious contention. Throughout the following year, the SNC held various meetings,[75] with the discussions focusing on power-sharing arrangements among the factions. Perhaps the most important achievement of this phase of the negotiation process was the decision, taken after prolonged debate at the Beijing meeting of 16–17 July 1991, to endorse Sihanouk as chairman of the SNC. However, the serious disagreement between Phnom Penh and the CGDK on the UN's role continued. Fearful that the UN might engage in an administrative takeover of Cambodia, the former still portrayed an extensive UN role as a violation of Cambodia's sovereignty. Demobilisation of Cambodian armed forces by the UN was considered unacceptable. Phnom Penh was at best prepared to countenance a small UN presence with a limited range of monitoring functions.[76]

Despite the obstacles to a detailed agreement between the factions, in autumn 1991 the political atmosphere was conducive to a second attempt at resolving the conflict. At the very least, there was now sufficient consensus among the factions' international backers, which could be used as leverage. At the invitation of the French Government, the Second Paris Conference convened on 21 October 1991. Legally, Cambodia was now represented by a single body, the SNC, although in practice all four factions were invited. The participants of the First Paris Conference were again all present.[77] The Conference resulted in the signing of four separate documents, which would provide the basis of an active UN presence in Cambodia: the Final Act; the Agreement on Political Settlement (with its 5 annexes); the Agreement on Cambodia's Sovereignty; and finally the Declaration on Rehabilitation.[78] Through these accords, the Cambodian factions formally invited the Security Council to establish a UN mission in their country.

The provisions of the Agreement signalled the actors' determination to solve the critical issue of consent once and for all. Throughout the four-year negotiation process, Phnom Penh had made it amply clear that it would not accept a UN 'takeover' of its governmental privileges. The obstacle associated with the Khmer Rouge position had been handled largely through Beijing's leverage and Sihanouk's appeasement. Both parties could at any moment withdraw their consent from the peace process.[79] The Agreement clearly indicated that the signature by the SNC members would commit all Cambodian parties and armed forces to the provisions of the Agreement.[80] It underlined that the SNC thereby delegated to the UN all powers necessary to ensure the implementation of the Agreement.[81] As a consequence, the authoritative interpretation of the Agreement, that is, judgements as to its content, would belong to the UN.

Considered in the light of the Congo and Cyprus experiences, where the parties to the conflict remained entitled to their own interpretation of the UN's mandate, this was a substantial assertion of the UN's normative authority. Uch Kiman, the Cambodian Secretary of State for Foreign Affairs, would later comment:

> The first and foremost feature of UNTAC was that it was a serious infringement on Cambodian sovereignty. This was probably the most bitter pill which we all had to swallow. For the sake of peace and national reconciliation, we accepted that the UN more or less run the local government and allowed it to organize general elections in a member state. We had to accept the 'Akashi Protectorate' and referred to the position held by H.E. Yasushi Akashi . . . as that of a 'Viceroy'. [82]

The Accords placed all administrative agencies, bodies and offices in the fields of foreign affairs, national defence, finance, public security and information under the direct control of UNTAC, and further empowered the UN to issue directives which would be binding on all Cambodian parties.[83] This aspect of the settlement package indicates a substantial enhancement of the UN's authority and functions, and stands in stark contrast to the Congo and Cyprus cases. In the Cambodian context, the UN was to all intents and purposes given a temporary trusteeship role in a legally sovereign country.

The mandate: sovereignty and human rights hand in hand

In contrast to the Congo and Cyprus missions, UNTAC's formal mandate took shape outside of the UN. It was specified in the Paris Accords rather than in a UN resolution. UNTAC was authorised by the Security Council mainly to implement 'the mandate envisaged in the agreements on a comprehensive political settlement to the Cambodia conflict'.[84] Once established, the future of the mission was almost exclusively determined by the Security Council in close interaction with the Secretary-General.[85] The role of the General Assembly in defining UNTAC's mandate or shaping its actions was minimal, and at best informal.

The extensive role prescribed for UNTAC was closely connected with both state-centric and human-centric principles:

> The States participating in the Paris Conference on Cambodia . . .
> In order to maintain, preserve and defend the sovereignty, independence, territorial integrity and inviolability, neutrality and national unity of Cambodia . . .
> Recognizing that Cambodia's tragic recent history requires special measures to assure protection of human rights, and the non-return to the policies and practices of the past,
> Have agreed . . .[86]

The incorporation of state-centric and human-centric principles to UNTAC's mandate was a way of reconciling the contradictory interests of the relevant players and resulted from a decade-long process of negotiation. Several factors contributed to UNTAC's assumption of human rights and humanitarian responsibilities. Although the influence of public pressure, mobilised espe-cially by western media and civil society organisations, is not negligible, two other factors were arguably more decisive in shaping the UN's normative pref-erences. First, in the aftermath of the Vietnamese intervention three key non-western players (Moscow, Hanoi and Phnom Penh) consistently appealed to the human rights discourse in pursuit of their strategy against the Khmer Rouge whose principal backer was Beijing. Secondly, the selective insistence by western governments, in particular the United States, on human rights issues made possible that a human-centric discourse be adopted as a way of reconciling the different interests of the direct and indirect parties to the conflict.

Influence of non-governmental actors

Following the regime change in Cambodia in 1978, western public opinion became increasingly critical of the atrocities committed by the Khmer Rouge. Calls were made with increasing frequency and intensity by media organs and NGOs to punish those guilty of massacres on the one hand, and to alleviate the ensuing humanitarian situation on the other. These calls attracted the atten-tion of western governments even before the fall of the Khmer Rouge regime. A policy paper, prepared by the US Department of State, mentioned by name such organisations as Amnesty International and the International Commission of Jurists, adding that the Department would be prepared to consider what useful role it could play, should any effort be undertaken by any organisation in relation to the human rights situation in Cambodia.[87]

On 3 March 1978, when the British Under-Secretary of State addressed the UN Commission of Human Rights, he made references to gross human rights violations reported by several informed organisations and media organs, including Amnesty International, *The Times*, the *Guardian*, and *Le Monde*.[88] In France, mounting criticism from the ranks of the parliament and from intellectual circles forced the government to clarify its policy in regard to Pol Pot's atrocities. The government had to publicly account for its failure to vote at the General Assembly in favour of the new Phnom Penh regime.[89]

NGO efforts to mobilise international support in order to correct Cambodia's past injustices, to provide humanitarian assistance, and to facili-tate socio-economic development persisted before and after the UNTAC period.[90] Systematic NGO involvement in the Cambodian crisis went through three phases until 1995: 'emergency' (1979–82), 'isolation' (1982–87), and 'transition and liberalisation' (1988–95).[91]

From the early 1980s, NGOs formed several consortia in Cambodia. The Oxfam–NGO Consortium, Agricultural Relief and Rehabilitation in Kampuchea (ARRK) and Partnership for Development in Kampuchea (PADEK) are among notable examples.[92] Perhaps the most important step in NGO involvement was the establishment of the Cooperation Committee for Cambodia (CCC) in April 1990. The membership of the CCC would increase from 25 to 47 in four months. By 1992, more than 70 international NGOs were active in Cambodia.[93]

Field activities of non-governmental actors were also complemented by advocacy campaigns. In 1986, 20 leading NGOs from Australia, Europe, Japan, and the United States,[94] for instance, formed an *ad hoc* coalition to raise the profile of the Cambodian issue worldwide.[95] They were categorical in their assessment of what was needed for Cambodia's recovery: first, a guarantee that the Khmer Rouge would not return to power; secondly, peace and stability to enable the people to pursue a normal social and economic life; thirdly, material aid, both for emergency use and for reconstruction; and finally, a greater degree of independence and self-determination.[96] Although it is not easy to suggest a causal link, it is safe to assume that such advocacy, greatly amplified by widespread media coverage, exerted indirect but substantial influence on the definition of UNTAC's normative basis. All four points would be addressed by the Paris Accords as well as by the Secretary-General's implementation plan.

Human rights rhetoric by Moscow, Hanoi and Phnom Penh

All along, a key bone of contention between the positions of Phnom Penh and the CGDK was the status of the Khmer Rouge. Phnom Penh as well as Vietnam insisted on labelling past Khmer Rouge actions as 'genocide'. The Pol Pot 'clique' could not be allowed to participate in Cambodian elections. By contrast, Sihanouk considered the role of the Khmer Rouge as the main stumbling block to Vietnamese colonisation of Cambodia, and argued that Hanoi simply wanted to eliminate this main obstacle to its expansionist plans. For their part, the Vietnamese and the Phnom Penh governments adopted a clear line of normative argument, according to which there had been no Vietnamese intervention in Cambodia's domestic affairs. What had occurred in Cambodia was the legitimate overthrow of an illegitimate government which had grossly and indiscriminately violated the human rights of its people – a sequence of events described as the 'logical development of the mass uprising of the entire Kampuchean people'.[97]

In the days before the Khmer Rouge turned to Beijing for support, the Soviet Union had categorically opposed a draft resolution at the UN Commission of Human Rights, calling for a 'thorough study of the human rights situation in

Democratic Kampuchea'. It had accused the United States and its allies of presenting biased information using the pretext of protecting human rights simply to undermine the prestige of the socialist states.[98] In the aftermath of the Vietnamese invasion, the Soviet position underwent strategic change.[99] Throughout the 1980s, it would argue, first, that the change of regime in Phnom Penh had taken place as a result not of Vietnamese intervention, but of civil war, and secondly, that the Khmer Rouge regime was guilty of genocide.

Central to Moscow's, Hanoi's and Phnom Penh's propaganda campaign was the emphasis on the 'genocide' committed by the Khmer Rouge. In the Secretary-General's opinion, the use of the word 'genocide' and 'genocidal' would raise the question of applicability of the Convention against Genocide. Neither the Khmer Rouge, nor their coalition partners in the CGDK, nor China would be willing to agree on a Cambodian settlement under these terms. An alternative phrase was, therefore, embraced in reference to the Khmer Rouge legacy: 'universally condemned policies and practices of the recent past'.[100] This phrase would be essentially retained in all subsequent discussions, and would find its way into the Paris Accords as well as subsequent UN resolutions on Cambodia.[101]

Although the Soviet Union began to contradict its earlier position by attacking the Pol Pot regime on human rights grounds, it remained consistent in its most characteristic normative preference, that is, the principle of non-intervention in domestic affairs. The Soviet Union was at the time itself the target of severe criticism over its human rights record. In a Security Council debate on the Vietnamese intervention, the Soviet Union held that the Khmer Rouge were overthrown by the Cambodian people through an internal revolution. There was therefore no need for the Security Council to take action, given that the situation involved 'a purely internal question of concern only to the people of that country'.[102] By implication at least, the view of the Soviet delegation was that the Security Council would have had a responsibility to act, had it been a case of external aggression. A civil war, however, was beyond the scope of Security Council action, even if it resulted in gross human rights violations. Significantly, this highly state-centric view would change on the eve of UNTAC's authorisation. By endorsing the Framewok Document the Soviet Union accepted the argument that the adoption by the UN of 'all appropriate measures'[103] could be justified either on the grounds that Cambodia's independence, sovereignty and territorial integrity were under threat or as a response to human rights violations.[104]

Selective western insistence on human rights

Persistent use of human rights discourse by western governments, albeit selectively, was yet another factor contributing to the definition of UNTAC's

194

objectives. These governments' unwillingness, supported by ASEAN and China, to deny the Khmer Rouge international recognition was essentially a strategic choice, which inevitably prompted accusations of hypocrisy from voices influential in shaping world opinion and from the Soviet bloc. President Carter, it should be remembered, had denounced the Khmer Rouge Government as the 'worst violator' of human rights, followed by a unanimous vote by the US House of Representatives to condemn the Cambodian regime.[105] The United States nevertheless voted in favour of seating the Khmer Rouge representative in the General Assembly,[106] and throughout the following decade, Phnom Penh would continue to be subjected to economic and diplomatic isolation, thereby exacerbating Cambodia's humanitarian catastrophe.

Once the major actors were determined to 'settle', if not end, the Cambodian conflict, the rhetorical western commitment to human rights proved useful, since it converged with Soviet and Vietnamese insistence on the importance of preventing Cambodia's return to its genocidal past. China, then, posed the main obstacle to the incorporation of human-centric normative discourse into the UN's job description. As early as May 1987 Deng Xiao Ping had provided the Secretary-General with an authoritative statement of the Chinese position on Cambodia.[107] It was true, Deng held, that 'Pol Pot made many mistakes, by no means small ones', but the Vietnamese invasion was a more serious mistake – 'by a long way'. He stressed that the internal mistakes of individuals could not compare with foreign invasion; that the principle of non-intervention had worldwide application; and that the Cambodian people should be allowed to solve their own problem themselves.

With growing international criticism following the events at Tienanmen Square, however, China's leverage was weakened, which may help to explain the softening of its position. In any case, China had as early as 1987 signalled a possible way of formulating a settlement. Although Deng insisted that the Khmer Rouge could not be excluded from the peace process, he suggested that China would not support a government headed by Pol Pot, only one by Sihanouk.[108] While exclusion of the Pol Pot group from the settlement would implicitly address other actors' human rights concerns, it would at the same time keep the issue of human rights in low profile.

Eventually, after a strong and successful advocacy, the United States would manage to decorate the Draft Agreement of the Permanent Five with ample references to human rights. Accordingly, the Agreement went beyond the Framework Document in that it required Cambodia 'to support the right of all Cambodian citizens to undertake activities which would promote and protect human rights and fundamental freedoms'. In addition, whereas the Framework Document had called merely for 'necessary measures' to be taken in order to observe human rights and prevent a return to the 'policies and practices of the past',[109] the Draft Agreement replaced the vaguer phrase 'necessary measures' with the stronger phrase 'effective measures'.[110]

The rhetorical language used pointed to Washington's capacity to translate its political agenda into accepted normative discourse. Because of determined Chinese insistence on full Khmer Rouge participation in the Cambodian settlement, exclusion of the faction from the process had not been possible. A second best objective from the US perspective was to minimise the Khmer Rouge influence, which was seen as antithetical to long-term US interests in Indochina. In the aftermath of Vietnam's withdrawal from Cambodia, the Khmer Rouge were no longer seen as serving American interests. Containment of the Khmer Rouge had become necessary, because the Soviet Union might otherwise terminate its continuing support for the burgeoning peace process. Moreover, it was not easy to include in the 'peace' process a faction which had been condemned for years for its genocidal practices. The United States could no longer afford to ignore the strong anti-Khmer Rouge sentiment in western public opinion.

The Final Act announced that the Paris Accords represented essentially an elaboration of the Permanent Five's Framework Document.[111] As for the overall conceptualisation, there was practically no difference between the Draft Agreements and the Accords. The former's human rights clauses were fully contained in the latter. The Agreement on Political Settlement recognised 'that Cambodia's tragic recent history requires special measures to assure protection of human rights, and the non-return to the policies and practices of the past'. In addition, Part III of the same instrument was specifically devoted to human rights.

The Permanent Five joint statement of 16 January 1990 had contemplated that a Supreme National Council might be the repository of Cambodian sovereignty during the transition process.[112] Provision 3 stated that the goal was self-determination for the Cambodian people through free, fair and democratic elections, with provisions 7 and 12 specifying to some extent the meaning of 'free and fair': the transition process should not be dominated by any of the Cambodian factions, and elections had to be conducted in a neutral political environment in which no party would be advantaged. Provision 14 further indicated that all Cambodians should enjoy the 'same rights, freedoms, and opportunities' to participate in the elections process.[113] The Charter principle of self-determination was now reintroduced in relative isolation from such state-centric concepts as 'territorial integrity' and 'political independence'. In the Cambodian context, the principle was interpreted more in terms of human-centric values, with the emphasis on political rights and civil liberties. In other words, self-determination was perceived more in relation to its 'internal' dimension, implying a people's right to freely determine their own political future.

196

UNTAC deployed

UN deployment in Cambodia was actually formalised prior to the signing of the Paris Accords. Upon the request of the SNC on 26 August 1991,[114] the deployment of a UN Advance Mission in Cambodia (UNAMIC) was authorised by the Security Council.[115] Its mandate had a powerful inter-state dimension formulated as 'cessation of foreign military assistance', that is, Vietnamese aid. UNAMIC was to assist in maintaining the cease-fire and to liaise with the SNC on the implementation of the Paris Accords.[116] In January 1992 UNAMIC's mandate was expanded to include an extensive mine clearance programme as well as road and bridge repairs.[117] The following month came the Secretary-General's detailed operational plan for the actual peacekeeping mission envisaged for Cambodia (UNTAC),[118] and the Security Council's authorisation of it.[119] UNTAC would soon absorb UNAMIC.

The Secretary-General's operational plan led to an elaborate mission structure of seven interlinked components:[120] military, civil administration,[121] electoral, police, human rights,[122] repatriation, and rehabilitation.[123] The operation was designed to proceed in four stages over two years. The 'Preparatory Phase' would be followed by a 'Cantonment and Demobilisation Phase', which, upon successful completion, would in turn give way to the 'Electoral Phase', and eventually the 'Post-Electoral Phase', bringing UNTAC's mandate to an end.

Perhaps the first difficulty UNTAC faced related to repatriation. The UN addressed this issue not only through UNTAC, but also through its expert organ, the UNHCR. There were more than 360,000 Cambodian refugees living along the Thai border. The majority of them preferred to stay in north-west Cambodia – reportedly because of their fear of renewed fighting – from where they could escape to Thailand if need arose.[124] Faced by this unwillingness to move, the UNHCR had to shift its repatriation policy, and on 20 May 1992 presented more attractive options to refugees, including land, building, cash, employment and family reunification possibilities.[125] Progress towards maintenance of peace and security required active handling of the socio-economic situation on the ground.

According to the Paris Accords, the four parties had to pursue a phased and balanced process of demobilisation of their military forces. This process was to be completed before the end of voter registration. Phase Two was scheduled to begin on 13 June, but the Khmer Rouge proved to be a major obstacle. It not only committed cease-fire violations, but also refused entry to UNTAC troops in the areas under its control.[126] Furthermore, it failed to provide information about its troops, equipment and mine fields – all of this on the grounds that Vietnamese forces were still operating in Cambodia. Unless they were totally withdrawn and their non-return ensured, the Khmer Rouge would not demobilise, disarm or leave aside security considerations. The other three parties expressed their readiness to begin with the Cantonment Phase. The Secretary-General recommended that as of 13 June 1992 UNTAC should proceed with the second phase regardless of the level of Khmer Rouge non-cooperation.[127] Not to do so, he argued, would seriously jeopardise the missions' functions, especially the organisation of elections.[128] This view was endorsed by the Security Council on 12 June 1992.[129]

Meanwhile, both Khmer Rouge non-cooperation and diplomatic attempts to overcome that non-cooperation continued. On 22 June 1992, an international conference was held in Tokyo, at which 33 countries pledged nearly US$900 million for Cambodia's recovery and an International Committee on the Reconstruction of Cambodia was created.[130] The conference also attempted to create an atmosphere more conducive to negotiation between the Cambodian parties. Socio-economic conditions were now explicitly underlined as a precondition of peace and security. All factions, except for the Khmer Rouge who maintained that the SNC was not able to exercise its powers, accepted the Tokyo proposals. Phnom Penh, the Khmer Rouge argued, was largely in control of the administrative structure. Ironically, it was not so much the UN's presence in Cambodia that the Khmer Rouge were now criticising as the *lack* of active involvement on the UN's part.

International determination to settle the internal conflict

The decision to proceed with Phase Two soon necessitated a more fundamental decision on whether or not the operation should be suspended altogether until all four factions complied with the Paris Accords.[131] The decision became increasingly unavoidable, as the lack of Khmer Rouge cooperation was causing comparable and growing hesitation on the part of the other factions. According to the UN plan, Phase Two had to be completed by 11 July 1992, but one day before the envisaged deadline only 13,500 out of a total of 200,000 Cambodian troops had been cantoned.[132]

September 1992 saw intensive diplomatic efforts to overcome the difficulties. Australia presented a paper underlining how the international community should now proceed.[133] In a statement the Security Council strongly reaffirmed its commitment to the principles of the Paris Accords.[134] On 30 September 1992, the KPNLF specified a set of conditions, which, once met, would remove the basis of any further Khmer Rouge non-cooperation. These moves culminated in SC Resolution 783 of 13 October 1992, which declared that the Cambodian election process would proceed as planned. UNTAC's much-contested Electoral Law had already been adopted on 5 August.[135] Despite the opposition of internal parties, the international actors were of the view that the rules of election should be determined by the UN, thereby re-confirming its authority.

In October and November, a series of unsuccessful diplomatic efforts were made by Thailand and Japan on the one hand,[136] and France and Indonesia on the other.[137] In his report of 15 November 1992, the Secretary-General informed the Security Council that Khmer Rouge cooperation had still not been ensured. By that time sporadic fighting was taking place between the Khmer Rouge and Phnom Penh forces, with the former launching assaults on ethnic Vietnamese, and even UNTAC personnel coming under attack.[138] On 30 November 1992, the Security Council resolved that elections for a constituent assembly would be held no later than May 1993. It insisted that the Khmer Rouge were not being 'excluded' from the election process – a long-standing Chinese concern. It was entirely up to the Khmer Rouge to decide whether or not they would participate. The rules of the game were already set and could not be changed. In line with this tougher stance, the Security Council was now intent on tightening the economic sanctions imposed on the Khmer Rouge.[139]

The Khmer Rouge problem aside, practically all the major parties 'engaged in a certain degree of misleading propaganda and political coercion during the registration/campaign period'.[140] In December 1992, the tension in the country increased, as cease-fire violations became more frequent. Apart from inter-factional clashes, Khmer Rouge forces detained UNTAC personnel on more than one occasion. The Khmer Rouge held that such incidents were provoked by UNTAC. In a letter to the Secretary-General, they argued that in all such instances, it was UNTAC personnel that had entered the zones under Khmer Rouge control without first informing them.[141] This view had a striking resemblance to Katanga's approach during the Congo crisis. However, unlike Hammarskjöld's strict adherence to the norm which required the parties' continuous consent, UNTAC was implementing a mandate that was based on a single all-encompassing consent.

By February 1993, it was Phnom Penh's turn to place obstacles in the path of UNTAC. Hun Sen's decision to initiate a military offensive against Khmer Rouge forces[142] caused growing dissatisfaction on the part of all parties, though their reasons differed.[143] On 4 January 1993, Sihanouk informed Akashi that the violent campaign against his party obliged him to cease all further cooperation with UNTAC. Hun Sen, for his part, demanded Chapter VII enforcement against the Khmer Rouge. While the Secretary-General was eventually able to appease both parties, they remained highly sceptical of the UN's role.

The electoral campaign in Cambodia began on 7 April 1993. The Khmer Rouge, having announced that it would not participate in the election, continued to charge the Vietnamese with aggression. The Phnom Penh faction used the state administration under its control to gain an advantage over FUNCINPEC and other parties. Boutros-Ghali points out that 'strong intervention by UNTAC' had been necessary to secure the release by the Phnom Penh faction of FUNCINPEC's broadcasting equipment.[144] While dealing with these difficult challenges to its authority, UNTAC, and especially Radio UNTAC, remained at the forefront throughout the campaign process.

Between April and mid-May 1993, violence intensified, with members of all factions, as well as several UNTAC personnel, being injured or killed.[145] Most of the victims, however, were of Vietnamese descent. By the end of April 1993, more than 21,000 ethnic Vietnamese had become refugees or displaced persons, including second- and third-generation Cambodian residents. Paradoxically, as of 30 March 1993, with the closure of the last refugee camp at the Thai border, UNTAC had successfully completed its original repatriation programme,[146] only to see a different refugee problem emerge, which it was either unable or unwilling to address. In Boutros-Ghali's words, 'the issue of the status of ethnic Vietnamese resident in Cambodia had not been provided for in the Paris Accords, and some within UNTAC's leadership were inclined to think of the situation as *an internal security* issue for Cambodian authorities to resolve.'[147] In other words despite the UN's clear involvement in an internal conflict in Cambodia, there were limitations or reservations as to the extent of such involvement. The overarching concern over the maintenance of *international* peace and security resurfaced now and again.

For election purposes, Cambodia was divided by UNTAC into three types of security zone: low-, medium- and high-risk zones. In Boutros-Ghali's words, 'the Cambodian parties had primary responsibility for maintaining the security of the zones they controlled'.[148] This was the limit of the UN's 'protectorate', normatively expected yet practically unsustainable. UNTAC even agreed to the request that some of the weapons cantoned by UNTAC be returned to the relevant factions. These, then, were the circumstances in which elections would be conducted.

The elections took place between 23 and 28 May 1993. Some 90 per cent of the nearly 4.2 million registered voters cast their votes. Khmer Rouge's boycott and threats proved highly unsuccessful. On 29 May 1993, the Secretary-General endorsed his Special Representative's assessment that the conduct of the elections had been free and fair.[149] The final vote tally was released on 10 June 1993. FUNCINPEC won 45.5 per cent of the votes and became the first party. Thereupon Phnom Penh raised accusations of irregularities and fraud in the elections, in which it had obtained 38 per cent of the votes.[150] The BLDP had come in third with less than 4 per cent of all votes.

On 16 June Sihanouk established an Interim Joint Administration, with

Prince Ranarriddh and Hun Sen as co-chairmen of the Council of Ministers. The Security Council restated that UNTAC's mandate would end upon the creation of a new Cambodian Government.[151] On 24 September UNTAC's mandate formally ended, signifying 'Cambodia's democratic transition to Neo-authoritarianism'.[152]

Concluding observations

Quite apart from the triangular geostrategic rivalry between China, the Soviet Union and the United States, regional tensions between Vietnam, China and ASEAN as well as the ideological intra-Khmer and ethnic Khmer–Vietnamese frictions had created within Cambodia a complex blend of mistrust and animosity. The normative basis of the UN's response to the Cambodia conflict emerged from a painfully slow process of informal bilateral and formal multi-lateral negotiations over more than a decade, in which the predominant concern was to accommodate the strategic interests of the actors involved.

The UN was able to assert its authority *vis-à-vis* Cambodia only when the key antagonists, though still deeply suspicious of each other, were finally reconciled, in the wake of a structural change in world politics, to putting an end to a protracted conflict that had consumed a great deal of resources, time and effort with little corresponding benefit. The end of the Cold War was presumably an important catalyst for this sequence of events. The UN suggested itself as a well placed mechanism through which these competing interests could be accommodated and it was given considerable leeway to exercise a relatively independent authority – in ways that might well set an irreversible precedent – in a conflict where diverse but powerful local, regional and global antagonisms had hitherto proved mutually reinforcing. This, of course, had a price tag attached to it. The principle of non-intervention, understood as absolute 'respect' for external state sovereignty, was effectively superseded.

As with the other cases we have examined, maintenance of international peace and security, with particular reference to regional stability, remained the primary international concern both before and during the Cambodia operation. The value attached to sovereignty manifested itself largely in the preoccupation with the promotion of its internal aspect which, in a sense, had to go hand in hand with internal self-determination as well as with protection and promotion of human rights in general. These principles were incorpo-rated into the composite notion of 'good governance'. The international community was also concerned with issues of socio-economic development, to a much higher degree than in any of the previous cases under considera-tion. Several UN and non-UN development projects were set in motion in tandem with the peacekeeping mission. Indeed, the socio-economic development objective was attached directly to the peacekeeping mandate under the rubric of 'reconstruction'.

A crucial factor in the UN's emphasis on human rights was the persistent moral pressure exerted by civil society organisations after the Khmer Rouge atrocities became known in the mid- to late 1970s. Arguably just as important was the significant overlap between the self-serving application of human rights discourse by western governments and three key non-western players, Moscow, Hanoi and Phnom Penh, who defended their position, partly with western 'audiences' in mind, as the legitimate and morally appropriate response to Khmer Rouge atrocities. On the other hand, the increasing NGO involvement in relief and reconstruction efforts throughout the 1980s brought along an emphasis on Cambodia's development.

Compared with the previous cases we have surveyed, Cambodia conveys a sense of 'comprehensiveness' in several respects. When authorised it became the largest UN mission ever deployed. It assumed multiple and complex tasks, involving extensive participation in the day-to-day running of the country. The evolution of the UNTAC concept was itself based on comprehensiveness, in the sense that the Jakarta Informal Meetings and the Paris process involved a great many interested actors and active participants. But what exactly does such comprehensiveness signify for the UN's role, beyond changing objectives and enhanced authority? Is it indicative of a new normative trend? If so, what is the underlying logic of this trend? We will now reflect on these questions.

NOTES

1 The estimated population of Cambodia in 1990 was 8,570,000: see IMF, *International Financial Statistics on CD-ROM* (Washington DC: series code 6870). The ratio of UNTAC's largest authorised strength to the local population was 25/10,000.

2 D. Sagar, 'Historical survey', in M. Wright (ed.), *Cambodia: A Matter of Survival* (Essex: Longman, 1989), p. 11.

3 Sihanouk, arguably the most colourful personality in post-War Cambodian politics, served Cambodia in different capacities: King, Prime Minister, Chief of State, and again King. Until 1963, Sihanouk adopted a policy of neutralism against the two blocs. Then, until 1967, he adopted a pro-Chinese and North Vietnamese line. At the height of the Chinese Cultural Revolution, he went back to neutrality. From the late 1970s, he became increasingly pro-Western: see Morris, *Why Vietnam Invaded Cambodia*, p. 46.

4 See Sagar, 'Historical survey', p. 23.

5 After he was removed from power, first, by the pro-American *coup*, and then by the Khmer Rouge, Sihanouk maintained good relations with China (and North Korea), which, although largely symbolic, would prove crucial for the international efforts towards a Cambodian settlement in the 1990s: see H. C. Mehta and J. B. Mehta, *Hun Sen: Strongman of Cambodia* (Singapore: Graham Brash, 1999), pp. 162–3.

6 Among the victims were Cambodia's Buddhist monks and ethnic minorities such as the Vietnamese, Thai and Cham Muslims: see Mehta and Mehta, *Hun Sen*, p. 258.

7 While up to 20 per cent of this number is estimated to have resulted from outright executions, the rest is attributed to the conditions created by the Khmer Rouge regime, including starvation and deportation: see J. F. Metzl, *Western Responses to Human Rights Abuses in Cambodia, 1975–1980* (Houndmills: Macmillan, 1996), p. xviii.

8 Former Thai Prime Minister Kraivichien reportedly accused Cambodia of intruding into his country 400 times between January and August 1977: see S. Peou, *Conflict Naturalization in the Cambodia War: From Battlefield to Ballot-box* (New York: Oxford University Press, 1997), p. 23.

9 See D. Roberts, 'More honoured in the breech: consent and impartiality in the Cambodian peacekeeping operation', *International Peacekeeping*, 4:1 (Spring 1997), 8.

10 Mehta and Mehta, *Hun Sen*, p. 258.

11 According to US estimates, the number of Vietnamese troops deployed in Cambodia reached 224,000 in 1979. By 1988, the number was reduced to about 100,000: see K. Berry, *Cambodia – From Red to Blue: Australia's Initiative for Peace* (Canberra: Allen & Unwin, 1997), p. 10.

12 Morris, *Why Vietnam Invaded Cambodia*, p. 16.

13 Morris, *Why Vietnam Invaded Cambodia*, pp. 161–6.

14 Morris, *Why Vietnam Invaded Cambodia*, pp. 170–96.

15 Morris, *Why Vietnam Invaded Cambodia*, pp. 209–15.

16 In April 1989, the regime would be renamed the State of Cambodia – SOC. This new regime would last *de jure* until the formation of the Supreme National Council in 1990, and *de facto* until after the Cambodian elections of May 1993.

17 Despite their uneasy relationship with Thailand, the Khmer Rouge had established diplomatic relations with all ASEAN members but Indonesia. Upon increasing tension with Vietnam, the Khmer Rouge further 'courted' ASEAN. By August 1978, the Khmer Rouge ensured diplomatic relations with Indonesia at the ambassadorial level: see Morris, *Why Vietnam Invaded Cambodia*, pp. 83–4.

18 Ratner, *The New Peacekeeping*, p. 142.

19 M. Alagappa, 'Regionalism and the quest for security: ASEAN and the Cambodian conflict', *Australian Journal of International Affairs*, 47:2 (October 1993), 199; and Mehta and Mehta, *Hun Sen*, p. 78.

20 See D. Chandler, 'Three visions of politics in Cambodia', in M. W. Doyle, I. Johnstone and R. C. Orr (eds), *Keeping the Peace: Multidimensional UN Operations in Cambodia and El Salvador* (Cambridge: Cambridge University Press, 1997), p. 49.

21 S. Lithgow, 'Cambodia', in K. Clements and R. Ward (eds), *Building International Community: Cooperating for Peace Case Studies* (St. Leonards: Allen & Unwin, 1994), p. 29.

22 See Alagappa, 'Regionalism and the quest for security', p. 196.

23 For an excellent account of the initial formation of western public opinion on the issue, see Metzl, *Western Responses*, especially pp. 46–65.

24 Ratner, *The New Peacekeeping*, p. 141.

25 J. P. de Cuéllar, *Pilgrimage for Peace: A Secretary-General's Memoir* (Basingstoke: Macmillan, 1997), p. 448.

26 See N. Sihanouk, *War and Hope: The Case for Cambodia* (London: Sidgwick & Jackson, 1980), p. 137.

27 Meanwhile, in March 1984, Australia and Vietnam worked out an agreement of principle consisting of five points: Vietnam's withdrawal from Cambodia; elimination of the Pol Pot group and creation of a safety zone along the Thai–Cambodian border; Cambodia's self-determination by elections; guarantee of security for the Chinese–Vietnamese, Chinese–Laotian and Thai–Laotian borders; and international

supervision of these provisions. ASEAN responded by arguing that the Cambodian conflict was between Vietnam and Cambodia, not ASEAN. Rafeeuddin Ahmed, the Special Representative of the Secretary-General, pointed out to Vietnam that ASEAN could not be expected to discuss the Chinese–Vietnamese and Chinese–Laotian borders with Vietnam; see de Cuéllar, *Pilgrimage for Peace*, pp. 450–1.

28 For a very comprehensive review, see Berry, *Cambodia*.

29 Mehta and Mehta, *Hun Sen*, p. 102.

30 Alagappa, 'Regionalism and the quest for security', p. 200.

31 Peou, *Conflict Naturalization in the Cambodia War*, p. 33.

32 And to a lesser, though by no means unimportant, extent the United States.

33 The UN Commission of Human Rights, for instance, had been discussing the matter since the late 1970s, albeit with a remarkable ineffectiveness.

34 On 22 October 1988, Khieu Samphan, the Khmer Rouge spokesman, indicated his support for the idea.

35 Provision 11 in the Khmer Rouge peace proposal of 22 November 1988.

36 See de Cuéllar, *Pilgrimage for Peace*, p. 455.

37 The statement issued at the end of the meeting emphasised both the 'withdrawal of Vietnamese forces within the context of an overall solution' and the 'prevention of the recurrence of genocidal policies and practices of the Pol Pot regime': see Jakarta Informal Meeting 2 'Consensus Statement', issued on 21 February by Indonesian Foreign Minister Ali Alatas, reproduced in McMillen (ed.), *Conflict Resolution in Kampuchea*, pp. 146–51.

38 Berry, *Cambodia*, pp. 12–13.

39 ASEAN foreign ministers, in contrast, called for a comprehensive settlement and effective UN supervision: see 'ASEAN Foreign Ministers' Call for a Comprehensive Political Settlement of the Kampuchean Problem' of 3 July 1989, available online at www.asean.org/general/ads1989/kampuchean_89.htm (13 April 2001).

40 According to the wording of the final document produced at the conclusion of the Second Paris Conference on Cambodia (The Final Act of the Paris Conference of 23 October 1991; see A/46/608-S/23177 of 30 October 1991), there was only one Paris Conference on Cambodia, and that conference was held in two sessions, the first from 30 July to 30 August 1989, and the second from 21 to 23 October 1991. In contrast to this official presentation of the events, here we will refer to two separate Paris Conferences on Cambodia just to make it clear that originally the conference was not contemplated in two sessions, and the second Conference may not have taken place at all, had circumstances not changed.

41 A. Acharya *et al.* (eds), *Cambodia – The 1989 Paris Peace Conference: Background Analysis and Documents* (Toronto: Centre for International and Strategic Studies, York University, 1991), pp. 125, 129 cited in M. Brown and J. J. Zasloff, *Cambodia Confounds the Peacemakers, 1979–1998* (Ithaca: Cornell University Press, 1998), p. 54.

42 De Cuéllar, *Pilgrimage for Peace*, p. 461.

43 Brown and Zasloff, *Cambodia Confounds the Peacemakers*, p. 56.

44 See de Cuéllar, *Pilgrimage for Peace*, pp. 460–2.

45 However, Prince Sihanouk and China would maintain in due course that more than 100,000 Vietnamese soldiers remained under disguise in Cambodia: see Brown and Zasloff, *Cambodia Confounds the Peacemakers*, p. 58.

46 GA Resolution 44/22 of 16 November 1989.

47 Evans' plan had been influenced by Stephen Solarz, the Chairman of the US House of Representatives Subcommittee on Southeast Asia, who had developed the idea of a UN 'interim administration': see G. Evans, 'Achieving Peace in Cambodia'.

48 The so-called (from the colour of its binding) 'Red Book' consisted of one overview paper, six working papers, and three supplementary papers: see *Cambodia: An Australian Peace Proposal* (Canberra: Department of Foreign Affairs and Trade, Commonwealth of Australia, Working Papers for the Informal Meeting on Cambodia, Jakarta, 26–28 February 1990).

49 Overview Paper, para. 2.

50 Overview Paper, para. 4.

51 Working Paper 1, para. 23; see also Working Paper 2, paras 27, 40.

52 The 'Sources of Authority for Government Structure' were summarised in 5 steps; see Working Paper 1, para. 10.

53 On 15 January and 16 March 1979, for instance, the Soviet Union had vetoed two draft resolutions condemning the Vietnamese intervention.

54 Brown and Zasloff, *Cambodia Confounds the Peacemakers*, p. 61.

55 Evans cited in F. Frost, *The Peace Process in Cambodia: Issues and Prospects* (Queensland: Centre for the Study of Australia–Asia Relations, Australia–Asia Papers No. 69, October 1993), pp. 5, 51.

56 See Working Paper 2, paras 27–8.

57 British Foreign Secretary Hurd stated that his Government welcomed the Australian proposal. The Permanent Five had agreed on the principles which should underpin a settlement. These included 'an enhanced role for the United Nations, the modalities of a peace-keeping effort in Cambodia, and the administrative structure during the interim period of United Nations involvement': see UK House of Commons, Hansard Debates, 26 March 1990, cols 29–30.

58 See Peou, *Conflict Naturalization in the Cambodia War*, pp. 41–2.

59 S/21087 dated 18 January 1990.

60 See S/21689 of 31 August 1990. By Resolution 668 of 20 September 1990, the Security Council endorsed the Framework Agreement, encouraged the continuing efforts of the Permanent Five, and conferred upon the SNC formal legitimacy.

61 The most important among these were the meetings of 11–12 February, 12–13 March, 25–26 May and 16–17 July 1990.

62 Yet it continued to insist on giving the SNC 'a status that would at least imply the dismantling of the Phnom Penh regime': de Cuéllar, *Pilgrimage for Peace*, p. 466.

63 S/21087, para. 4.

64 S/21087, para. 6.

65 S/21087, para. 11.

66 S/21087, para. 8.

67 S/21087, para. 10.

68 S/21087, para. 9.

69 De Cuéllar, *Pilgrimage for Peace*, p. 465.

70 De Cuéllar, *Pilgrimage for Peace*, pp. 464–5.

71 De Cuéllar, *Pilgrimage for Peace*, p. 470.

72 For the *communiqué*, see S/21985 of 6 December 1990.

73 Soon after, ASEAN would 'fully support an enhanced role for the United Nations in Cambodia' and call for a 'Supreme National Council representing all shades of political opinion that could administer Cambodia in the interim period through existing administrative structures in conjunction with the United Nations': see *Joint Statement of the ASEAN Foreign Ministers on the Cambodian Problem* of 23 July 1990, available online at www.aseansec.org/general/ads1990/afm_cam90.htm (13 April 2001).

74 According to the adopted formula, 6 members were appointed from the Phnom Penh Government, and 2 members each from FUNCINPEC, the KPNLF and the PDK.

75 Important meetings included those of 21–22 December 1990 (Paris), 24–26 June 1991 (Pattaya), 16–17 July 1991 (Beijing) and 26–29 August 1991 (Pattaya).

76 During the SNC meeting of 24–26 June 1991, all parties agreed that the UN should supervise the cease-fire. However, Phnom Penh still refused a strong UN military presence in Cambodia: see Peou, *Conflict Naturalization in the Cambodia War*, pp. 44–5.

77 This time Yugoslavia had replaced Zimbabwe in its capacity as the chairman of the NAM.

78 The full titles are, respectively, the Final Act of the Paris Conference on Cambodia; the Agreement on a Comprehensive Political Settlement of the Cambodian Conflict; the Agreement Concerning the Sovereignty, Independence, Territorial Integrity and Inviolability, Neutrality, and National Unity of Cambodia; and the Declaration on the Rehabilitation and Reconstruction of Cambodia.

79 Actually this is precisely what would happen at different stages of the UNTAC operation.

80 Agreement on Political Settlement, para. 28.2.

81 Agreement on Political Settlement, para. 6.

82 In his 'Cambodia: our experience with the United Nations', *Pacifica Review*, 7:2 (Oct/Nov. 1995), 62.

83 Annex 1 to the Agreement on Political Settlement, Section B, para. 1.

84 SC Resolution 745 of 28 February 1992; operative para. 1.

85 After the signature of the Paris Accords, as Ratner points out, most states held that Cambodia was the UN's problem, that is the Secretary-General's problem: see Ratner, *The New Peacekeeping*, p. 161.

86 Agreement on Political Settlement, preambular paras 1 and 10.

87 Telegram of the Secretary of State to all East Asian and Pacific Diplomatic Posts (June 1976) cited in Metzl, *Western Responses*, p. 62 n. 154.

88 Metzl, *Western Responses*, p. 95.

89 Metzl, *Western Responses*, p. 179.

90 For an overview of World Vision's activities from 1970 to 1996, see J. Sarma *et al.*, 'World Vision in conflict and peace: a perspective from Cambodia', *Pacifica Review*, 8:2 (Nov/Dec. 1996), 69–79.

91 For an overview, see J. Bennett *et al.*, *Meeting the Needs: NGO Coordination in Practice* (London: Earthscan Publications, 1995), pp. 168–73.

92 See Bennett *et al.*, *Meeting the Needs*, pp. 175–6.

93 Bennett *et al.*, *Meeting the Needs*, pp. 177–9.

94 These included such well known organisations as Community Aid Abroad, Oxfam, and the Quakers.

95 E. Mysliwiec, *Punishing the Poor: The International Isolation of Kampuchea* (Oxford: Oxfam, 1988), p. ix.

96 Mysliwiec, *Punishing the Poor*, p. 52.

97 S/PV.2108 of 11 January 1979, p. 13.

98 E/CN.4SR.1469 and E/CN.4/SR.1473 cited in Metzl, *Western Responses*, p. 96 n. 197.

99 The change in the attitude of the socialist bloc is noted by Sihanouk in his *War and Hope*, p. 104.

100 De Cuéllar, *Pilgrimage for Peace*, pp. 452–4.

101 See GA Resolution 44/22 of 16 November 1989 and SC Resolution 745 of 28 February 1992.

102 S/PV.2108 of 11 January 1979, p. 2.

103 A phrase that alludes to enforcement measures under Chapter VII.

104 S/21689 of 31 August 1990, para. 36.

105 *Congressional Record of the United States*, 25 April 1978, p. 11337 cited in Metzl, *Western Responses*, p. 113 n. 120.

106 It was a decade later, during the Bush administration, that the United States finally withdrew recognition from the CGDK, though without extending recognition to the Phnom Penh Government: see Alagappa, 'Regionalism and the quest for security', pp. 201–2.

107 De Cuéllar, *Pilgrimage for Peace*, pp. 454–5.

108 De Cuéllar, *Pilgrimage for Peace*, p. 454.

109 *Framework Document*, Section 4, para. 24.

110 A/46/61-S/22059 dated 11 January 1991; a point noted in Peou, *Conflict Naturalization in the Cambodia War*, pp. 150–1.

111 Para. 10.

112 S/21087 of 18 January 1990.

113 Although no direct relationship was established between the envisaged UN mission and the principles by which a settlement should be reached, it is possible to argue that the Permanent Five document did embody an understanding of UN impartiality, where the contents were in need of further elaboration. What would 'domination' by any one party entail? What were the rights, freedoms and opportunities that all parties were supposed to enjoy under a guiding principle of 'sameness'?

114 See A/46/494-S/23066 of 24 September 1991.

115 SC Resolution 717 of 16 October 1991.

116 UNAMIC's deployment began on 9 November 1991; see Report of the Secretary-General on UNAMIC, S/23218 of 14 November 1991.

117 SC Resolution 728 of 8 January 1992.

118 S/23613 of 19 February 1992.

119 SC Resolution 745 of 28 February 1992.

120 The number of international and Cambodian personnel required to accomplish the tasks would be 21,000 and 56,000 respectively: see Report of the Secretary-General, S/23613 of 19 February 1992.

121 The civil administration component had the authority to issue 'binding directives': see M. W. Doyle, 'Authority and elections in Cambodia', in Doyle, Johnstone and Orr (eds), *Keeping the Peace*, p. 137.

122 Doyle observes that, 'Never before had a UN peacekeeping operation assumed so intrusive and authoritative a mandate to implement universal human rights.' See Doyle, 'Authority and elections in Cambodia', p. 146.

123 Several studies, which concentrate usually on the operational aspects of UNTAC, find it useful to offer separate reviews for each of these components. Examples include Brown and Zasloff, *Cambodia Confounds the Peacemakers*, pp. 95–129 and Ratner, *The New Peacekeeping*, pp. 169–85. For our purposes there is no need to provide such an assessment.

124 By the end of April 1992, not more than 6,000 persons had returned to Cambodia. In the subsequent three months, the number of returning refugees reached 130,000.

125 See United Nations, *The United Nations and Cambodia, 1991–1995* (New York: UNDPI, 1995), pp. 19–20.

126 The Secretary-General reported that on one occasion even his Special Representative and the Force Commander had been denied entry: see United Nations, *The United Nations and Cambodia*, p. 17.

127 See S/24090 of 12 June 1992.

128 One consideration was that the elections should be held before Cambodia's rainy season.

129 See S/24091 of 12 June 1992.
130 The participants were the Permanent Five, all nine members of today's ASEAN, all but two members of today's EU (Greece and Luxembourg were absent), Australia, Canada, India, Japan, New Zealand, Norway, South Korea, Switzerland, the European Community (in its collective capacity) and the Special Representative of the Secretary-General. The biggest donors would be Japan with US$200 million and the United States with US$135 million.
131 Meanwhile, by 15 July the civil administration component had established offices in all 21 provinces. By September 1992, UNTAC was almost fully established throughout Cambodia. In the area of finance, for instance, as of early September 1992, financial controllers were present in each of the ministries, in the National Bank of Cambodia, and in Phnom Penh's provincial administrations: see United Nations, *The United Nations and Cambodia*, p. 22.
132 United Nations, *The United Nations and Cambodia*, p. 24; see also S/PV.3099 of 21 July 1992, p. 18.
133 Australian paper entitled 'Cambodia: next steps' (16 September 1992).
134 S/24587 dated 25 September 1992.
135 The first electoral law was drafted in April 1992. The CGDK partners, with an anti-Vietnamese Khmer sentiment, strongly opposed this draft, claiming that it gave 'Vietnamese' suffrage. However, the rewritten draft too did not meet these factions' notion that political participation should be based on ethnic criteria: see Roberts, 'More honoured in the breech', p. 9.
136 The Security Council, in its Resolution 783, had requested these two countries to continue their unrelenting diplomatic efforts.
137 The Secretary-General requested the Co-Chairmen of the Paris Conference to undertake consultations.
138 Boutros-Ghali's depiction of the political climate in November 1992 is noteworthy: see United Nations, *The United Nations and Cambodia*, p. 26, para. 62.
139 See United Nations, *The United Nations and Cambodia*, p. 27, para. 65.
140 United Nations, *The United Nations and Cambodia*, p. 29, para. 70. For a concise analysis, see K. Frieson, 'The politics of getting the vote in Cambodia', in S. Heder and J. Ledgerwood (eds), *Propaganda, Politics, and Violence in Cambodia: Democratic Transition under United Nations Peace-keeping* (New York: M. E. Sharpe, 1996), pp. 183–207. Between 5 October 1992 and 31 January 1993, during the period of voter registration, about 4.6 million Cambodians registered to vote. This figure represented nearly all of the eligible voters outside of Khmer Rouge-controlled areas. UNTAC was largely denied access to the areas under Khmer Rouge control. However, according to estimates, those areas did not contain more than 5 per cent of the total Cambodian population anyway: see United Nations, *The United Nations and Cambodia*, p. 29, paras 69–70.
141 Letter dated 20 December 1992 from Khieu Samphan to the Secretary-General: see United Nations, *The United Nations and Cambodia*, pp. 246–8.
142 See United Nations, *The United Nations and Cambodia*, p. 34, para. 80. In fact, two main streams of violence were detectable: the first by Phnom Penh against FUNCINPEC, the second by the Khmer Rouge against the ethnic Vietnamese: see M. Plunkett, 'The establishment of the rule of law in post-conflict peacekeeping', in Smith (ed.), *International Peacekeeping*, p. 71.
143 See United Nations, *The United Nations and Cambodia*, pp. 35–6 (para. 87), and 249–51.
144 United Nations, *The United Nations and Cambodia*, p. 39, para. 93.
145 At the end of the mission, total fatalities of UNTAC were 78: see UN webpage at www.un.org/Depts/DPKO/Missions/untac.htm (15 September 1997).

146 All nine refugee camps at the Thai border were finally closed.

147 United Nations, *The United Nations and Cambodia*, p. 42, para. 99; emphasis added.

148 United Nations, *The United Nations and Cambodia*, p. 43, para. 104.

149 S/25879 dated 2 June 1993.

150 S/25879 dated 2 June 1993. Phnom Penh's allegations were practically ignored by UNTAC: see the Report of the Secretary-General, S/25913 of 10 June 1993, especially paras 9–12.

151 SC Resolution 860 of 27 August 1993.

152 S. Heder cited in W. Shawcross, *Deliver Us from Evil: Warlords & Peacekeepers in a World of Endless Conflict* (London: Bloomsbury, 2000), p. 184.

9

Reflections on international normative change

HE NORMATIVE CONNECTION between the UN and intra-state conflicts is
not static. It is a matter of continuous redefinition and reinterpretation
as can be usefully observed in the context of intra-state peacekeeping
environments. One of our contentions in this study is that, in the space of just
three decades – that is, from the early 1960s to the early 1990s – the normative basis of UN peacekeeping in intra-state conflicts has evolved unevenly but
appreciably in terms of both objectives and authority, with the shift in the
pattern of prescribed functions emerging as one important indicator of this
change.

Objectives were conceptualised here with reference to four key principles
enshrined in the UN Charter, namely peace and security, state sovereignty,
human rights and socio-economic development. Authority, on the other
hand, was conceptualised in a four-dimensional way, to encompass the depth
and breadth of peacekeeping functions, the requirement of consent, the UN's
normative competence to make judgements, and the implementation of decisions. Within this conceptual framework, we developed an analysis of the
collective expectations of the international community, focusing specifically
on the objectives and authority of the UN in relation to intra-state peacekeeping environments in the two specified time periods.

As a first step, we established that both international normative prescriptions and the UN as actor had evolved under the influence of structural
changes in world politics. The early 1960s and the early 1990s were critical
thresholds in the post-1945 period, each with its own particular power configuration and corresponding ideational framework. Against this backdrop, we
analysed how the general political and normative complexion of the post-
1945 world order had evolved in the context of intra-state peacekeeping.

The focus, especially in our detailed case studies, was on three interrelated
considerations, the elaboration of which would pave the way for a comprehensive examination of normative change. For each specified time period, we

set out to discern the differences separating the positions of various actors, and their impact on the normative basis of the UN's involvement in intra-state conflicts. We then sought to identify the relationship between the most influential normative positions and the interests that they reflected and often, but not always, reinforced. In other words, we attempted to characterise the nexus between interests and normative preferences. Finally, we tried to explore how major normative differences were reconciled, resolved, or somehow synthesised. In other words we subjected to careful scrutiny the crystallisation of the dominant normative prescriptions surrounding the UN's role in peacekeeping environments. Building on these three considerations, we examined how the normative basis of intra-state peacekeeping had changed from the early 1960s to the early 1990s.

On the available evidence, our analysis suggests that the UN's main objective, namely maintenance of '*international* peace and security' lost little of its salience over time, although the way that objective was interpreted may have undergone considerable change. Objectives were conceived more and more in terms of an integrated approach to the UN's peace and security function. An implicit distinction was in due course drawn between the 'external' and 'internal' dimensions of state sovereignty. In the absence of 'external' threats, protection of 'external' sovereignty was progressively downplayed as an objective in favour of promotion of 'internal' sovereignty, which in turn became closely interlinked with promotion of human rights and socio-economic development.[1]

On the authority front, too, a significant change could be detected. Developments with respect to all four dimensions of authority had a cumulative effect which became especially striking in the rising intensity of UN involvement in intra-state conflicts. While in the 1960s authority for the management of intra-state conflicts was deemed to rest directly with the parties to the conflict, the tendency in the 1990s was for that authority to be located with increasing frequency and acceptance in the UN. In the quest for a more independent mechanism of conflict management, the UN revealed itself as the most plausible option. Though motivations varied considerably in each case, regional and global players, and to a lesser degree intra-state parties, came to view the UN as uniquely placed to assume this role. The UN, in other words, was now seen as a plausible though temporary and partial political authority, capable, in normative terms, of overseeing, and seeking compliance with, the 'rules of the game'.

Normative change in a historical structural context

Having reached this stage in our analysis, it may be useful to reflect a little more closely on an elusive but unavoidable question. If it is true to argue that the objectives and authority ascribed to the UN acquired new meaning, what might this imply for the evolution of the international political landscape from the 1960s to the 1990s and perhaps beyond? After all, discerning continuities and discontinuities is one thing, fully grasping its logic quite another, and understanding its wider implications another still. It is at this stage that our other contention becomes clearer, namely that the normative change we have detected can be usefully understood in terms of a complex interaction between material, ideational and institutional factors in a historical structural setting, which has a good deal of forward momentum.

The Congo was in many ways the Somalia of its time. 'Never again another Congo' prevailed as the international motto for nearly thirty years. How might this be explained? In contrast to the dominant preoccupation in the peacekeeping literature, issues of 'success' and 'failure' have not been the primary focus of this study. Yet one cannot help but ask in the light of our analysis, whether the international reluctance to create space for UN peace-keeping in the aftermath of the Congo operation stemmed from ONUC's 'failure' to accomplish its mission. Despite all the difficulties and complexities in the theatre of conflict, judged by several criteria, ONUC was by no means an unmitigated failure, especially in the light of such relatively recent disasters as Bosnia, Rwanda and Sierra Leone. Thanks largely to active UN involvement, the internal conflict did not escalate to the point of international (regional or global) confrontation. A modicum of internal law and order was established; the political process in the country was revitalised; and eventually, in accordance with the dominant wish of the international community, the Congo's territorial integrity was preserved. What is more, ONUC's casualties were citizens neither of the United States nor of another great power – all the more reason, one might have thought, for an expansive approach to UN peacekeeping to ensue.

Instead, a 'Congo syndrome' emerged, that was clearly visible in Cyprus and elsewhere. In Cyprus, France and the Soviet Union did not favour UN intervention. It is arguable that the United States, too, would have been less than enthusiastic about UN peacekeeping, had the crisis developed between an American and a Soviet proxy rather than between two parties with special ties to American regional allies. In a sense, Cyprus was a 'backward' step so far as enlargement of political space for UN action was concerned, as indeed it was for the redefinition of its normative basis. The terms of UN involvement were carefully designed, camouflaged in convenient ambiguity, to ensure that the Congo episode would not repeat itself. In this sense, ONUC may be regarded as an isolated phenomenon. The Congo mission did not usher in a new 'phase'. There was nothing quite like it either immediately before or immediately after, or indeed for some time to come.

In a sense, what happened in the Congo was a testing of the geopolitical power play in all its dimensions – material, ideational and institutional. Prior to the ONUC episode, the full extent of the structural contradictions and tensions impinging on peacekeeping had not yet been revealed. In the Congo episode, the Soviet Union initially favoured the 'central' government, though it would subsequently change its attitude to one of favouring the 'legitimate' government. The United States initially favoured its (neo)colonialist allies, but over time adopted a position closer to that favoured by the Third World. All other actors, to varying degrees, had to redefine their stance. These contradictory preferences were not, however, *merely* the policy 'choices' of rational actors. Neither did they reflect primarily processes of social learning and internalisation in the wake of prior normative commitments. Rather, they developed under the influence of the prevailing structural constraints. The tensions and contradictions inherent in the structural configuration were perhaps most visible in the contortions of the Secretaries-General of the time, who had enormous difficulty in reconciling 'peacekeeping principles' with the prevailing material and ideational configurations in the peacekeeping environment. Inescapably, the normative 'resolution' that emerged in such an inhospitable environment was merely momentary, certainly in no sense definitive or even indicative of a possible new trend.

In the space of three decades, the international system experienced a number of structural shifts, if not outright transformation, in both material and ideational terms. Several contradictions inherent in the existing historical structure manifested themselves in ways conducive to change. Just to mention one example, the adoption of human rights discourse in the international arena, as we have seen, was partly the result of the East–West antagonism, with each side trying to gain leverage over the opponent by appealing to a wider audience. Nor was the North–South axis of conflict without its own contradictions. Unity and disunity went hand in hand in the geographically expanded South.

Perhaps the most important dialectic common to both axes of conflict was the relationship between state and non-state players. As Falk reminds us in reference to the Third World's socio-economic aspirations, which can be characterised as a unifying tendency in the South, 'even without resistance from the centers of capital in the North, there were problems with this essentially statist vision of global economic reform ... tending to stabilise inhumane governance at the state level'.[2] Although such contradictions had not fully played themselves out, they were strong enough by the late 1980s to have a substantial impact on the structure of the international system. Again, Falk is illuminating here. Two historical conditions in the post-Cold War years characterised the period of 'transition to geogovernance'.[3] The first was the removal of 'any pattern of strategic antagonism in the North' (mainly the Cold War), whereby the North was left in control of the management of global power and resources and as 'the source of ideological cohesion'. Second, and for our purposes more important, was 'the seeming appropriation by the US government of the United Nations, especially the Security Council, as an instrument of geopolitical legitimation and public mobilization, at least in some situations'. This seeming appropriation involved, as Falk immediately adds, 'a reshaping of geopolitics, *but also . . . a path toward geogovernance*'.[4] In other words, an intentional (or, given that it operates under structural constraints, 'presumably' intentional) policy choice may well have led to unintended outcomes and consequences. Put still differently, the treatment of the UN as an instrument may have led to the development of the UN as actor in its own right. It may have gone even further and brought about the beginnings of a 're-institutionalisation' of the UN.

In the context of our analysis the same idea may be usefully, and perhaps more graphically, expressed with the benefit of Cox's triangular framework. In a nutshell, the changing geopolitical material configurations (understood primarily in terms of economic, political and military power) were accompanied, though not necessarily with the same rhythm or at the same speed, by an ideational change as observable in the relative ascendancy of such values as human rights and socio-economic development on the international platform. For a long time, however, the institutional corner of the triangle (for our purposes, the UN as 'institution') lagged behind. At a critical historical juncture, in the early 1990s, the changing material and ideational attributes combined to form a 'hegemonic' historical structure which heavily influenced international normative preferences, yet still lacked a fully corresponding institutional framework.[5]

'Institutional' implications of 'normative' change?

In this study we have problematised the UN as 'actor' rather than 'institution', keeping in mind that the attributes of the UN as actor are closely connected to the UN as institution – to a higher degree than is the identity of any other international actor. Few observers would disagree that the behaviour of the UN is obviously and necessarily constrained and facilitated by the Charter. We have already argued, in addition, that the job description of the UN as actor – whether in intra-state peacekeeping or any other sphere of activity – is influenced by the material and ideational characteristics of the international environment in which it operates. More specifically, the role and conduct of the UN (in a sense, the UN's 'identity' as actor) is constrained and facilitated by the international community's *interpretations* (ideas/values) of the Charter (institutionalised ideas/values) within a given power configuration (material capabilities).

The change we have detected in the normative basis of intra-state peacekeeping is, then, but one manifestation of the international community's evolving interpretation of the UN as 'institution'.[6] At its inception, the UN stood as a symbol for collective security and inter-governmental regulation. The impression we gain from the intra-state peacekeeping since the early 1990s is, however, rather different. Apart from what the UN actually does or does not do, and how it does or does not do it, there is little doubt that it tries to fulfil a different set of collective expectations – not necessarily expectations that represent a complete break with the past, but expectations which nonetheless represent significant modification, adaptation and development. Ideas of collective security and inter-governmental regulation are still very much part and parcel of the UN's identity. Yet, at least implicitly, there is more that is expected of the UN, not least the notion that it is an active participant in the task of governance at different levels. By the mid-1990s, the UN, it seems, was seen as an agent not only of global regulation, but of regional coordination and even local supervision. Increasingly it came to be seen as a source of authority that could legitimately pronounce on the standards which governance had to observe – a trend implicit in the very notion of 'good governance'.

Thus far the argument has proceeded by way of conceptual abstraction. But what of the evidence to be gleaned from more recent developments? In Kosovo, the conflict which had escalated after the abolition the Province's autonomous status eventually prompted a NATO bombing campaign against the new Yugoslavia between March and June 1999. The assessment, planning and implementation stages of NATO's intervention occurred with negligible reference to the Security Council.[7] It would seem, at least at first sight, as if, in the wake of the unipolar moment, a US-led coalition had effectively sidestepped the UN and tried to impose its unilateral decision. Yet is this all that happened? In the immediate aftermath, the UN was called upon to play a role in domestic governance. Why else would the UN be asked to coordinate the post-bombing interim administration in Kosovo?[8]

In East Timor, following the UN-organised ballot and the subsequent eruption of violence, the Security Council authorised an Australian-led multinational force (INTERFET) to restore peace and security and to facilitate humanitarian assistance operations.[9] In this episode, Australia no doubt pursued its regional foreign policy (with the blessing of the United States), while a transnational coalition of civil society organisations pursued either their human rights programmes or their anti-Indonesian political agendas. The fact remains that it was the UN that was called upon to fill the political space created by Indonesia's withdrawal.[10] The legitimacy of action, which Australia and others needed, was acquired through UN authorisation and involvement. Equally striking is the often overlooked fact that the UN successfully pressed Indonesia, certainly not the weakest of states, to give its consent to a coercive Chapter VII operation in what it still regarded as 'its' territory.[11]

From one vantage point, then, our study confirms the obvious, namely that international actors, especially major powers, continued in the early 1990s to treat the UN as an instrument – a policy option – in the pursuit of interests, just as they did in the early 1960s.[12] Not surprisingly, UN peace-keeping, the UN activity which perhaps best symbolises the 'UN as actor' (with its blue helmets, flag, equipment, headquarters and relatively distinctive mode of action), was called upon by a loose coalition of western/northern states to perform a diverse range of activities in a geographically dispersed set of south-ern countries. The UN was given the task of dealing with 'complex emergencies' in a number of 'failed states'. Arguably, the 'complex emergen-cies' and 'failed states' rhetoric was itself part and parcel of the emerging hegemonic power configuration of the 1990s, and reflected as much a partic-ular (hegemonic) 'image of reality' as the 'reality in itself'.[13]

Be that as it may, the key point is that international actors continued to treat the UN, and UN peacekeeping, as an instrument of policy that could be utilised at a suitable historical moment to achieve desired outcomes. Taken at face value this observation may not seem particularly startling. What is strik-ing, however, is that the UN gradually became the almost 'automatic' option for an international community needing to respond to multiple intra-state conflicts. More frequent application of the UN peacekeeping mechanism – let alone the changes that peacekeeping has undergone – was no doubt one manifestation of this. Rightly or wrongly, the UN was now viewed as the organisation best equipped to manage political and societal breakdown in conflict-torn states. To put it simply but not inaccurately, whenever some-thing went drastically wrong within a state, the UN was somehow expected to be actively engaged, indeed to take the lead, in the search for a solution. The UN's interventionism, its deepening involvement in the business of gover-nance, was met with increasing acceptance, even encouragement. The authority assigned to the UN and the integrated objectives it was expected to pursue did not end with Namibia and Cambodia. Nor, for that matter, with Bosnia and Rwanda. Kosovo and East Timor also pointed to the changing collective expectations of the UN. Do we detect a trend here? It would as yet be foolhardy to draw categorical conclusions in the affirmative – especially given the nebulous scenery created by September 11. What can be said is that high expectations placed in the UN have thus far survived the enormous difficulties in its path,[14] which is not to say that the UN's evolving authority has ever matched its evolving purpose.

Nevertheless, when ECOWAS announced that it would withdraw its peacekeeping force from Sierra Leone, the Security Council was subjected to mounting pressure for the authorisation of an expanded UN presence there.[15] Whether deemed successful or not, the UN Assistance Mission to Sierra Leone (UNAMSIL) was certainly authorised under a Chapter VII mandate to facilitate, among others, humanitarian relief efforts, support free and fair elections, and more generally strengthen the political process. The second Congo mission (MONUC), too, had a Chapter VII mandate with a clear emphasis on human rights and humanitarianism. Notwithstanding the slowing pace of UN action, the normative expectations that crystallised in the early 1990s do not appear to be losing momentum. If indeed the specified three decades have seen material and ideational change, with institutional change lagging behind, it may well be the case that the international community is still grappling with the task of constructing an institutional framework compatible with the new material and ideational configurations.

In responding to crises of peace and security (understood broadly to encompass man-made humanitarian catastrophes) the international community has a wide spectrum of choices and methods at its disposal. Yet this does not change the fact that it is actually confronted with two major sensible options – especially with respect to intra-state conflicts: to intervene effectively or not to intervene at all. The latter option, though at times tempting, may itself prove rather costly given the long-term ramifications for security and stability, in both political and socio-economic terms, locally as much as regionally and even globally. Effective intervention, however, raises the awkward question: whose intervention is likely to be effective? In the first place, unilateral intervention, at least since Vietnam, has proven politically difficult to execute for western states, especially the United States, unless immediately recognisable vital interests are at stake as is exemplified by the post-September 11 'war on terrorism'. Moreover, even the most determined unilateral intervention falls short of being truly effective, if for no other reason than its narrowly defined focus on immediate outcomes of the operation and its almost guaranteed failure to address multidimensional long-term consequences of the intervention. The only other option remains 'multilateral' intervention, although the multilateralism in question may be frequently limited in scope/geography and far from universal.[16] For the moment such intervention appears feasible given that the South's capacity to oppose western hegemony remains limited and that the internal contradictions within the West/North have yet to offset the dominant unipolar power configuration.

Still, the question remains: what 'kind' of multilateral response? Who or which entity is best suited to manage conflicts, and, eventually, guarantee a degree of international stability? The UN readily suggests itself as the plausible option. On the one hand, it gives legitimacy to the policy preferences of major powers which somehow coexist. On the other, it makes it possible for each major stake-holder in any given conflict to contribute, however marginally, to the decision-making process. It is not surprising, then, that the late 1990s witnessed a continuation of the emerging international mindset that has guided the peacekeeping formula in Angola, Cambodia and elsewhere in the immediate aftermath of the Cold War.

There is, of course, no guarantee that this 'trend' will continue, or that it is immune to tensions and contradictions, especially given that it is subject to structural constraints and opportunities. Nor is its desirability beyond criticism. Yet the evidence suggests that the UN is increasingly called upon to 'govern' what might otherwise become ungoverned or ungovernable political space – whether at the local, regional or global levels or at their intersection. The UN's evolving governance function, however, does not fit neatly into traditional frameworks of governance. Rather it assumes complex territorial as well as non-territorial qualities, and proceeds on the basis of painfully difficult normative 'resolutions' or, at least, 'syntheses' that constantly interact with changing power configurations on the world stage. Placed in a historical structural setting, this may be suggestive of the slow but continuing institutionalisation of new ideas, values, expectations, and patterns of behaviour. The contemporary world may be in the process of creating a new mosaic of complex, fluid and interlinked forms of governance, in which the UN is admittedly only one, though uniquely placed, actor which reflects, influences, and, above all, gradually re-institutionalises the changing international normative landscape.

NOTES

1 The Secretary-General would declare that 'there is complementarity between the processes related to the *Agenda for Development* and the *Agenda for Peace* . . . Development cannot be attained in the absence of peace and security or in the absence of respect for all human rights and fundamental freedoms.' See B. Boutros-Ghali, *An Agenda for Development: With Related UN Documents* (New York: United Nations, 1995), paras 3–4.

2 Falk, *On Humane Governance*, p. 28.

3 Falk, *On Humane Governance*, pp. 85–6.

4 Falk, *On Humane Governance*, p. 86; emphasis added.

5 From this perspective, the latest proposals for a new and/or expanded Security Council may be interpreted as the international community's search for appropriate re-institutionalisation.

6 This in turn may be a manifestation of the evolving multilateralism, understood as a 'deep organising principle' rather than an institution *per se*: see Knight, *A Changing United Nations*, p. 38.

7 As was the case with the Iraqi situation, however, the Kosovo operation took place in the context of several UN resolutions dealing with the Kosovo crisis, including SC Resolutions 1160, 1199, 1203.

8 Following the withdrawal of FRY security forces from Kosovo, and subsequent suspension of NATO air operations, the Security Council established an international civilian administration in Kosovo (UNMIK), which has been vested with all legislative, executive and judicial powers in the territory it administers: see SC Resolution 1244 dated 10 June 1999.

9 SC Resolution 1264 of 15 September 1999.

10 SC Resolution 1272 of 25 October 1999 would authorise an integrated, multi-dimensional peacekeeping operation fully responsible for the administration of East Timor during its transition to independence: UNTAET.

11 Following the visit of a Security Council mission to Jakarta and Dili in September 1999, Indonesia agreed to accept the international community's assistance offer. The ensuing SC Resolution 1264 of 15 September reaffirmed 'respect for the sovereignty and territorial integrity of Indonesia', not of East Timor: see preambular para. 8. Furthermore, the resolution made reference to 'peaceful and orderly transfer of authority in East Timor [from Indonesia] to the United Nations': see operative para. 8.

12 Whether the 'interests' in question are those as would be defined by hardline 'realists' or those that may have emerged from a process of mutual constitution as would be defined by 'constructivists' need not detain us here. Similary, the interests may well be national or sectional.

13 An influential IGO (the OECD) and an influential NGO (Oxfam) alike could be seen to adopt the 'complex emergency' rhetoric; see, respectively, OECD, *Guidance for Evaluating Humanitarian Assistance in Complex Emergencies* (London: Overseas Development Institute and OECD Development Assistance Commitee, 1999), and Oxfam International, *Improving the UN's Response to Complex Emergencies* (Washington, DC: Position Paper, November 1997). For 'failed states', see A. A. Mazrui, 'The failed state and political collapse in Africa', in O. A. Otunnu and M. W. Doyle (eds), *Peacemaking and Peacekeeping for the New Century* (Lanham, MD: Rowman & Littlefield, 1998).

14 Consider the UN's changing role *vis-à-vis* Afghanistan immediately before, during and after the fall of the Taliban regime in the aftermath of September 11.

15 For instance, Kofi Annan pressed for the authorisation of a sizeable force.

16 For an emphasis on this understanding of multilateralism, see in general J. G. Ruggie (ed.), *Multilateralism Matters: The Theory and Praxis of An Institutional Form* (New York: Columbia University Press, 1993), and in particular Friedrich Kratochwil's contribution to the same volume.

SELECT BIBLIOGRAPHY

Abi-Saab, G., *The United Nations Operation in the Congo 1960–1964* (Oxford: Oxford University Press, 1978).

Adrian, P., *Peacemaking and Peacekeeping in Angola 1988–1994* (Geneva: Institute Universitaire des Hautes Etudes Internationales, 1994).

Alagappa, M., 'Regionalism and the quest for security: ASEAN and the Cambodian conflict', *Australian Journal of International Affairs*, 47:2 (October 1993), 189–209.

Alger, C. F. (ed.), *The Future of the United Nations System: Potential for the Twenty-first Century* (Tokyo: United Nations University, 1998).

Allsebrook, M., *Prototypes of Peacemaking: The First Forty Years of the United Nations* (Essex: Longman, 1986).

Alston, P. (ed.), *The United Nations and Human Rights: A Critical Appraisal* (Oxford: Clarendon Press, 1995).

Amate, C. O. C., *Inside the OAU: Pan-Africanism in Practice* (London: Macmillan, 1986).

Anstee, M., 'Angola: the forgotten tragedy, a test case for UN peacekeeping', *International Relations*, 11:6 (December 1993), 495–511.

Anstee, M., *Orphan of The Cold War: The Inside Story of the Collapse of the Angola Peace Process, 1992–93* (London: St. Martin's Press, 1996).

Australian Department of Foreign Affairs and Trade, *Cambodia: An Australian Peace Proposal* (Canberra: Department of Foreign Affairs and Trade, Commonwealth of Australia, Working Papers for the Informal Meeting on Cambodia, Jakarta, 26–28 February 1990).

Balch-Lindsay, D. and Enterline, A. J., 'Killing time: the world politics of civil war duration, 1820–1992', *International Studies Quarterly*, 44 (2000).

Ball, S. J., *The Cold War: An International History, 1947–1991* (London: Arnold, 1998).

Ball, W. G., *The Past Has Another Pattern: Memoirs* (New York: W. H. Norton, 1982).

Baran, P. A., *The Political Economy of Growth* (New York: Monthly Review Press, 1957).

Beitz, C. R., *Political Theory and International Relations* (Princeton, NJ: Princeton University Press, 1979).

Bennett, J. *et al.*, *Meeting the Needs: NGO Coordination in Practice* (London: Earthscan Publications, 1995).

Berry, K., *Cambodia – From Red to Blue: Australia's Initiative for Peace* (Canberra: Allen & Unwin, 1997).

Betts, R. F., *France and Decolonisation 1900–1960* (Houndmills: Macmillan, 1991).

Beyerlin, U., 'Sanctions', in Wolfrum, R. and Philipp, C. (eds), *United Nations: Law, Policies and Practice* (Dordrecht: Martinus Nijhoff Publishers, 1995).

Bloomfield, L. P., 'Peacekeeping and peacemaking', *Foreign Affairs*, 44:4 (1966), 672–82.

Bloomfield, L. P., 'Political control of international forces in dealing with problems of local instability', in Waskow, A. J. (ed.), *Quis Custodiet? Controlling The Police in a Disarmed World* (Washington, DC: Peace Research Institute, 1963).

Bloomfield, L. P. (ed.), *The Power to Keep Peace: Today and in a World Without War* (Cambridge, MA: The MIT Press, 1971).

Blum, Y. Z., *Eroding the United Nations Charter* (Dordrecht: Martinus Nijhoff, 1993).

Borton, N. and Taner, V., 'Strengthening U.S. Government humanitarian action in Africa' (Washington, DC: Center for Strategic and International Studies, Working Paper, April 2001).

Booth, W. J., James, P. and Meadwell, H. (eds), *Politics and Rationality* (Cambridge: Cambridge University Press, 1993).

Boutros-Ghali, B., *An Agenda for Development, with Related UN Documents* (New York: United Nations, 1995).

Boutros-Ghali, B., *An Agenda for Peace: Preventive Diplomacy, Peacemaking and Peace-keeping* (New York: United Nations, 1992).

Boutros-Ghali, B., *An Agenda for Peace, 2nd edn with the New Supplement and Related UN Documents* (New York: United Nations, 1995).

Boutros-Ghali, B., 'Empowering the United Nations: historic opportunities to strengthen world body', *Foreign Affairs*, 72:5 (1992), 89–102.

Braillard, P. and Djalili, M-R., *The Third World and International Relations* (London: Frances Pinter, 1986).

Bratt, D., 'Peace over justice: developing a framework for UN peacekeeping operations in internal conflicts', *Global Governance: A Review of Multilateralism and International Organizations*, 5:1 (Jan–Mar 1999), 63–81.

Brown, M. and Zasloff, J. J., *Cambodia Confounds the Peacemakers, 1979–1998* (Ithaca: Cornell University Press, 1998).

Brown, M. E. (ed.), *The International Dimensions of Internal Conflict* (Cambridge, MA: The MIT Press, 1996).

Camilleri, J. A. and Falk, J., *End of Sovereignty?: The Politics of A Shrinking and Fragmenting World* (Aldershot: Edward Elgar, 1992).

Carey, H. F., Book Review of '*Security Council Decision-Making: the Case of Haiti, 1990–1997, by David Malone, Oxford: Clarendon/Oxford University Press, 1998*'; circulated by ACUNS discussion group at 'acuns-io@lists.yale.edu' (Tue, 15 June 1999 12:25:18 –0400).

Carnegie Commission on Preventing Deadly Conflict, *Final Report* (Washington, DC: Carnegie Corporation of New York, 1997).

Center for Systemic Peace, *Major Episodes of Political Violence, 1946–1998*, available online at http://members.aol.com/CSPmgm/warlist6.htm (17 June 2000).

Chamberlain, M. E., *The Longman Companion to European Decolonisation in the Twentieth Century* (London: Longman, 1998).

Chopra, J. (ed.), *The Politics of Peace-Maintenance* (Boulder, CO: Lynne Rienner, 1998).

Chopra, J. and Weiss, T. G., 'Sovereignty is no longer sacrosanct: codifying humanitarian intervention', *Ethics and International Affairs*, 6 (1992), 95–117.

Clements, K. and Ward, R. (eds), *Building International Community: Cooperating for Peace Case Studies* (St. Leonards: Allen & Unwin, 1994).

Clerides, G., *Cyprus: My Deposition* (Nicosia: Alithia, 1990).

Collins, C. and Weiss, T. G., 'An Overview and Assessment of 1989–1996 Peace

Operations Publications' (Providence, RI: The Thomas J. Watson Jr. Institute for International Studies, Occasional Paper No. 28).

Collins, C. J. L. 'The Cold War comes to Africa: Cordier and the 1960 Congo crisis', *Journal of International Affairs*, 47:1 (Summer 1993), 243–69.

Commission on Global Goverance, *Our Global Neighbourhood: The Report of the Commission on Global Governance* (New York: Oxford University Press, 1995).

Community Aid Abroad, *Learning the Lessons: United Nations Interventions in Conflict Situations* (Melbourne: Community Aid Abroad, December 1994).

Cox, R. W. with Sinclair, T. J., *Approaches to World Order* (Cambridge: Cambridge University Press, 1996).

Damrosch, L. F. (ed.), *Enforcing Restraint: Collective Intervention in Internal Conflicts* (New York: Council on Foreign Relations Press, 1993).

Daniel, D. C. F. and Hayes, B. C. (eds), *Beyond Traditional Peacekeeping* (New York: St. Martin's Press, 1995).

Darwin, J., *Britain and Decolonisation: The Retreat from Empire in the post-Cold War World* (Houndmills: Macmillan, 1988).

de Cuéllar, J. P., *Pilgrimage for Peace: A Secretary-General's Memoir* (Basingstoke: Macmillan, 1997).

de Jonge Oudraat, C., 'Intervention in Internal Conflicts: Legal and Political Conundrums' (Washington, DC: Carnegie Endowment for International Peace, Working Paper No. 15, August 2000).

Dessler, D., 'Constructivism within a positivist social science', *Review of International Studies*, 25 (1999), 123–37.

Diehl, P. F., 'Forks in the road: theoretical and policy concerns for 21st century peace-keeping', *Global Society: Journal of Interdisciplinary International Relations*, 14:3 (July 2000), 337–60.

Diehl, P. F., *International Peacekeeping* (Baltimore, MD: Johns Hopkins University Press, 1993).

Diethelm, R., *Das Friedenssicherungssystem der Vereinten Nationen in der Mitte der 90er Jahre* (St. Gallen: ETH Forschungsstelle fur Internationale Beziehungen, Beitrag Nr. 7, Juni 1996).

Donaldson, R. H., 'The Soviet Union in South Asia: a friend to rely on?', *Journal of International Affairs*, 34:2 (Fall/Winter 1980/81).

Doyle, M. W., 'Authority and elections in Cambodia', in Doyle, M. W., Johnstone, I. and Orr, R. C. (eds), *Keeping the Peace: Multidimensional UN Operations in Cambodia and El Salvador* (Cambridge: Cambridge University Press, 1997).

Doyle, M. W., Johnstone, I. and Orr, R. C. (eds), *Keeping the Peace: Multidimensional UN Operations in Cambodia and El Salvador* (Cambridge: Cambridge University Press, 1997).

Dreyer, R., *Namibia and Southern Africa: Regional Dynamics of Decolonization, 1945–90* (London: Kegan Paul International, 1994).

Duncan-Jones, A., 'The civil war in Cyprus' in Luard, E. (ed.), *The International Regulation of Civil Wars* (London: Thames & Hudson, 1972).

Dunne, T. and Wheeler, N. J. (eds), *Human Rights in Global Politics* (Cambridge: Cambridge University Press, 1999).

Durch, W. J., 'Keeping the peace: politics and lessons of the 1990s', in Durch, W. J.

(ed.), *UN Peacekeeping, American Politics, and the Uncivil Wars of the 1990s* (New York: St. Martin's Press, 1996).

Durch, W. J. (ed.), *UN Peacekeeping, American Politics, and the Uncivil Wars of the 1990s* (New York: St. Martin's Press, 1996).

Durch, W. J. (ed.), *The Evolution of UN Peacekeeping: Case Studies and Comparative Analysis* (London: Macmillan, 1994).

Dyer, H. C., *Moral Order/World Order: The Role of Normative Theory in the Study of International Relations* (Houndmills: Macmillan, 1997).

Eide, A., 'Peace-keeping and enforcement by regional organizations', *Journal of Peace Research*, 3 (1966), 125–45.

Ekpebu, L. B., *Zaire and The African Revolution* (Ibadan: Ibadan University Press, 1989).

Esman, M. J. and Telhami, S. (eds), *International Organizations and Ethnic Conflict* (Ithaca: Cornell University Press, 1995).

Evans, G., *Cooperating for Peace: The Global Agenda for the 1990s and Beyond* (St. Leonards: Allen & Unwin, 1993).

Evans, G., 'Achieving peace in Cambodia' (Paper presented to the Hague Centennial Peace Conference on Dispute Settlement, Humanitarian Law and Disarmament, University of Melbourne, 20 February 1999).

Falk, R. A., *Human Rights Horizons: The Pursuit of Justice in A Globalizing World* (London: Routledge, 2000).

Falk, R. A., *On Humane Governance: Toward A New Global Politics* (University Park, PA: The Pennsylvania State University Press, 1995).

Falk, R. A. (ed.), *The International Law of Civil War* (Baltimore, MD: Johns Hopkins Press, 1971).

Fetherston, A. B., *Towards A Theory of United Nations Peacekeeping* (London: Macmillan, 1994).

Findlay, T., *The New Peacekeepers and the New Peacekeeping* (Canberra: The ANU, Department of International Relations, Working Paper No. 1996/2, May 1996).

Forbes, M. and Hoffman, M., *Political Theory, International Relations, and the Ethics of Intervention* (New York: St. Martin's Press, 1993).

Franck, T. M. and Carey, J., 'Working paper: the role of the United Nations in the Congo – a retrospective perspective', in Tondel Jr., L. (ed.), *The Legal Aspects of the United Nations Action in the Congo* (New York: Oceana Publications, 1963).

Frost, F., 'The Peace Process in Cambodia: Issues and Prospects' (Queensland: Centre for the Study of Australia–Asia Relations, Australia–Asia Papers No. 69, October 1993).

Frost, M., *Toward a Normative Theory of International Relations: A Critical Analysis of the Philosophical and Methodological Assumptions in the Discipline with Proposals toward A Substantive Normative Theory* (Cambridge: Cambridge University Press, 1986).

Frye, W. R., *A United Nations Peace Force* (New York: Oceana Publications, 1957).

Gaer, F. D., 'Reality check: human rights NGOs confront governments at the UN', in Weiss, T. G. and Gordenker, L. (eds), *NGOs, the UN, and Global Governance* (Boulder, CO: Lynne Rienner, 1996).

Galtung, J., 'Three realistic approaches to peace: peacekeeping, peacemaking, peace-building', in *Impact of Science on Society*, 26:1/2 (1976), 103–15.

Gazioglu, A. C., *Two Equal and Sovereign Peoples: A Documented Background to the Cyprus Problem and the Concept of Partnership* (Nicosia: CYREP, 1997).

Gazioglu, A. C. and Demirer, M. A. (eds), *Cyprus: The Island of Sustained Crises*, 2nd edn, (Nicosia: CYREP, 1999).

George, R. P. (ed.), *The Autonomy of Law: Essays on Legal Positivism* (Oxford: Clarendon Press, 1996).

Gibbs, D. N., *The Political Economy of Third World Intervention: Mines, Money, and U.S. Policy in the Congo Crisis* (Chicago, IL: The University of Chicago Press, 1991).

Gordon, J. K., *The United Nations in the Congo: A Quest for Peace* (New York: Carnegie Endowment for International Peace, 1962).

Government of Canada, *Towards A Rapid Reaction Capability for the United Nations* (Ottawa: September 1995).

Heder, S. and Ledgerwood, J. (eds), *Propaganda, Politics, and Violence in Cambodia: Democratic Transition under United Nations Peace-keeping* (New York: M. E. Sharpe, 1996).

Heiberg, M. (ed.), *Subduing Sovereignty: Sovereignty and the Right to Intervene* (London: Pinter, 1994).

Heller, A., *A Philosophy of Morals* (Oxford: Basil Blackwell, 1990).

Heye, C., 'United Nations peacekeeping – an introduction', in Moxon-Brown, E. (ed.), *A Future for Peacekeeping?* (Houndmills: Macmillan, 1998).

Higgins, R., *United Nations Peacekeeping: Documents and Commentary*, vols 1–4 (London: Oxford University Press, 1969, 1970, 1980, 1981).

Hoffman, S., *Duties Beyond Borders: On The Limits and Possibilities of Ethical International Politics* (Syracuse, New York: Syracuse University Press, 1981).

Hoffman, S., 'The politics and ethics of military intervention', *Survival*, 37 (Winter 1995/96), 29–51.

Hood, S. J., 'Beijing's Cambodia gamble and the prospects for peace in Indochina', *Asian Survey*, 30:10 (October 1990), 977–91.

Hopkinson, N., *Humanitarian Intervention?* (London: HMSO, Wilton Park Paper 110, 1996).

Hoskyns, C., *The Congo Since Independence: January 1960–December 1961* (London: Oxford University Press, 1965).

Hughes, C., *UNTAC in Cambodia: The Impact on Human Rights* (Singapore: Institute of Southeast Asian Studies, 1996).

Huntington, S. P., *The Clash of Civilizations and The Remaking of World Order* (New York: Simon & Schuster, 1996).

International Peace Academy, *The Peacekeeper's Handbook* (New York: Pergamon Press, 1984).

James, A., *Britain and the Congo Crisis, 1960–63* (Houndmills: Macmillan, 1996).

James, A., *The Politics of Peace-keeping* (London: Chatto & Windus, 1969).

Jensen, E. and Fisher, T. (eds), *The United Kingdom – The United Nations* (Houndmills: Macmillan, 1990).

Jordan, R. S. (ed.), *Dag Hammarskjöld Revisited: The UN Secretary-General as a Force in World Politics* (Durham, NC: Carolina Academic Press, 1983).

Joseph, J. S., *Cyprus: Ethnic Conflict and International Concern* (New York: Peter Lang, 1985).

Joseph, J. S., *Cyprus: Ethnic Conflict and International Politics – From Independence to the Threshold of the European Union* (Houndmills: Macmillan, 1997).

Juergensen, O. T., 'Repatriation as Peacebuilding and Reconstruction: The Case of Northern Mozambique, 1992–1995' (Geneva: UNHCR, Working Paper No. 31, October 2000).

Kalb, M. G., *The Congo Cables: The Cold War in Africa – From Eisenhower to Kennedy* (New York: Macmillan, 1982).

Kaloudis, G. S., *The Role of the U.N. in Cyprus from 1964 to 1979* (New York: Peter Lang, 1991).

Kanza, T., *Conflict in the Congo: The Rise and Fall of Lumumba* (Middlesex: Penguin Books, 1972).

Katzenstein, P. J. (ed.), *The Culture of National Security: Norms and Identity in World Politics* (New York: Columbia University Press, 1996).

Katzenstein, P. J., Keohane, R. O. and Krasner, S. D. (eds), *Exploration and Contestation in the Study of World Politics* (Cambridge, MA: The MIT Press, 1999).

Kent, A., *China, The United Nations, and Human Rights: The Limits of Compliance* (Philadelphia, PA: University of Pennsylvania Press, 1999).

Keohane, R. O., 'International institutions: two approaches', *International Studies Quarterly* 32 (1988), 379–96.

Kiman, U., 'Cambodia: our experience with the United Nations', *Pacifica Review*, 7:2 (Oct/Nov. 1995).

Klotz, A., *Norms in International Relations: The Struggle against Apartheid* (Ithaca: Cornell University Press, 1995).

Knight, W. A., *A Changing United Nations: Multilateral Evolution and the Quest for Global Governance* (Houndmills: Palgrave, 2000).

Knudsen, T. B., 'Humanitarian intervention revisited: post-Cold War responses to classical problems', *International Peacekeeping*, 3:4 (Winter 1996).

Kratochwil, F. V., *Rules, Norms and Decisions: On the Conditions of Practical and Legal Reasoning in International Relations and Domestic Affairs* (Cambridge: Cambridge University Press, 1989).

Kratochwil, F. and Mansfield, E. D. (eds), *International Organization: A Reader* (New York: HarperCollins College Publishers, 1994).

Krauthammer, C., 'The unipolar moment', *Foreign Affairs*, 70:1 (1990/91), 23–33.

Krška, V., 'Peacekeeping in Angola (UNAVEM I and II)', *International Peacekeeping*, 4:1 (Spring 1997), 75–97.

Ku, C. and Diehl, P. F., *International Law: Classic and Contemporary Readings* (Boulder, CO: Lynne Rienner, 1998).

Kyle, K., *Cyprus: In Search of Peace* (London: Minority Rights Group International, 1997).

Laberge, P., 'Humanitarian intervention: three ethical positions', *Ethics and International Affairs*, 9 (1995), 15–35.

Leaver, R. and Richardson, J. L. (eds), *Charting the post-Cold War Order* (Boulder, CO: Westview, 1993).

Lefever, E. W., *Crisis in the Congo: A United Nations Force in Action* (Washington, DC: The Brookings Institution, 1965).

Lefever, E. W., *Uncertain Mandate: Politics of the U.N. Congo Operation* (Baltimore, MD: The Johns Hopkins Press, 1967).

225

Lodico, Y. C., 'A peace that fell apart: the United Nations and the war in Angola', in Durch, W. J. (ed.), *UN Peacekeeping, American Politics, and the Uncivil Wars of the 1990s* (New York: St. Martin's Press, 1996).

MacQueen, N., 'Peacekeeping by attrition: the United Nations in Angola', *The Journal of Modern African Studies*, 36:3 (1998), 399–422.

Marks, S. P., 'Elusive justice for the victims of the Khmer Rouge', *Journal of International Affairs*, 52:2 (Spring 1999), 691–718.

Mazrui, A. A., *Africa's International Relations: The Diplomacy of Dependency and Change* (Boulder, CO: Westview Press, 1977).

McCoubrey, H. and White, N. D. *International Organizations and Civil Wars* (Aldershot: Dartmouth, 1995).

McDonald, R., 'The Problem of Cyprus' (London: IISS, Adelphi Paper No. 234, Winter 1988/89).

McGinnis, M. D., 'Policy substitutability in complex humanitarian emergencies: a model of individual choice and international response', *The Journal of Conflict Resolution*, 44:1 (February 2000), 62–89.

McGregor, C., 'China, Vietnam, and the Cambodian conflict: Beijing's end game strategy', *Asian Survey*, 30:3 (March 1990), 266–83.

McKay, V., *Africa in World Politics* (Westport, CT: Greenwood Press, 1974).

McSweeney, B., *Security, Identity and Interests: A Sociology of International Relations* (Cambridge: Cambridge University Press, 1999).

Mermin, J., *Debating War and Peace: Media Coverage of U.S. Intervention in the post-Vietnam Era* (Princeton, NJ: Princeton University Press, 1999).

Metzl, J. F., *Western Responses to Human Rights Abuses in Cambodia, 1975–1980* (Houndmills: Macmillan, 1996).

Miller, L. B., *World Order and Local Disorder: The United Nations and Internal Conflicts* (Princeton, NJ: Princeton University Press, 1967).

Mills, K., *Human Rights in the Emerging Global Order: A New Sovereignty?* (Houndmills: Macmillan, 1998).

Morris, S. J., *Why Vietnam Invaded Cambodia: Political Culture and the Causes of War* (Stanford, CA: Stanford University Press, 1999).

Mortimer, R. A., *The Third World Coalition in International Politics* (New York: Praeger, 1980).

Moxon-Brown, E. (ed.), *A Future for Peacekeeping?* (Houndmills: Macmillan, 1998).

Munck, G. L. and Kumar, C., 'Civil conflicts and the conditions for successful international intervention: a comparative study of Cambodia and El Salvador', *Review of International Studies*, 21:2 (April 1995), 159–81.

Murphy, C. N., 'Global governance: poorly done and poorly understood', *International Affairs*, 76:4 (2000), 789–803.

Myrdal, G., *Development and Underdevelopment: A Note on the Mechanism of National and International Economic Inequality* (Cairo: National Bank of Egypt, 1956).

Nardin, T. and Mapel, D. R. (eds), *Traditions of International Ethics* (Cambridge: Cambridge University Press, 1992).

Necatigil, Z. M., *Our Republic in Perspective* (Nicosia: Tezel, 1985).

Nicholson, M., *Causes and Consequences in International Relations: A Conceptual Study* (London: Pinter, 1996).

OECD, *Guidance for Evaluating Humanitarian Assistance in Complex Emergencies* (London: Overseas Development Institute & OECD Development Assistance Committee, 1999).

Otunnu, O. A. and Doyle, M. W. (eds), *Peacemaking and Peacekeeping for the New Century* (Lanham: Rowman & Littlefield, 1998).

Oxfam International, *Improving the UN's Response to Complex Emergencies* (Washington, DC: Position Paper, November 1997).

Paris, R., 'Broadening the study of peace operations', *International Studies Review*, 2:3 (Fall 2000), 27–44.

Peceny, M. and Stanley, W., 'The promotion of liberal norms in United Nations efforts to resolve civil wars' (Paper prepared for the 95th Annual Meeting of the American Political Science Association, GA, September 2–5, 1999).

Peck, C., *Sustainable Peace: The Role of the UN and Regional Organizations in Preventing Conflict* (Lanham, MD: Rowman & Littlefield, 1998).

Pei-heng, C., *Non-Governmental Organizations at the United Nations: Identity, Role, and Function* (New York: Praeger, 1981).

Peou, S., *Conflict Naturalization in the Cambodia War: From Battlefield to Ballot-box* (New York: Oxford University Press, 1997).

Popper, K. R., *The Poverty of Historicism*, 2nd edn (London: Routledge and K. Paul, 1960).

Price, R., 'Moral norms in world politics', *Pacifica Review*, 9:1 (1997), 45–72.

Price, R. M., *The Chemical Weapons Taboo* (Ithaca: Cornell University Press, 1997).

Quane, H., 'The United Nations and the evolving right to self-determination', *International and Comparative Law Quarterly*, 47:3 (July 1998), 537–72.

Ramsbotham, O., 'Humanitarian intervention 1990–5: a need to reconceptualize?', *Review of International Studies*, 23 (1997), 445–68.

Ratner, S. R., *The New Peacekeeping: Building Peace in Lands of Conflict after the Cold War* (New York: St. Martin's Press, 1995).

Rawls, J., *A Theory of Justice* (London: Oxford University Press, 1973).

Raymond, G. A., 'Problems and prospects in the study of international norms', *Mershon International Studies Review*, 41 (1997), 205–45.

Rikhye, I. J., *The Theory and Practice of Peacekeeping* (London: C. Hurst & Co., 1984).

Rikhye, I. J. and Skjelsbaek, K. (eds), *The United Nations and Peacekeeping: Results, Limitations and Prospects: The Lessons of 40 Years of Experience* (London: Macmillan/International Peace Academy, 1990).

Risse, T., Ropp, S. C. and Sikkink, K. (eds), *The Power of Human Rights: International Norms and Domestic Change* (Cambridge: Cambridge University Press, 1999).

Roberts, A., 'Humanitarian war: military intervention and human rights', *International Affairs*, 69:3 (1993), 429–49.

Roberts, A. and Kingsbury, B., *Presiding over A Divided World: Changing UN Roles, 1945–1993* (Boulder, CO: Lynne Rienner, 1994; IPA Occasional Paper Series).

Roberts, D., 'More honoured in the breech: consent and impartiality in the Cambodian peacekeeping operation', *International Peacekeeping*, 4:1 (Spring 1997), 1–25.

Robertson, C. L., *International Politics since World War II: A Short History* (Armonk, NY: M. E. Sharpe, 1997).

Rosenau, J. N., *Along the Domestic–Foreign Frontier: Exploring Governance in a Turbulent World* (Cambridge: Cambridge University Press, 1997).

Rosenau, J. N., *The United Nations in a Turbulent World* (Boulder, CO: Lynne Rienner, 1992).

Rosenau, J. N. and Durfee, M., *Thinking Theory Thoroughly: Coherent Approaches to An Incoherent World* (Boulder, CO: Westview Press, 1995).

Ruggie, J. G., 'Human rights and the future international community', *Daedalus*, 12:4 (Fall 1983), 93–110.

Ruggie, J. G. (ed.), *Multilateralism Matters: The Theory and Praxis of An Institutional Form* (New York: Columbia University Press, 1993).

Ruggie, J. G., 'The UN and the collective use of force: whither or whether?', *International Peacekeeping*, 3:4 (Winter 1996), 1–20.

Sagar, D., 'Historical survey', in M. Wright (ed.), *Cambodia: A Matter of Survival* (Essex: Longman, 1989).

Sambanis, N., 'The United Nations operation in Cyprus: a new look at the peacekeeping–peacemaking relationship', *International Peacekeeping*, 6:1 (Spring 1999).

Shapcott, R., 'Solidarism and after: global governance, international society and the normative "turn" in international relations', *Pacifica Review*, 12:2 (June 2000), 147–65.

Shawcross, W., *Deliver Us from Evil: Warlords & Peacekeepers in A World of Endless Conflict* (London: Bloomsbury, 2000).

Shue, H., *Basic Rights: Subsistence, Affluence, and U.S. Foreign Policy* (Princeton, NJ: Princeton University Press, 1980).

Siekmann, R. C. R., *Basic Documents on United Nations and Related Peace-keeping Forces*, 2nd edn (Dordrecht: Martinus Nijhoff, 1989).

Sihanouk, N., *War and Hope: The Case for Cambodia* (London: Sidgwick & Jackson, 1980).

Sikkink, K., 'Transnational politics, international relations theory, and human rights', *Political Science & Politics*, 31:3 (September 1998).

Simmons, P. J., 'Learning to live with NGOs', in *Foreign Policy*, 112 (Fall 1998).

Singer, P., *Ethics* (Oxford: Oxford University Press, 1994).

SIPRI Yearbook 1994–1999 (Oxford: Oxford University Press, published annually).

Smith, H. (ed.), *International Peacekeeping: Building on the Cambodian Experience* (Canberra: Australian Defense Studies Centre, 1994).

Smith, H., 'Prospects for peacekeeping', in Smith, H. (ed.), *International Peacekeeping: Building on the Cambodian Experience* (Canberra: Australian Defense Studies Centre, 1994).

Smouts, M-C., 'The General Assembly: grandeur and decadence', Taylor, P. and Groom, A. J. R. (eds), *The United Nations at the Millennium: The Principal Organs* (London: Continuum, 2000).

Soo, T. S., *The Malayan Special Force in the Heart of Africa* (Malaysia: Palanduk Publications, 1989).

Stedman, S. J., *International Actors and Internal Conflicts* (New York: Rockefeller Brothers Fund, 1999).

Stedman, S. J., 'Spoiler problems in peace processes', *International Security*, 22:2 (Fall 1997), 5–53.

Stegenga, J. A., *The United Nations Force in Cyprus* (Ohio: Ohio State University Press, 1968).

Stephenson, C. S., 'NGOs and the principal organs of the United Nations', in Taylor, P. and Groom, A. J. R. (eds), *The United Nations at the Millennium: The Principal Organs* (London: Continuum, 2000).

Stern, P. C. and Druckman, D. (eds), *International Conflict Resolution After The Cold War* (Washington, DC: National Academy Press, 2000).

Tamkoç, M., *The Turkish Cypriot State: The Embodiment of the Right of Self-Determination* (London: K. Rustem & Brother, 1988).

Taylor, P. and Groom, A. J. R. (eds), *Global Issues in the United Nations' Framework* (Houndmills: Macmillan, 1989).

Taylor, P. and Groom, A. J. R. (eds), *The United Nations at the Millennium: The Principal Organs* (London: Continuum, 2000).

Thakur, R., 'Human rights: Amnesty International and the United Nations', *Journal of Peace Research*, 31:2 (1994), 143–60.

Thakur, R. and Thayer, C. A. (eds), *A Crisis of Expectations: UN Peacekeeping in the 1990s* (Boulder, CO: Westview, 1995).

Um, K., 'Cambodia in 1989: still talking but no settlement', *Asian Survey*, 30:1 (January 1990), 96–104.

UNHCR, *Background Paper on Refugees and Asylum Seekers from Angola* (Geneva, October 1994).

UNHCR, *The State of the World's Refugees: Fifty Years of Humanitarian Action* (Oxford: Oxford University Press, 2000).

UNIDIR, *Managing Arms in Peace Processes: Cambodia* (New York: United Nations, 1996).

UNIDIR, *Small Arms Management and Peacekeeping in Southern Africa* (New York: United Nations, 1996).

United Nations, *The Blue Helmets: A Review of United Nations Peace-keeping* (New York: UNDPI, 1985).

United Nations, *The Blue Helmets: A Review of United Nations Peace-keeping* 2nd edn (New York: UNDPI, 1990).

United Nations, *The Blue Helmets: A Review of United Nations Peace-keeping* 3rd edn (New York: UNDPI, 1996).

United Nations, *United Nations Action in the Field of Human Rights* (New York: United Nations, 1980).

United Nations, *The United Nations and Cambodia, 1991–1995* (New York: UNDPI, 1995).

United Nations, *The United Nations and El Salvador, 1990–1995* (New York: UNDPI, 1995).

United Nations, *The United Nations and Mozambique, 1992–1995* (New York: UNDPI, 1995).

United Nations, *The United Nations and Rwanda, 1993–1996* (New York: UNDPI, 1996).

United Nations, *The United Nations and Somalia, 1992–1996* (New York: UNDPI, 1996).

United Nations, *The United Nations and the Iraq-Kuwait Conflict, 1990–1996* (New York: UNDPI, 1996).

Urquhart, B., 'The United Nations in 1992: problems and opportunities', *International Affairs*, 68:2 (April 1992), 311–19.

Valkenier, E. K, 'Great power economic competition in Africa: Soviet progress and problems', *Journal of International Affairs*, 34:2 (Fall/Winter 1980/81), 259–68.

Vance, C. R., *Hard Choices: Critical Years in America's Foreign Policy* (New York: Simon & Schuster, 1983).

Vickery, M., *Cambodia: A Political Survey* (Canberra: The Department of Political and Social Change, Research School of Pacific and Asian Studies, ANU, 1994).

Vincent, R. J., *Nonintervention and International Order* (Princeton, NJ: Princeton University Press, 1974).

Warner, D. (ed.), *New Dimensions of Peacekeeping* (Dordrecht: Martinus Nijhoff Publishers, 1995).

Weiss, H. F., *Political Process in the Congo: The Parti Solidaire Africain during the Independence Struggle* (Princeton, NJ: Princeton University Press, 1967).

Weiss, T. G., Forsythe, D. P. and Coate, R. A. *The United Nations and Changing World Politics* (Boulder, CO: Westview, 1997).

Weiss, T. G. and Gordenker, L. (eds), *NGOs, the UN, and Global Governance* (Boulder, CO: Lynne Rienner, 1996).

Weissman, S. R., *American Foreign Policy in the Congo 1960–1964* (Ithaca: Cornell University Press, 1974).

White, N. D., *The United Nations and the Maintenance of International Peace and Security* (Manchester: Manchester University Press, 1990).

Young, C., *Politics in the Congo: Decolonization and Independence* (Princeton, NJ: Princeton University Press, 1965).

Yuan, J., 'Multilateral intervention and state sovereignty: Chinese views on UN peace-keeping operations', *Political Science*, 49:2 (January 1998), 275–95.

INDEX